PUTTING THE CART

BEFORE THE HORSE

Putting The Cart Before The Horse:

Contested Nationalism and the Crisis of the Nation-State in Somalia

Edited by
Abdi M. Kusow

The Red Sea Press, Inc.
Publishers & Distributors of Third World Books

P.O. Box 1892 P.O. Box 48

Trenton, NJ 08607 Asmara, ERITREA

The Red Sea Press, Inc.

Publishers & Distributors of Third World Books

P.O. Box 1892		P.O. Box 48
Trenton, NJ 08607		Asmara, ERITREA

Cover design: Roger Dormann
Typesetting: Jerusalem Typesetting

Library of Congress Cataloging-in-Publication Data

Putting the cart before the horse: contested nationalism and the crisis of
the nation-state in Somalia / edited by Abdi Kusow.
 p. cm.
Includes bibliographical references and index.
 ISBN 1-56902-202-x (hardcover) -- ISBN 1-56902-203-8 (pbk.)
 1. Nationalism--Somalia. 2. Somalia--Politics and government. I.
Kusow, Abdi.

 DT403.25.P88 2004
 967.7305'3--dc22

2004014126

To my wife,

Alangti Aw Umur Mad Aliyow;

and to Loo-ma-oyayaasha (those for whom no one sheds tears over their
death and destruction or to whom no one gives credit to their contributions in the making of the Somali nation) wherever they are.

Acknowledgement

This book would not have materialized without the moral and intellectual support of family and friends. Ali Jimale Ahmed shared his wisdom and critical gaze throughout the project. It was, in fact, in the constant conversation with him that the idea of the book was born, and from that moment on provided cheerful encouragement and supportive criticism. I owe a tremendous debt to my good friend and mentor, David Russell Maines, for his undying support. He has been there whenever I needed him. To Linda Benson for making my family and I truly welcome to the Benson-Maines home. Lenny Markovitz, Peter Kivisto, Yacob Fisseha, and Vincent Khapoya have shown a particularly keen appreciation of my work over the years. I owe them a special gratitude.

I also wish to acknowledge the contributions of a number of colleagues and friends, Hassan Mahadallah, Mohamed Haji Mukhtar, Ahmed Qasim Ali, Abdulkadir Arif, Abukar Arman, Abukar Balle, Dr. AbdiNur Mohamed, Abdullahi Osman (Xirey), Omar Raghe, Nur Barre, Abdiaziz Abukar (Baffo), Malaq Mukhtar Mohamed Adan, Omar Eno, Mohamed Eno, and Nur Abdi Hussen; my colleagues at Oakland University, Peter Bertocci, Judith Brown, Lindsay Cooper, Jennifer Dierickx, James Dow, Jay Meehan, Linda Morrison, Lynetta Mosby, Terri Orbuch, Jo Reger, Cindy Schellenbach, Gary Shepherd, Suzanne Spencer-Wood, Richard Stamps, and particularly Kathy Barrett for their support over the years. I am grateful to Linda Fortin for editing an earlier version of the manuscript; and to Christina Gonzalez for standardizing the footnotes, and for transcribing and scanning the images in Chapter Two.

Thanks to my brothers, Abdullahi Jasaaye, Ali Atore, Ahmed Katara, and Isak Kusow; sisters Fartumo and Rukia Kusow; brother in-laws, Mahamud Mohamed (Bono), Adan Bulle, Ali Omar, Mad Karin Omar, Mowlid Omar, and Abdi Omar; sister in-laws, Shukri Jamac, Fadumo Abukar, Fadumo Omar, and Nacima; uncle/brother Ali Abdi Semed Aw Muxumed; and my nieces and nephews for their unconditional love. To my late father, *Alangki Aw Kusow Edeng* whose deep understanding of the hidden meanings of everyday things, and appreciation of every day people, along with my mother, *Ina Cabdi Semed Aw Muxumed* whose love and straight forward approach to life gave me an early and a committed sense of the importance of critical awareness, particularly as it relates to *those whose voices are unacknowledged*. I owe them more than I could possibly repay. A special and a deep sense of appreciation must go to my father in-law, *Alangki Aw Mad Aliyow*; and my mother in-law, *Alangti Aw Nurow Emed*, for their unconditional love, and for truly adopting me as their own.

To my Luley, however, must go the greatest appreciation. She has remained true to me despite my constant obsession with writing rather than living and enjoying life; and to my children, Karima, Omar, and Abbas for being such wonderful children.

Contents

Preface

CONVENTIONAL SOMALI HISTORIOGRAPHY IS MAINLY derived from the assumption that the society has been and remains a nation *sui-generis, a priori,* or what Somalis call *Muqadas* (holy) nation. The most revealing expression of this sentiment is found in Laitin and Samatar's (1987) book title, *Somalia: A Nation in Search of a State*.[1] This title, as it were, represents a long line of research that depicts the society as a *self-same nation*, downplays, and sometimes violently oppresses any mention of social and political faultlines. The only acknowledged political and social faultlines, according to *self-same nation* thesis, are those that resulted from *Faragelin Shisheeye* (foreign intervention) otherwise colonialism both European and what Somalis habitually refer to *Gumaysiga Madow* (black colonists).[2] If colonial actors are not blamed, moreover, the breakdown of the Somali moral fiber, according the *self-same nation* thesis, is traced to the actions of one or another post-colonial regime which allegedly pitted hitherto harmonious and homogeneous clans against each other, and thereby, destroyed the cultural and spiritual values of the society leading to the present crisis.[3] More importantly, this historiography articulates the making of the Somali nation as the result of the *Darwiish* anti-colonial resistance movement which supposedly rescued the nation from the British overlords, in the case of Mohamed Abdulle Hassan; and Ahmed Gurey, in the case of *Gumaysiga Madow*, while conveniently ignoring the contributions of the peasant masses, women; and in general, what I would call *Lo-ma-oyayaasha*, those for whom no one sheds tears over their death and destruction; and to whom, no one gives credit to their contributions in the well-being of the nation.

For the methodologically and theoretically informed scholar, however, articulating the making of the Somali nation through the activities of the *Darwiish*; and more importantly, locating the social faultlines of the nation on *Fragelin Shisheeye* (foreign intervention) or individual dictators alone is, to paraphrase Ahmed, shouting "wolf" when the predator is not, in fact, "wolf", but one of the sheep.[3] This kind of historiography is, moreover, analogous to "the tale of the African peasant who was stopped by a traveler in a large car and asked the way to the city, who responded after reflecting on the matter a while, 'if I were you, I wouldn't start from here.'[4] Somali historiography, in other words, starts from where the African peasant warned against by concentrating on one or another kind of foreign intervention, or the invention of a single variant nationalism. The point is not to dismiss the effects of colonialism or post-colonial regimes on the traditional structures of the Somali society, or any other colonized people for that matter. However, we suggest that conceptualizing the idea of *Somaliness* in terms of mere interactions between colonial overlords and undifferentiated local masses may not be sufficient cause to have had totally disrupted the supposed Somali traditional tree under which its pleasant shadows all social and legal problems were amicably resolved. It is not, either, to dismiss the recent scholarship that has tried to engage Somali historiography through multiple causal factors, including, but not limited to resource problems (Omar and De Waal 1993; Besteman and Cassanelli 1996) racial and ethnic cleavages (Besteman 1996; Eno 1996; Menkhause 1989), or class-based exploitations (Samatar, 1989; Little 1996).[5] Taken together, these arguments are very instructive in furthering our understanding of the causes and the consequences of the current Somali social faultlines. However, they are very limited in that they do not specify the sociological conditions that may have paved the way for certain groups to expropriate land, exploit, stigmatize, and/or racialize certain segments of the society. In other words, they fail to appropriate the ideological narratives through which the act of land expropriation, racialization, or class cleavages have been legitimized.

One scholarship that has tried to understand Somalia for what it is, and not what it ought to be is that which is articulated in *The Invention of Somalia,* edited by Ali Jimale Ahmed (1995).[6] The chapters in that volume lay out the most credible starting point for what I refer to as the "contradiction between *master and empirical narratives of Somaliness*," and provide a far more delineated understanding of the current crisis in Somalia. The collection of chapters in *The Invention of Somalia,* for example, introduce issues of legitimation and contested identities, and thereby provide fresh ontological and conceptual framework through which contemporary Somali social realities can be understood. The central argument put forth in the *The Invention of Somalia* is that the notion of *Somaliness* and therefore Somali nationalism, like all identities, are socially constructed, and are therefore liable to counter interpretations.

The essays in this volume contribute to that project and suggest that a more meaningful historiography is one that can appreciate the multiple, often contested, and sometimes oppressed voices that exist within the social boundary of the nation. The book is specifically intended to further move Somali historiography beyond the *self-same nation theory* and focus instead on contested identities and conflict of interpretations as a possible framework for understanding the current social and political realities in Somalia. Consequently, the essays in this volume underline the multiple and often contested meanings of *Somaliness,* and collectively attempt to begin to clear the terrain for a new theoretical analysis of Somali society. In the first chapter, Kusow argues that the fundamental problems that inform much the of the social crisis in Africa, and Somalia in particular, result from "contested narratives." By "contested narratives," he means a condition of interpretive conflict between the simultaneous existence of two major paradigms, lineage (national/master) versus territorial (empirical) narratives – of *Somaliness* – that involve relationships among people, place, and the history on which nationalism is predicated. The first paradigm is based on founding myths that have no application to the everyday realities of the people. These myths, nonetheless create: 1) a symbolic and narrative-based processes that privilege certain categories and cultural meanings that delimit the social boundary of *Somaliness* by defining who belongs and who does not, and 2) establishes an invented core cultural center upon which the notion and the boundary of *Somaliness* is drawn. This paradigm constructs the social boundary of *Somaliness* in terms of lineage priorities and on the elevation of regional and localized traditions and, then camouflages them as national symbols and values. The territorial narratives, on the other hand, demarcate the social boundary of *Somaliness* not in terms of lineage, but rather on economic, moral, and territorial priorities. As simple as the territorial narratives may seem, in actuality, they discredit the notion of *the self-same nation* by embracing the existence of multiple voices and the increasing identity assertions of previously suppressed social identities, including but not limited to language, caste, gender, and/or racialized social groups. The contested ways in which the two paradigms organize and structure social relations, and therefore, the social boundary of *Somaliness,* we argue, create what Paul Ricoeur characterized as a *conflict of interpretations*, and result in what Habbermas referred to as *legitimation crisis.*[7]

The remaining chapters of the book are organized into four thematic areas. The first theme is a critical re-reading and re-writing of earlier misrepresentations of Somali history and nationalism. Employing Linguistic approaches to the past, Mohamed Nuuh Ali, reconstructs the social and economic developments of the past three millennia in the Eastern Horn of Africa. His is a more complex picture of Somali historical developments than the pastoral-based oral tradition that has been the stable of Somali historiography since the turn of last century. Cedric Barnes deals with the misrepresentations of the nation and therefore Somali nationalism. Focusing on the *Jigjiga* area, he calls our attention to how earlier scholars have emphasized high politics while overlooking the political and economic circumstances of local populations. By high politics, Barnes refers to the earlier understanding of "the division of the Somalilands either "as the triumph of Ethiopian independence or the betrayal of the hopes for Somali unification and the repartition of the Somali nation by the very same forces of imperialism, which overlooked the political and economic circumstances of the local populations concerned." Barnes provides a solid argument that links Somali nationalism to local economic circumstances.

Hassan Mahaddala's essay contributes further to the overall assertion of this book that there is nothing *Muqads* (holy) about Somali nationalism. Mahadalla critically analyzes the canonical categories of language, Islam, history, and the tradition upon which much of the historiography of Somali nationalism has been articulated, and refers to it as *pithless nationalism* – one with no particular and identifiable foundation, except that which is socially constructed.[8] Had there been an *a priori Somaliness* that transcends other differences, as some would like us to believe, the existence of Djibouti as a nation separate and distinct from the holy union begs for an explanation. What about the so-called Somaliland's bid to secede from the union? Is it based on differences of language, religion, or culture, or the oppressive acts of the Siyad Barre regime on the people of Hargeisa? Alternatively, is it because of differences, British versus Italian, in colonial history? Whatever *Somalilandness* as opposed *to Somaliness* may be based, it sure defies what brother Lewis has been telling us for more than half a century now. Similar arguments can be made about the Somali communities both in Kenya and Ethiopia as exempli-fied by their reaction to Hussein Aideed's 2002 interview with IRIN, in which he implied his desire to unify all the Somali communities under one flag, and to which both communities reacted angrily, and rejected his comment outright. All of these comments attest to the fact that, like all communities and nations, the Somali na-tion is, in some profound sense, to borrow from Benedict Anderson, an "imagined community" and that such an imagination is determined by the prevailing social and economic circumstances and not by any predetermined categories of similari-ties and/or differences.[9] In other words, Somaliland's claim to an identity distinct from the rest of the Somali regions is equally dubious as the claim of the *sui-generis* Somali nation to which the leaders of today's Somaliland have contributed to and played a big role in its concoction.

Mohamed Mukhtar continues the undoing of the *Darwiish* nationalism and colonial resistance by introducing hitherto hidden and ignored accounts of the nationalist resistance movements in southern Somalia. Mukhtar's essay provides a more inclusive picture of the different anti-colonial movements and thus a more global understanding of Somali nationalism and the making of the modern Somali nation. What nationalist historiographers and therefore the equation of Somali nationalism as the result of the *Darwiish* activities cannot explain is the many

xiv

nationalist and anti-colonial resistance movements that have emerged in many parts of the country's modern history, including the 1890–1907 Gosha movement, the *Banadir Resistance Movement* from 1888–1921, and the well-known *Awaysia Movement* led by Sheikh Aweys. In fact, one can argue that the *Darwiish* movement played an insignificant part of the nation's overall social and political history. The majority of social movements, colonial resistance or otherwise, involved in the making of the modern Somali nation occurred outside the *Darwiish* sphere. More importantly, though, the history of modern Somalia dates at least one thousand years before the British colony occupied northern Somalia. Somali societies have interacted with cultures as far away as China and India and have resisted different foreign powers, including the Portuguese, Egyptian, and Omani in the *Banadir* Coast. All of these occurred much earlier than the *Darwiish* movement. Even if the idea of Somali nationalism were understood in terms of European colonial resistance alone, one would have to account for the fact that Somali interaction with European colonialism took place more in relation to the Italian colony than the British occupation of northern Somalia. This is, again, not to dismiss the role of the *Sayyid*, but to reject the elevation of his movement as the only meaningful site for understanding Somali nationalism and colonial resistance.

The next three chapters amplify what we mean by contested social identities and social exclusions. An informative example of what we mean by contested narratives is exemplified in Ladan Affi's chapter title derived from that famous Somali proverb, *Rag Waa Shaah, Dumarna Waa Sheeko* (men drink tea, while women gossip). Here, Ladan shows that despite the fact that this proverb was intended to characterize Somali women as mere circulators of gossip who contributed nothing to the economic and social well-being of the nation; it is men who have contributed nothing but the destruction of the nation. Ladan continues to argue that Somali women have not only been written out of the history of the nation, but that they are now beginning to debunk existing views as they claim the right to be heard, participate, and confront conventional understanding of Somali realities produced by males. In a slightly different way, Rima Berns McGown extends Ladan's argument by examining Somali gender identities and conflicts in the diaspora through what she aptly characterized as transformative Islam. She specifically examines how Somalis in exile have not only become significantly more religious than they had been in their homeland, but in the process, reconstituted new ways of practicing Islam which in turn transformed social relations and interactions between husband and wife as well as children and their parents. One of the most significant implications of this changed environment, according to Berns McGown, is that gender roles have shifted such that women increasingly hold more power than before within households. Such transformations have brought previously taboo issues such as the role of women in the household, premarital and extra marital affairs to the forefront. Accordingly, one of the most significant transformations of the Somali society in the Diaspora is the change of power and status from men to women. According to Berns McGown, it is the women who have been most likely to have found work, support their families, and in many situations, have been at the forefront in the re-imagination of Islam within the family in the now predominantly Judeo-Christian societies in which they find themselves.

Omar Eno's essay, "Landless Landlords and Landed Tenants," represents the first work about slavery in Somalia written by a Somali scholar. It attempts to dispel the contention that the majority of the *Bantu/Jarer* populations of Southern Somalia are slaves imported from East Africa. On the contrary, writes Eno, "oral traditions as well as available archival records indicate that the majority of the *Bantu/Jarer* people occupied their present location as far back as the tenth century." More importantly, though, Eno's essay shows how a significant segment of the Somali population has been reduced to second a class citizen status, and placed outside the social boundary of *Somaliness*.

The next topic pertains to issues of resources and resource misappropriations. Written with a sharp sociological eye, and of course, from first-hand experience based on more than a decade's work on development projects as a civil and hydraulic engineer, Ali provides a sociological analysis of how land misappropriation remains one of the most salient obstacles to achieving a fair and more durable political and social structure. Ali's argument is a clear departure from earlier works that used resources as an important factor in understanding the current Somali crisis in that he marshals a rich data along with an actual experience on the ground. In a similar vein, Arif provides a historical analysis of how monitory systems inherited from the colonial administration and adopted by successive post-colonial Somali regimes coupled with shifting policies and erratic management systems ultimately collapsed the Somali banking system.

Finally, we belief that the relevance of any scholarship, and Somali scholarship not being an exception, requires its students to pursue ideas that earlier generation did not, and perhaps could not imagine for whatever reason(s), and to continuously make it more in touch with the every day realties of the people to which it tries understand. The collection of the essays in this volume, we hope, will make a small contribution towards realizing that goal.

Notes

1. David Laitin and Said Samatar, *Somalia: A Nation in Search of State* (Boulder CO: Westview Press, 1987).
2. The reference here is to the expansionist ambitions of the successive Ethiopian regimes. Ethiopian regimes have as well accused Somalia of similar expansionist tendencies.

What is not acknowledged in these allegations and counter allegations, however, is the suffering of the every day people in both counties.

3. Mohamed Dahir Afrax, "The Mirror of Culture: Somali Dissolution Seen Through Oral Expression," in Ahmed I. Samatar, ed., *The Somali Challenge: Form Catastrophe to Renewal* (Boulder, CO: Lynn Rienner Publishers, 1994).

4. Ali J. Ahmed, *Daybreak is Near: Literature, Clans, and the Nation-State in Somalia* (Lawrenceville, NJ: The Red Sea Press, 1996).

5. Kawame Anthony Appiah, *In My Fathers House: Africa in the Philosophy of Culture* (New York: Oxford University Press, 1992), p. 26.

6. Catherine Bestemen and Lee V. Cassanelli, eds., *The Struggle for Land in Southern Somalia: The War Behind the War* (Boulder: Westview Press, 1996); Peter D. Little "Conflictive Trade, Contested Identity: The Effects of Export Markets on Pastoralists of Southern Somalia" in *African Studies Review* 39, no 1 (1996); Rakiya Omar and Alex de Waal, *Land Tenure, The Creation of Famine, and Prospects for Peace in Somalia* (London: Africa Rights, Discussion paper, no 1, 1993), Abdi I. Samatar, *The State and Rural Transformation in Northern Somalia* (Madison: University of Wisconsin Press, 1989); Omar Eno, *The Historical Roots of the Somali Tragedy and the Vulnerable Minority Groups, particularly the Bantu/Jarer*, Paper presented to the *African Studies Annual Conference*. Orlando, Florida, 1995; Kenneth Menkhause, *Rural Transformations and the Roots of Underdevelopment in Somalia's Lower Jubba Valley*, Ph.D. Diss., University of South Carolina, Columbia, South Carolina, 1989)

7. Ali J. Ahmed, ed., *The Invention of Somalia* (Lawrenceville, NJ: The Red Sea Press, 1995).

8. Paul Ricoeur, *The Conflict of Interpretations: Essays in Hermeneutics* (Evanston: Northwestern University Press, 1974); for a more extensive discussion of *Legitimation Crisis,* see Jurgen Habbermass, *Legitimation Crisis,* Trans. T. McCarthy (Boston: Beacon Press, 1973).

9. Peter Berger and Thomas Luckmann, *The Social Construction of Reality* (New York: Doubleday, 1966).

10. Benedict Anderson, *Imagined Communities: Reflections on the Origins and Spread of Nationalism* (New York: Verso, 1983).

Chapter One

Contested Narratives and The Crisis of the Nation-State in Somalia: A Prolegomenon

Abdi M. Kusow
Oakland University, Rochester, Michigan

THE PURPOSE OF THIS CHAPTER is to a sketch a preliminary outline for a new perspective through which the social structure and the ultimate source of the social conflict in Somalia can be viewed, framed, and analyzed. This perspective starts from the ontological assumption that the fundamental problems that inform much of the social crisis in Africa, and Somalia in particular, result from "contested narratives." By "contested narratives," I mean a condition of a conflict of interpretations between the simultaneous existence of two major paradigms – lineage versus territorial narratives, of *Somaliness,* involving the relationship among people, place, and the history on which nationalism is predicated. The first paradigm is based on state-sponsored idealistic images and founding myths that have no practical application to the everyday realities of the people. This paradigm constructs the social boundary of *Somaliness* on the basis of lineage priorities, or what Ahmed referred to as "imagery reflective of the pastoralist *modus vivendi,*[1] otherwise locally known as *Maandeeq,* and camouflaged as national symbols and values. These priorities and values, as it were, privilege certain cultural meanings that delimit and define who belongs and who does not in the *Maandeeq* social boundary of *Somaliness.* The second paradigm (the territorial narrative) constructs the social boundary of *Somaliness* not on lineage/*Maandeeq* priorities, but rather on economic, moral, and territorial priorities. The contested ways in which the two paradigms (narratives)

organize and structure social relations, and therefore, the social boundary of *Somaliness* create what Habbermas characterized as legitimation crisis.[2] Accordingly, I argue that the current social crisis in Somalia must be seen as a war over contested ideas and social identities, i.e., a conflict of interpretations.[3]

The first part of the chapter examines the assumptions, and therefore the social and political implications of the lineage-based narratives. In this section, I specifically analyze how the lineage narrative permanently excludes certain segments of the society from the social boundary of *Somaliness*, while it simultaneously includes and excludes others. The second part deals with the assumptions of the territorial narrative and how it structures the social boundary of *Somaliness* in ways diametrically opposed to those of the lineage narrative, while the final section provides some concluding remarks. I must point out, however, that the purpose of this essay is not to lend authenticity to either of the paradigms, but to simply delineate the ontological assumptions that inform each narrative and how the two assumptions ultimately confronted each other on the ground leading to the current crisis. As the title indicates, the chapter is decidedly theoretical and the categories used are as simply heuristics, and therefore, must be understood as such. A more detailed analysis of the arguments and categories used in this chapter will appear in a forthcoming project.

Lineage-Based Narratives

The lineage-based narratives follow from the premise that the Somali founding ancestor originated from southern Arabia, settled in the northeastern region of the country, and married a local Somali woman. This union, according to the narrative, started what later became the source of contemporary Somali society, and by extension its national identity.[4] As simple as it may seem, the above narrative establishes two ontological points: (1) an original, Muslim and non-indigenous founding ancestor and, (2) an original dispersal point. The first part of the narrative establishes the Somali ancestor as an immigrant from Southern Arabia who practiced Islamic values, otherwise Arab and Muslim. The second part of the narratives locates the original landing as well as the settlement place of the founding ancestor in the northeastern region of the country. Each dimension of the narrative constructs a social boundary of *Somaliness* that includes certain segments and clans and excludes others from the social boundary of *Somaliness*. For example, the Islamic aspect of the ancestor removes, those (Midgaan, Yibir, to mention only a few) who initially retained pre-Islamic cultural traditions and values and stigmatizes them as less than noble. The implied *Arabness* of the ancestor removes those allegedly accused of having African ancestry. This aspect of the narrative effectively removes the *Bantu/Jarer* Somalis from the social boundary of *Somaliness*. Taken together, the original founding ancestor and the original dispersal point construct a social boundary of *Somaliness* by enacting "a process of simultaneous exclusion and inclusion." Certain groups are explicitly and permanently placed outside this boundary, while others are included, or excluded depending on the prevailing political arrangements and power structures. In what follows, I will discuss the process of exclusion and inclusion through caste, race, and lineage-based categories.

Caste-Based Exclusion

Since the Somali mythical ancestor is narratively considered to have migrated from southern Arabia, and because Islamic values dictated the new moral values of the society, the first task of the narrative was to engage in the violent removal of non-Islamic cultural traces and heritages and those who refused to become part of the social boundary of this new *Somaliness*. According to this narrative, during the arrival of the founding ancestor, there existed in the land a vicious magician king who ruled the country. This king was a ruthless one who terrorized the people, raped women, killed innocent children, and in general exploited the people until the founding Somali ancestor, with the help of Saint *Aw Barkhadle*, caused two mighty hills to close on him. This event created the distinction between the noble and non-noble groups.

The articulation of noble versus non-noble categories is also enacted through another narrative which contends that the ancestors of both the noble and non-noble caste were two biological brothers who, otherwise, differently reacted to the advice of their father regarding the moral conditions under which one can consume un-Islamic slaughtered mead or one from an already dead animal. The narrative reads, before the brothers set out on a long journey, their father advised them that in case they became hungry at any time during the journey, they should eat whatever they find, even if it was the meat of a dead animal. However, the father warned that when they reach their final destination, they should force themselves to vomit in order to cleanse their souls of the negative elements that the non-*halaal* meat may have left behind. As the narrative goes, midway through the journey, the brothers became so hungry that they ate the meat of a dead animal. However, after they reached their final destination, the younger brother followed his father's advice and forced himself to vomit, while the older bother refused to do so. What happened after that is well known: the descendants of the younger brother became the nobles, while those of the older brother became outcasts.

Despite its mythical quality, though, this narrative has been very successful in effectively marginalizing and stigmatizing a significant portion of the Somali society as having an unholy origin. These groups are variously known as *Yibir*, *Midgaan*, or *Tumaal*, and to this day, they remain outside the social boundary of *Somaliness*. Social intercourse of all forms, including marriage, with any member from caste group is quietly discouraged. They are, in essence, considered as socially polluting in ways, not one dissimilar to that of the untouchables in India. Drawing from this narrative, a number of scholars have spent a great deal of energy studying either their speech patterns or their blood type to corroborate the narrative. The most important example of such undertaking is Goldsmith and Lewis's (1958) serological examination to determine whether genetic differences existed between what they categorized as noble versus the caste groups. Goldsmith and Lewis, of course, did not find any differences between the two samples, but insisted that the results were tainted by the small sample size from the caste (53) as opposed to the somewhat larger sample from the nobles (1,000). They implied that had they used a larger sample from the caste group, they would have arrived at a different conclusion. What is more important here, though, is not whether they found any differences between the two samples, but that the research itself was intended to verify pseudo-scientifically the claims of the lineage narrative.[5]

Racialized Exclusions

The other group permanently removed from the *Maandeeq* social boundary of *Somaliness* is the so-called *Bantu/Jarer* Somalis. At one level, the narratives concerning the *Jarer* Somalis did not require such an elaborate narrative system as that of the caste groups because of their supposed African-like physical appearance which allegedly makes them distinguishable from the Somali one, whatever that may mean. They are referred to as *Adoon*, meaning slave, or *Jarer*, meaning "hard textured hair." In other situations, they are referred to as *Gosha* (people of the rain forest), or *Reer Shabelle* (people of Shabelle river). Despite the variations in naming, though, all such references are derogatory in nature because they are, according to the lineage narrative, associated with African-like physical characteristics, slave status, or with primitive and uncivilized mode of existence in the impenetrable tropical rain forests around the *Jubba* and *Shabelle* rivers of southern Somalia. Beyond the alleged physical and location-based stigmatization, though, the *Jarer* people are stigmatized, and in some cases, violently oppressed by the narrative that that they originated from imported slaves from East Africa during the nineteenth century, which further facilitated their social exclusion from the boundary of *Somaliness*.

The idea of racial exclusion is applied to the so-called *Banadiri* groups as well. The *Banadiri* is collectively known as *Gibil Cad* (white skin). According to the lineage narrative, the *Jarer* Somalis are accused of being too African, while the *Banadiri* Somalis are considered too light to be Somali. Moreover, the original homeland of the Jarer is said to have been somewhere in Africa, while that of the Banadiri groups is located somewhere in the Arabian Peninsula, Portugal, or Persia depending on the whim of the narrator. The Jarer and the *Banadiri* Somalis, however, belief that they have lived in Somalia as long as other Somalis did, if not longer. For example, according to Luling, one *Jarer* respondent in Afgoi told her,

"Our ancestors were born here, they did not come here." Moreover, Luling points out that all the basic cultural values of the *Jarer* indicate a long tradition of cultural association with the river rather than a labor force recently imported from outside the country.[6] The implication of the counter narrative, which suggests that the Jarer people are indigenous Somalis, underscores the core of the argument of this paper, which is that the existence of indigenous *Jarer* Somalis in Somalia prior to the Somali arrival is bound to challenge the lineage narrative that strips them of any claim to land holdings in Somalia. The *Jarer*, caste, and the *Banadiri* have now started to organize themselves around their own identities in lines, not one, dissimilar to that of the black power movements among African Americans in the 1960s. More important, these attempts reveal the contested nature of *Somaliness*, or to use Paul Ricour's phrase, the "conflict of interpretations" that exist in Somalia today.[6] It shows the increasing confidence of previously stigmatized groups or individuals who have earlier been forced not to reveal their identities, lest they pollute the social environment. It further attests to the changing political climate and the radically shifting power structures in Somalia today as is reflected by the increasing political assertiveness of hitherto unrecognized groups who, since the Reewing Reistence Army's (RRA) defeat of Aideed's occupation of Baidoa, rediscovered their own political voices. These assertions are starting to redefine the social boundary of *Somaliness* in ways that politician, commentators, and social historians could not have imagined just a decade ago.

The process of simultaneous exclusion and inclusion is not limited to those permanently removed from the social boundary of *Somaliness*, but affects the so-called major clan family groupings too. In what follows, I will discuss how the lineage narratives structure the relationship between and among the so-called major clans. I will then provide examples of how the basic tenets of the lineage narrative are contradicted by the territorial narrative's alternative definition of the social boundary of *Somaliness*. I will then provide some concluding remarks intended to summarize and elevate the preceding comments into a more theoretical level.

Segmentary-Based Exclusion

So far, I have been concerned with how the Islamic and Arabian aspects of the narrative effectively and permanently removed the Caste and the *Bantu/Jarer* groups from the social boundary of *Somaliness*. This process, as I have pointed earlier, is very simple in that the narrative claims that those who retained pre-Islamic cultural values and those accused of having African-like physical features are simply not Somalis and therefore excluded from the social boundary of the nation. The most complicated construction of the social boundary of *Somaliness*, however, pertains to the narrative aspect that attempts to structure the relationship between and among the so-called major Somali clan family groupings through a system of simultaneous exclusion and inclusion. The process of simultaneous inclusion and exclusion is articulated in what I refer to as "the degrees of distance and/or closeness" from the common ancestor or the supposed original dispersal point. The degree of distance or closeness is organized along spatial and a social dimensions. The social dimension refers to the degree to which groups claim direct lineage from the mythical founding ancestor and the degree to which they represent the supposed core cultural values of the *Maadheeq* nation. The genealogical location of a particular clan on the lineage chart determines its position in the social hierarchy, and therefore, its degree of *Somaliness*. The basic premise of the social dimension is that the further away a clan is removed from the founding ancestor genealogically, the lower that clan is located in genealogical hierarchy, and therefore, the lower its social status. Spatially, it refers to the geographic distance a particular clan family is removed from the supposed original landing place of the original ancestor, or dispersal point. The basic premise of the spatial dimension is that the further south a clan family is located, the further away it is from the mythic origins and therefore the lower in the social hierarchy. Several binary opposition categories operate on these dimensions that either include or exclude certain groups from the social boundary of the lineage-based *Somaliness*. Specifically, the state-sponsored official Somali language and literature is a major element through which the lineage narratives enact the degrees of distance and closeness from the social boundary of *Somaliness*. The state- sponsored language and poetry is based mainly on the speech of those that claim to have descended from the original ancestor and dispersal point. The further south one moves, according to the lineage narrative, the less likely the language is thought to embody any mystical or aesthetic values. It is also from this alleged core cultural area that provided, according to the narrative, what Saadia Touval referred to as "The Heroes of Somali Nationalism." According to Touval, the two most important figures of Somali nationalism, Imam Ahmed Ibn Ibrahim al Ghazi and Sayyid Mohamed Abdulle Hassan, came from the region of the lineage narrative.[7] Another category pertains to the degree to which a particular clan is considered as nomadic. According to the narrative, Camel herding is the most dignified mode of production, and the degree of *Somaliness* is gauged through it. All other modes of production, from fishing to agriculture, are by comparison, despised. More important, the notion of pastoral nomadism versus all other modes of production has been one of the most important principles of social differentiation in Somalia. It cuts across all regions and segments of the society from the nation to the clan and sub-clan. Whether one observes Baidoa or Bossaso, one quickly learns that pastoralism is more valued than other modes of production. However, as we will see later, this way of understanding *Somaliness* is facing another and equally powerful counter-narrative – that of territorial priorities.

Perhaps the most important category through which the lineage narrative attempted to define and delimit the social boundary of *Somaliness* pertains to the way the Somali lineage chart is presented. Unlike those who, as I have mentioned earlier, are totally excluded from the social boundary of *Somaliness*, the lineage narrative structures social relations among the so-called Somali clan family groupings by designating certain clans as direct descendents, and therefore, more Somali than others. The degree of *Somaliness* is determined by how far lineage-wise a particular clan group is away from the original ancestor, which, when combined with spatial distance, that is – how far geographically a particular clan is away from the narrated original dispersal point, creates what I refer to as a "Segmentary Lineage Stratification System" or "simultaneous exclusion and inclusion." For example, in the port city of Kismanyo, the lineage narrative divides the entire population of the city and its surroundings into two oppositional categories – Harti and the Giir-Giir. The lineage narrative defines the term Giir-Giir as having multiple stripes/identities and denotes a lack of specifically identifiable and valued social identity or direct lineage to the original ancestor, and the Harti, as the direct descendents of the original ancestor.

The distinction between direct and indirect connection to the *Maandeeq* original ancestor is based on the premise that only those affiliated with the *Maandheeq* nation are the direct descendents of the original ancestor. The rest, according to the lineage narrative, consist of clan groupings that do not claim direct *Abtirsi* to the original ancestral line, but sometimes contain small groups (sub-clans) who may have diverged from the original lineage and dispersal point and later intermarried with and adopted the cultural patterns of the indigenous groups that preceded them in the area. The narrative suggests that these small immigrant groups later served as the elite segments within those clans, and still maintain contact with their original source and serve as middleman groups between the Northern and Southern clans. This is what allowed the lineage narrative to claim that certain sub-clans within the Hawiye and Digil and Mirifle are Darood by original lineage. This process is known in Baidoa as *Geeki Mariidi* (in the old days). The phrase, according to the *Reewing*-speaking Somalis, underscores an elaborate system that attempts to portray their clan structures as simply resulting from the amalgamation of individuals and groups that originally resulted from the great Somali North-South migration. The *Rewing*, according to the lineage narrative, migrated from the north, settled in the interriverine regions, adopted the social and economic patterns of the indigenous populations they encountered, and finally assimilated them into their clan systems and developed a unique sense of clan identity. In order to proof this, the lineage narrative translated the name *Rewing* into *Rahanwayn* which, according this narrative, means a large and diverse congregation, or a place with abundance in land and pasture.[8] That is why, according to the lineage narrative, the area attracted many groups and individuals from different clan families who later formed what has become known as the *Rahanwayne* confederation organized along territorial-based kinship systems, instead of the traditional Somali lineage-based systems which is supposedly common among other clan groups.

The narrative claim that certain sub-clans within the larger Somali clans diverged from the original dispersal point is also applied to a number of Hawiye, Banadiri, as well as Jarer sub-clans. At the center of this process is an elaborate system, though now defunct, that attempted to impose the cultural values, symbols, mode of production, and speech patterns of certain segments of the society on the entire Somali population in a descending order starting from the supposed original settlement of the original ancestor. Almost all the social and historical events as well as notable events and figures of the nation are said to have either originated or taken place in certain regions of the country. This assimilative process is, in many ways, made possible by the fact that the sponsors of the lineage-based narratives directly or indirectly controlled most of the post-colonial Somali political structures. More important, such processes are not limited to a particular clan or situation, but is part of a larger phenomenon common among larger clan groups as a way of enhancing their political power through what Somali describe as *Toleyn* (to be incorporated into a particular clan). Regardless of "who claims whom," however, the general pattern is that the more southerly a particular clan is spatially located, the more likely they are claimed by a northern cousin clan. Those who are claimed are seen as having no meaningful lineage structure of their own, and are therefore, implicitly accused of being outside the boundary of the lineage-based *Somaliness*.

Territorial-Based Narratives
The territorial narrative, on the other hand, constructs the social boundary of *Somaliness* in terms of social, economic, and territorial priorities and values. Social values, according to the territorial narrative, functions along several dimensions, the most important of which, is the degree of anarchy displayed by a particular clan or found in a particular regional setting. The degree of anarchy is determined in terms of South-North and the central assumption is that the further north one observes, the more it becomes clear that the rules of social, political, and individual engagements is determined by urban nomadism. Urban nomadism, according to the territorial narrative, is a condition in which the idea of nobility and proper social values is measured by the tip of the gun; or through what Richard Burton unfortunately referred to as "Turbulent Republicanism," and sadly embraced by Somalis as a sign of nobility. On the other hand, the further south one observes, according to the territorial narrative, the more the rules of social relations are dictated by peacefulness and respect for social authority and communal collaboration.

The turbulent republicanism of the lineage narrative, according to the territorial narrative, is revealed by a dialogue that supposedly occurred between the late

Mohamed Rajis, a well known Somali lawyer, and a certain warlord at one of the more than the dozen Somali reconciliation conferences held over the past decade. One of the warlords informed Rajis, during one of those meetings, that since his clan did not have an armed militia, he had no right to be in their company, let alone be part of the power-sharing discussions. Rajis responded, according to the narrative: "if this were the only criterion for one's inclusion in the social boundary of *Somaliness*, and the right to take part in the reconciliation conference, then, I will go back to Somalia, kill few innocent people and come back, at which point, he said, I am sure you will accept me as a true member of the community." The conflict of interpretations between the two paradigms is also revealed in the well-known Somali folk story of a nomad burglar and an urban dweller in Mogadishu. The nomad burglar went to the house of a family in Hamar-Wayne in the middle of the night to steal a cow. While the burglar was untying the cow, the wife of the owner saw him through the window and informed her husband of the unfolding event, to which the owner replied, it is OK, don't worry, he will bring it to the market tomorrow, and there I will buy it from him. To the eyes of the lineage narrative, these stories are part of a national comedy circulated through and shared in the local tea houses and *chat* chewing sessions, and are intended to characterize the reaction of the owner of the cow, and by extension, those who do not follow a *Maandheeq* mode of production, as cowards and morally weak.

The territorial narrative, however, interprets the above dialogue or the encounter between the burglar and the owner of the cow from a different ontological framework. The territorial narrative asserts that it is, in fact, the burglar and the warlord in the Rajis narrative, and by extension, the moral foundation of the lineage narrative that suffers from lack of cultural sophistication and issues of civil morality. The following narrative related to me by a colleague who interviewed a number of *Bantu/Jarer* Somalis from Afgoe illustrates the point as the following: A certain prominent *Bantu/Jarer* in Afgoe who, after the human atrocities committed by one of the militia occupying the city, attempted to organize an armed group to stop the atrocities. Before he was able to mobilize his militia, however, a word about his intentions was leaked to the *Bantu/Jarer* religious and traditional leaders. The leaders, according to the narrative, warned him not to follow up with his activities and informed him that it was not their custom to take part in activities that may result in the lose of human lives, no matter how much injustice will be exacted on them.[8]

Beyond the moral priorities, though, the territorial narrative constructs the social boundary of *Somaliness* on territorial priorities. Here, the territorial narratives shift the social category of understanding from lineage to a territorial priority. It constructs the process of exclusion and inclusion based on who owns what ancestral land, where, and how. The process of exclusion and inclusion employed by the territorial narratives, unlike that of the lineage narrative, is determined through the degree to which a particular clan owns a collectively acknowledged and clan delimited ancestral homeland. The assumptions of the territorial narrative are as old as the lineage-based narrative. One can, in fact, make the argument that the 1969 military coup was not about saving the nation, but rather, a result of Siyad Barre's reading of the writing of the territorial narratives on the wall. This is what led Siyad Barre to reorganize the regional map of the nation by subdividing certain regions and adding more, in order to make sure that the motives of the territorial narrative were never realized. Since the civil war, however, the moral assumptions of the territorial narrative have gained an almost national folk status. The question of who owns what, where, and how, is based on the distinction between what is locally known as *Mudnaan iyo Asal* (originality and priority to ownership of the land) versus *Xuraysato* (takers of the land by force).[9] The underlying assumption behind this distinction is the perceived existence of true owners of land versus newcomers who have taken the land by force. In fact, the question of who owns Kismanyo, Baiadoa, Mogadishu, Beled-wayne, Jowhar, and Hargeisa, are now part of contemporary vernacular and are analyzed in coffee houses in Nairobi, Toronto, Mogadishu, as well as in Somali Internet Forums, in the same intensity. The following forum discussion in Jowhar.com represents one of the typical assumptions that inform the basic assertions of the territorial priority narrative. Here, one forum participant asks: "Who owns Jowhar originally, who is the largest clan statistically? Who is the group that is culturally and collectively recognized as the original owner of the city? I do not mean *Cida Xuraysatey* (those who took it by force)."[10] Similar discussions involving who owns Belet-Wayne, Hargeisa, Kismanyo, Gedo, Mogadishu or Baidoa are carried in the Puntland, Arlaadi, Ruunkiinet, and Somalitalk forums. Thus, the multiple and contested ways of defining the social boundary of *Somaliness* and the fact that neither the *Maandeeq* nor the territorial narratives embodied the necessary infrastructure to impose a durable hegemonic domination on the other led to what Paul Ricour referred to as a conflict of interpretations.

Conclusion

The purpose of this essay is to further move Somali scholarship beyond the *self-same nation theory* and introduce the notion of *contested identities* as a possible framework for understanding the current social and political realities on the ground. I argue that the social structure of the Somali society has historically contained two oppositional narratives; a mythical-based state supported lineage-based narrative and an equally powerful territorial narrative. The lineage narrative operates from the premise that the Somali society is essentially homogeneous and fundamentally egalitarian society. However, it implicitly creates a process that privileges certain categories and cultural meanings that delimit the boundary of *Somaliness* by defining who belongs and who does not and who is privileged and who is not by establishing a core cultural center upon which the notion and the boundary of *Somaliness* is measured.

The territorial narrative, on the other hand, constructs the social boundary of *Somaliness* neither on genealogy nor on the existence of a cultural core, but rather on social, moral, and territorial priorities. It assumes that the Somali society is homogeneous on an abstract idealized level, but in its everyday reality, consists of different groups with different social values and modes of production. As simple as it may seem, this narrative discredits the notion of the a priori nation by acknowledging the existence of previously oppressed social identities, including but not limited to language, caste, and/or racialized social identities. In other words, those suppressed groups are no longer accepting their fate. Another reason for the crisis is that the idea of segmentation has been totally misconstrued in that both the state and Somali scholars have portrayed lineage segmentation as essentially egalitarian, while in reality it embodies an explicit social hierarchy. In short, clan differentiation in Somalia takes the form of social stratification. These clan-based hierarchies produce similar stratification arrangements as that found in racial and ethnic societies. In other words, it determines who gets what, when, and where. The current Somali civil war must, therefore, be seen as a contradiction between the territorial and state-supported lineage-narrative culture.

Such theorizing may be unsettling to some of our Somali and *Somalist* colleagues who have spent the better part of their academic careers engaged in what I would call *a revive and rescue mission* intended to recreate a supposedly glorious and *self-same* Somali past, rather than a more objective historiography. It might as well make the everyday Somali who has been led into the false conscious belief that if s/he acknowledges the existence of multiple as well as oppressed voices, the nation will collapse. The simple answer is to say that the nation has already collapsed. My point, however, is that the existence of multiple voices is not necessarily a threat to national cohesiveness, and the best way to ensure a long lasting political and social stability is to embrace both the nation and its fragments at the same time and in the same degree. The key criterion that determines whether or not a society can flourish as a nation depends on the degree to which individuals and groups are included in the social, political, and economic boundaries of the nation. Once all individuals and groups are included their likelihood of feeling and acting as participants in the making of the nation increases, and that will in turn, increase the social and political stability of the nation.

A note on the relationship between scholarship and those who produce it is in order here. What I have in mind, of course, is the academic as well as the everyday Somali habit of interpreting scholarship, not on the merit of the words on the pages they read, but rather on the social characteristics of the author. I remember some time ago, at the *1994 African Studies Conference* in Toronto, Canada, a prominent scholar who specializes in Somali affairs (Professor Z) asked me, after learning that a group of Somali scholars were holding an academic conference intended to critically challenge the *self-same* Somali historiography, whether I was one of that group, to which I responded in the affirmative. Scholars Z reflected on my response for a moment and said, well, are you from the South, to which, I again said yes, and explained that I was specifically born in Baidoa. The scholar again thought for a moment and said, "I understand." To this scholar, my biography simply explained the reason why I was part of that group. Of course, this kind of thinking is not limited to this particular individual, but rather is a well-known phenomenon in which Somali scholars as well as lay individuals try to locate the geographical and social origins of the author before evaluating their work on the merit of its contents.

To be fair, this problem is not just a Somali one, but rather, part of a general academic dilemma pertaining to value positions. As Howard Becker expresses it "To have values or not to have values: the question is always with us." Implicit in Becker statement is whether or not value-free scholarship is ever possible. Becker argues that since social scientists are frequently part of the social worlds of the people they study, and it is impossible to do "research that is un-contaminated by personal and political sympathies; [therefore the real] question is not whether we should take sides, since we inevitably will, but rather whose side are we on."[11] The idea of clarifying whose side are we on is critical in doing research in a socially charged country like Somalia where political arrangements are being re-worked as we speak, and different groups openly present conflicting views of who has the right to define the social boundary of *Somaliness*. In such an environment, clearly, those who write about it are also, rightly or wrongly, implicated in the process and therefore are obligated to clarify their ontological positions.

For the purpose of this chapter, and in the spirit of saving Professor Z from the arduous task of figuring, once again, the ontological biases of this particular scholar, I like to tell her/him whose side I am on. I am on the side of adding voice to the history of hitherto unappreciated experiences and contributions of what I will call *Loo-ma-oyayaasha*. The concept *Loo-ma-oyayaasha* literally means "those for whom no one sheds tears over their death and destruction or to whom no one gives credit to their contributions in the making of the nation." It originated as a local phrase to capture the experiences of those known as the un-armed groups during the height of the Somali civil war. More generally, though, it encompasses those who are not included in the *Mandeeq-based* social boundary of *Somaliness*. It captures the experiences of rural and urban peasants, the poor, women, the stigmatized and the genealogically unaffiliated folks. This is not to suggest, however, that *Loo-ma-oyayaasha*, as a concept, is intended to capture another seamless homogeneous entity. In fact, I would like to suggest that it also contains multiple and contested voices such that the questions we ask in the future are not about, for example, how Somali women, peasants, and the poor have been written out of the history of nation, but which Somali women, or peasant groups are written out. In other words, I am also on the side of critically analyzing all aspects of the Somali people such that my only preconceived notion is that social arrangements are not necessarily what they seem to be on the surface. I realize this endeavor is not an easy task and requires scholars to adopt a new methodological looking-glass, so to speak, and to find information from multiple sources and analyze data more critically by examining what the nation is, instead of what it ought to be.

Notes

1. Ali J. Ahmed, DayBreak is Near...Literature, Clans, and the Nation-State in Somalia (Lawrenceville, NJ: The Red Sea Press, 1996)

2. Jurgen, Habbermass, *Legitimation Crisis*, Trans. T McCarthy (Boston: Beacon Press, 1973)

3. Paul Ricoeur, *The Conflict of Interpretations: Essays in Hermeneutics* (Evanston: Northwestern University Press, 1974).

4. The original assumptions behind the contemporary Somali origin Narratives can be traced back to the pre-Islamic religions of the Cushitic-speaking peoples of the Horn of Africa. These religions were organized around ancestors endowed with supernatural powers, and who allegedly descended from the sky. These supernatural entities were widely known in the region as *Waaq* (Sky God) and variously found on certain trees by locals who later encouraged them come down by offering them gift mainly young women for marriage. The coupling of the Sky God and the local women were probably used to provide answers to question and uncertainties about the origin of human beings. However, with the introduction of Islam, and particularly in the case of Somalis, the central plot of the pre-Islamic narratives-the Sky God and the tree were replaced with Southern Arabia as the original home of Islam, and the original birthplace of the Somali ancestor as well. For a discussion of these narratives, see Abdalla Mansur, "The Nature of the Somali Clan System," in Ali Jimale Ahmed, ed., *The Invention of Somalia* (Trenton, New Jersey: The Red Sea Press, 1995); See also Abdi M. Kusow, "The Somali Origin: Myth or Reality," in Ali Jimale Ahmed, ed., *The Invention of Somalia* (Trenton, New Jersey: The Red Sea Press, 1995), 81–99; and Viginia Luling, "The Man in the Tree: A Note on Somali Myth," *Proceedings of the 3rd Somali Studies Congress*, Rome, Italy, 1986

5. Goldsmith, K. and Lewis I.M. "A Preliminary Investigation of the Blood Groups of the 'Sab' Bondsmen of Northern Somalia", *Man* VIII (1958): 188–190.

6. Luling, Virginia, *Somali Sultanate: The Geledi City-State over 150 Years* (London: HAAN, 2002); Luling, Virginia. (n.d). "The Origins of the 'Bantu' People of the Shabelle: The Implications of Some Rituals." Unpublished Manuscript.

7. Paul Ricoeur, The Conflict of Interpretations: Essays in Hermeneutics

8. Touval, Saadia, Somali Nationalism: International Politics and the Drive for Unity in the *Horn of Africa* (Cambridge: Harvard University Press, 1964).

9. Personal Communication with Omar Eno, 2003.

10. Anonymous, RE: Magalada Jawhar Yaa Isla leh, June 1, 2003. Baravanet Forum, Retrieved on July 31, 2003, http://pub13.bravanet.com/forum/fetch.php?usernum=10781 18870&msgid=14327$mode/

11. Becker, Howard, "Whose Side are We?" *Social Problems* 14:239–247.

Chapter Two

Somali History: Linguistic Approaches To The Past

Mohamed Nuuh Ali

THE EASTERN HORN, running from the east side of the Ethiopian Rift to the Indian Ocean and the Gulf of Aden, is a vast region of varied climate, soils and terrain. The western edges are highlands, once forested, with sufficient rainfall for agriculture in all its forms. Much of the east is low and dry country. This eastern area has two major divisions: the Northern Horn (northern Somalia and Jabuuti) in which the higher terrain runs east-west, has a general elevation of less than 500 meters above sea level, except certain northwestern areas which reach up to 2,000 meters. Rainfall is higher in those northwestern parts, from 400 to 800mm a year. There are extremely arid sub regions in the north: the Bari and Nugaal (northeast) regions of Somalia receive 50 to 100mm of rainfall a year. By contrast, Muddug, in the middle of the Eastern Horn, gets about 200mm a year. The southern-most region between the rivers gets 600mm a year. There, the soils vary from sandy and infertile to black and quite fertile. Further inland, between the highlands to the west and the southern agricultural regions lays another belt of dry lands, receiving less than 400mm of rain.

This variety of terrain, climates and soils prompted different human adaptations among cultivators, pastoralists and hunter-gatherers. These adaptations in turn spurred complex social and economic interactions among the region's societies. But up until now historical studies of the Eastern Horn have tended to focus on recent centuries, and on geographically more limited perspectives than that of the whole region. This project will seek to reconstruct the broad outlines of social and economic developments of the past three millennia in the varied world of the Eastern Horn.

The primary source will be linguistic evidence drawn from different varieties of Soomaali now spoken through most of that region. These data will be used, first to reconstruct the internal relationships of the Soomaali language groups and from this to infer the patterns of social divergence and movement of people; secondly, to reconstruct the vocabulary of culture and economy at the different stages of history as revealed by the previous exercise; and thirdly to infer interactions among societies from the patterns of word-borrowing. The later stages of this social and economic history will overlap in to the eras when there are other sources of evidence, especially the oral, or where available, written sources.

Background

The most extensive treatment today of Soomaali historiography has been undertaken by anthropologists (Cerulli, 1931; I.M. Lewis, 1960, 1979). Their work has been founded largely upon two types of sources, viz. oral traditions and Arabic documents. H. Lewis (1966) and Turton (1975) have shown that I.M. Lewis (1960) and Cerulli (1931) relied upon oral tradition from a restricted area of the Soomaali nation, so that their work overemphasized the participation of Arabs and the role of the Oromo in the emergence of Soomaali nationality. Not only was the oral tradition collected by these two unfortunately limited to the extreme northwest and extreme east of the Soomalli-speaking world, where the presence of Arabs has been more marked than in other Soomaali areas, but neither Cerulli nor I.M. Lewis distinguished between strata in the traditions they did use.

H. Lewis and Turton also recognize the inadequacy of these two types of sources when used alone for the reconstruction of Soomaali pre-colonial history. It is possible to improve upon the anthropologists' work and to carry the story much further back in time by distinguishing and historically analyzing, as they have not, the genetic (Cushitic) and borrowed elements of the Soomaali language. The use of this kind of evidence becomes possible when linguistic methods are the primary research tool.

Early Documentary Sources

The history of the Soomaali speaking peoples has commonly been seen as a history of contacts between Africa and the Arabian Peninsula. And this effect is largely the result of the nature of the sources (Arab documents, oral traditions) upon which Soomaali historiography, as spearheaded by I.M. Lewis (1960) and E. Cerulli (1957–1959), has so far focused on events that took place during roughly the past thousand years, while tending to neglect historical events prior to those contacts. One is that this period is accessible to the historian, since there are some written accounts, stemming mostly from Arab travelers and Ethiopian records. The other is the nature of Soomaali traditions collected.

Historical writing on the Eastern Horn, both in the earlier colonial period and since independence in 1960, has been dominated by political concerns. Colonial historians directed their attention to historical processes of expansion, occupation, and conflict – processes which affected orderly administration and the stabilization of frontiers. Research directed to such ends was not without scholarly merit. Oral traditions and ethnographic information gathered by these early colonial historians have provided modern historians with many fruitful insights into Soomaali culture and society. However, most colonial researchers were not historians by training, and their work could not be expected to deal systematically with historical problems that lay manifestly beyond the scope of colonial administration and development.

While the causes and nature of Soomaali pastoral movements are important themes in Soomaali history, attempts to document them do not tell us very much about how Soomaalis adapted to the various environments they came to inhabit. Linguistic research over the past quarter century has disproved the idea that Soomaalis originated in the northern regions of the Horn and have been expanding southward ever since. It is now widely accepted that the earliest Soomalli speakers lived in what is today southeastern Ethiopia and that subsequent migrations have taken groups of them both north and south at different points in the past. Despite what this suggests about the long-term presences of Soomaali communities in the Horn, there is still a tendency to emphasize the expansionary movement of the Soomaali population as a whole, at the expense of the less dramatic processes of social and economic change that took place within the various regions of the peninsula. Colonial historiography, preoccupied with frontiers of expansion, has produced a somewhat one-dimensional image of early Soomaali history. The regional diversity of the Horn suggests that it is time to look at patterns of change over more circumscribed areas and to supplement migration studies with greater attention to social and economic history, ethnogenesis and ecological adaptation.

The first clear written reference to the Soomaalie speaking people is found in the writing of the thirteenth century geographer Ibn-Said which says that Merka, which consisted of more than fifty villages, was the capital of one of the Soomaali ethnic groups. The next references to the Soomaali-speaking peoples are contained in a song of King Yeshaq of Abbyssinia, who reigned from 1414 to 1429. In this song the name Soomaali is first recorded. It thus places Soomaalis quite far north and as resisters of Abyssinian expansion during this period, if not earlier.

A third early document containing recognizable referent to Soomaaali groups is an Arabic chronicle dealing with the Jihad wars of Axmed Gurey against the Abyssinian imperialism. The Soomaali groups mentioned in the Futuh-al-Habasha are generally ones, which still inhabit northwestern Somalia. The evidence of this work written between 1540 and 1550 is therefore a good indication that the composition of the Soomaali population of northwest Somalia has not changed significantly since then. Again this datum accords with the linguistic evidence placing the northern Soomaali settlement before the fifteenth century. But what should be noted here is that the Arabs were not until very recently aware of the differences between the Ethiopic and the Cushitic-speaking peoples in Northeast Africa. The fragmentary, general descriptions of the documents cannot tell anything about the early history of the Soomaali speaking peoples, and they do not lead either to or away from the hypotheses of major population movements. They only give an impression of the stability in the Horn of African in both the ways of life and the occupations of certain Soomaali communities.

Oral Traditions

By utilizing the earlier documents as secondary sources and the oral traditions are primary sources, some scholars, particularly Cerulli and I.M. Lewis, have supposed that the Soomaali speaking peoples originated in the northern part of their present areas and have been spreading south at the expense of Oromo, whom they presumed were the first Cushitic speaking occupants of the Horn. These Oromo who moved south were thought in their turn to have dislodged Bantu-speaking peoples from the Webi Shebeelle area.

Until the mid-1960s, it was commonly thought that the pre-Soomaali cultivating peoples of the Jubba-Shebeelle region were speakers of Bantu languages like those who have long inhabited much of Kenya and Tanzania to the south. So far archaeology and linguistics have no actual evidence of a Bantu settlement along the banks of Jubba and Shebeelle (Turton, 1975), even though there are Swahili speaking communities in Baraawa and the Bajuuni Islands along the coast. The survival of those two societies up to now can perhaps be explained by their fishing occupation, which filled, an ecological gap, since the other surrounding Soomaali-speaking communities were not competing with them. There are also Swahili and Zigula speaking people in the Jubba River farming areas but they seem to have settled more recently, perhaps during the eighteenth and nineteenth centuries (Turton, 1975).

Those scholars who have accepted traditional history as a framework for the actual history of the Soomaali and supported or modified it by reference to documentary and other evidence of varying reliability acknowledge, as do many educated Soomaali, that many of the traditional references to Arab ancestry will not stand careful scrutiny and are probably a function of the desire of the deeply Islamic Soomaali to link themselves to the people of the Prophet. Those who question the basic framework acknowledge that there has been substantial Arab influence and even, on occasion, and infusion of Arab blood. They do, however, question whether the point of origin of the Soomaali was in the north, as even the modified version of traditional history implies, and they have queried the pre-Soomaali presence of the Oromo in much of present day Somalia. This reconstruction described migrations throughout the Horn of Africa in terms of shunting movements in which pressure always come from the north. The oral traditions of the Soomaali pastoralists seemed to corroborate and indeed add detail to this reconstruction.

Recent Views

On the basis of linguistic evidence supported by a critical reading of documentary sources, anthropologist Herbert S. Lewis (after Fleming, 1964) argued in the mid-1960s that the point of origin of the speakers of the Eastern Cushitic languages, of which Soomaali is one and Oromo another, lay in southern Ethiopia and northern Kenya. Lewis suggested further that the Soomaali began their expansion to the north and east substantially before the Oromo and that there were Soomaali groups in southern Somalia as early as the twelfth century, three to four centuries before there is any clear record of Oromo presence in the area. In this he has since been supported by the work of E.R. Turton. In Lewis' view Soomaali groups preceded the Oromo in the north; sections of the Oromo moved, respectively, north and east beginning in the fifteenth and sixteenth centuries. According to H.S. Lewis, early written sources suggest a picture that is entirely compatible with population stability and the hypothesis that the Soomaali were already established in much of their present-day territory several centuries before the first recorded use of the name in the fifteenth century. Lewis also argues that the Soomaali traditions concerning their origins are suspect: first, because of the great time depth involved; secondly, because their claim that they came from the north can be seen as a necessary accompaniment to their rationalization of descent from Arabian migrations. Moreover, a close inspection of Soomaali traditions of clashes with the Oromo reveals a more confused picture than might at first be expected. Most of these traditions are to be found among Soomaali communities that are known to have experienced constant contact with the Oromo for nearly 300 years, during which time there were innumerable disputes over the control of grazing territories and water.

The ultimate origins of the Soomaali and their earliest movements were still matters of scholarly dispute in the mid-1970s, as were the characteristics of the peoples who preceded them in the areas that they occupied and who were absorbed into the Soomaali-speaking societies.

Soomaali Language Classification

To study such early periods of Soomaali history, there are essentially two academic disciplines: archaeology and historical linguistics. As yet there is no archaeological evidence available for this project, though there are indications in rock art, Stone

Age implements and possibly in rock shelters, which seem to indicate the potential for archaeological research. In the absence of much archaeological data as yet, linguistic evidence will be employed here to reconstruct the early history of the Soomaali speakers. The ideal correlation of the two kinds of evidence must wait for future research.

The first step is to establish the genetic relationships of the languages of the region whose history one wants to study. Since genetic relation among languages implies a common source language spoken in a single (though possible socially or economically plural) speech community, understanding the distribution of genetically related languages is a major step in tracing the patterns of dispersion of that original community and beginning to search for the factors which might have led to the diffusion of their language among other peoples. Historical linguistics has been shown to be an effective tool at the disposal of the culture historian, but until recently researchers in Northeaster Africa have failed to take advantage of this. Through the use of the principles of historical linguistics, and especially of migration and dispersal theory as developed and used by Sapir (1916) and others, and as applied by Fleming (1964), Bender (1971), Ehret (1974, 1976), Sasse (1975) and Heine (1978) to the Horn, it is possible to derive from linguistic data hypotheses as to the centers of origin and dispersal of speech communities and the directions of population movements and ethnic expansions. As will be demonstrated here, some application of this type of evidence has already been made in work that has transformed the historical picture of the Horn.

The Soomaali language belongs to the Afroasiatic family. Within this family, Soomaali is a member of the Cushitic subfamily whose original homeland must be sought on the Ethiopian Highlands (Ehret, 1976:93). Along with Afar-Saho and Oromo, among others, Soomaali is derived from the lowland sub branch of the Eastern branch of Cushitic. Within Lowland Eastern Cushitic, Soomaali forms one division of a sub branch called Omo-Tana. Hans Juergen Sasses summarizes the early history of the Omo-Tana group thus:

> "The presence of Somali-like languages so far away from the homeland of the Somali people clearly demonstrates that the ancestors of the Somali speaking tribes (communities) once occupied a territory far more to the southwest than modern Somalia. Indeed the present location of Rendille and Baiso suggests that proto-Somali speakers formerly inhabited a broad belt stretching from the eastern shore of Lake Rudolf on the west along the present state border of Kenya to the Juba and Tana regions on the east and extending northwards into southern Ethiopia. In a word, it seemed that a Somaloid community was superceded by the intrusion of Borana Gallas (Oromo) and other ethnic groups…" (Sasses, 1975:1)

This conclusion was first suggested by Harold Fleming (1964:35–92), who called Soomaali and its closely related languages "macro-Somali," and later by Bender (1971), who called the group "Somaloid." It contradicts earlier views according to which the Soomaali people originated in the northern part of their present territory.

The geographical distribution of the present day spoken languages requires indeed that the ancestral home land of the Omo-Tana speaking people has to be located in the boundary areas of Ethiopia, Kenya and Somalia, Since all Omo-Tana languages, with the exception of Soomaali II (or Sam) languages (see below), are spoken between Lake Abaya and Lake Turkana, it must be argued that the homeland of the Omo-Tana speaking people was in roughly this area. As the present distribution of the network of historical relationships among the East Cushitic languages suggests, it is perhaps also around this general areas that the origin of the earlier proto-Lowland Eastern Cushitic population, and probably the still earlier proto-Eastern Cushitic speaking community, has to be placed.

The early Western Omo-Tana apparently arose in the areas between Lake Stefani and Lake Turkana. Two of the communities of this grouping, the Arbore, expanded south about a thousand years ago, following the eastern shore of Lake Turkana up to its southern end, and among the societies they encountered and interacted with, was a group of fishing peoples living along the lake who took up their language, called today Elmolo. In more recent times there has been a spread of Rendille and Sambuur from the east and south respectively, and these groups absorbed the presumed pastoral ancient Elmolo community. The only Elmolo left still speaking the language in this century were a group of probably subordinate fishing communities along the lake itself.

Soomaali languages and dialects, which form the eastern branch of Omo-Tana (following Ehret and Ali, 1983), are by far the more widely spoken Omo-Tana group. The total number of Soomaali speakers exceeds six million. Most of them live in the Republic of Somalia, where Soomaali is the national and official language. Other areas inhabited by Soomaali speakers are the Republic of Jabuuti, western Somalia, and the Northwestern Province as well as the Tana area of Kenya.

The Soomaali dialect classification followed here is that of Ehret and Ali (1984), which is based on three linguistic criteria. A first set of criteria came from cognate counting of the core vocabulary of 100 words, including such items as numbers and parts of the body generally deemed by linguists to be especially resistant to change and borrowing, taken from 40 Soomaali languages and dialects. Using this list, a lexicostatistical comparison was undertaken of each member language or dialect to all others in order to calculate how many words they share in common, as a percentage measure of how closely related they are to one another. Secondly, and more conclusively, sound change histories and patterns of lexical innovation were examined to corroborate, refine and revise the internal branching within Soomaali arrived at from the cognation patterns. The genetic sub classification of the Soomaali languages and dialects was constructed by gathering the most closely related subgroups into larger subgroups, and so on until the following family tree was reconstructed.

Evidence of word borrowing between two languages can be used to posit historical interaction between the speakers of the two languages, since borrowing normally occurs when people speaking two languages interact directly with one another. The Soomaali languages and dialects have a number of different sets of loanwords, indicating that their speakers have interacted with different peoples at different times. By identifying these sets and arranging them sequentially when possible, one can reconstruct these patterns of historical interaction. Defining the time periods in which loan words are incorporated into a particular dialect yields significant information concerning the history and context of physical interaction and absorption of ideas and technologies.

The tree diagram shows the various stages of Soomaali language history. Thus Soomaali-I is the branch of Omo-Tana containing Bayso and Jiiddu as one sub branch and what Heine (1978) called Sam as the second sub branch; Soomaali-II is Heine's Sam, composed of Rendille as one sub branch and Soomaali-III as the second sub branch. Soomaali-III contains the remainder of the Soomaali languages and dialects, such as Garree-Aweer, Tunni, Baardheere, and Soomaali-IV, the later itself dividing into Maay and Banaadir-Northern subgroups.

In its earliest stage, the proto-Soomaali language differentiated into two major branches: Bayso-Jiiddu and Somaali-II. The cognation percentages of this split, leaving aside contact-affected scores, focus on the low to mid 40s. In the second stages, Soomaal-II diverged into Rendille and Soomalli-III, a division marked by cognation percentages on the low to mid-50s, similar in range to the breakup of Bayso-Jiiddu at 54%. In the third stage of development, Soomaali-III divided into (A) Garree-Aweer (B) Jubba (Tunni and Baardheere), and (C) Soomaali-IV. The cognation percentage for this divergence runs from the high 50s to the low 60s. Soomaali-IV further diverged into Maay and Banaadir-Norther subgroups with lowest cognation percentages centering around the mid-60s, and finally the Banaadir-Northern branch separated into the more recent Banaadir, Baraawa, Jowhar and Shebeelle-Northern subgroups with minimum cognation percentages in the mid–to high-60s.

The result of this classification is that is establishes the proposal that Bayso and Rendille are closely related to Soomaali proper, first suggested by Fleming (1964:83). It also confirms the partial classification of Heine, which demonstrated with substantial linguistic evidence that the closes related languages to what was then thought of as "Soomaali" are Aweera and Rendille. We do accept the wider connection of the Soomaali and Omo-Tana groups as postulated by Sasse (1975:19) and Heine (1978:9–10), namely that there is an Omo-Tana division of Lowland East Cushitic to which Soomaali in all its varieties belongs. We differ, however, with Sasse and Heine regarding their division of Omo-Tana into Western, Northern and Eastern groupings. Instead we have divided Omo-Tana into Western and Soomaali. In our classification Western includes Arbore, Dasenech and Elmolo,

Table 1

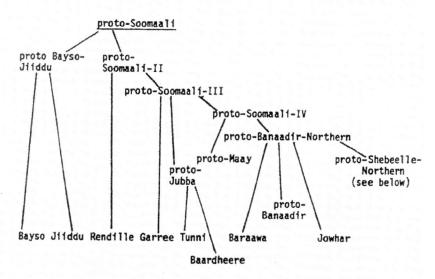

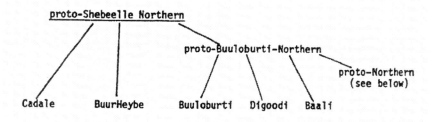

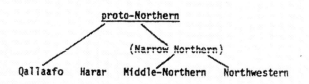

while Soomaali includes Bayso-Jiiddu and Soomaali-11 or Sam. But while our classification reconfirms the linguistic arguments of Heine and Fleming, it differs significantly in scope, taking into account dialects and languages not dealt with in any of these earlier classifications (see Table 1).

Discussion and Concluding Themes

From the preceding discussions a primary outline has emerged of development in the Easter Horn, the areas between the Rift Valley and the Indian Ocean, over the period from about 1000 BC to 1500 of the present era. The main source of insight into this history has been linguistic. Language is a diachronic record: a given sample of any language must embody, most visibly in its lexicon, elements of the past of its speakers and the traces of past contacts between that language and other languages. Systematic study of its relationships provides the context and controls for analyzing that evidence. The Soomaali tongues, as the primary languages of the region, have provided the focal bodies of data.

As vehicles of past contacts among peoples, the lexicons of these languages necessarily contain loanwords that, properly recognized, reveal interactions between Soomaali and non-Soomaali communities on the one hand, as well as intra-Soomaali relations. The treatment of such loans presented here show the power of linguistic evidence for historical reconstruction: the history of this region has emerged as the layers of loans and re-loans, and the identities of donor groups, were identified, sifted and ordered into a series of ethnic interactions. The language history of Soomaali reveals a series of amalgamations of peoples of different backgrounds, who together comprise Soomaalis today.

Unlike linguistic evidence, lineage histories are localized: they are exclusivist because they distinguish a group of people from their neighbors on the basis of some locally important criterion. Such a criterion gets elevated, via the institutionalization of lineage histories, into something culturally primary: into a group concern that obscures historical connections between groups. Of necessity, such lineage histories are limited in time depth: the memory of the community's traditions telescopes chronology, blurring ancient events into a pastiche of more recent themes. Here oral traditions have been utilized to enrich some of the more recent portions of this chronicle.

At the outset of the period studied, ca 1000 BC, much of the Eastern Horn was a food collecting area. That is, there were undoubtedly fishing villages at the coast (for which we have as yet no evidence), and certainly hunter-gatherers in the preponderance of the lowland areas of the Northern Horn and southern Somalia. There were three major centers of food production: a Northern Horn cattle-raising area, a similar lowland, a southern Somalia settlement, and at the far west a band of cool, rainy highland grain-cultivating lands, where the crops were finger millet, teff, wheat and barley. From the linguistic evidence, the Northern Horn populations spoke a language only loosely specifiable as North Lowland East Cushitic, and the pastoral southern lowland communities were Dahaloan Southern Cushitic speakers. The proto-Soomaali lived then at the southern extremity of the highland zone which lay just east of the Rift Valley.

By the early first millennium AD, the proportion of Horn residents practicing food production probably had grown. This growth would have come about in part through the migration of Soomaali-i and Soomaali-ii speakers, in search of increased foraging for their cattle. When these peoples settled in the less rainy lowland areas of Southern Somalia, their grain crop appears to have been the more suitable sorghum.

In the course of Soomaali peregrinations, the Jiiddu followed the Jubba River southward into areas populated by Dahaloan livestock-raisers, while the proto-Soomaali-ii expanded south as far as the edges of present northern Kenya, where they encountered Nilo-Saharan people The Jiiddu, at least, absorbed the Southern Cushites they met. The question to be asked is: why did the Soomaali come to predominate in those areas they penetrated, which already hosted food-producing populations? Both the lexical evident and the geographical indications, i.e., the greater aridity of these new climes, point to the possibility that more intensive livestock-raising might have had a part in enabling the Soomaali ethnic identity to prevail in such encounters.

The follow millennium was characterized by one special development, the advent of camel culture. While the presence of the camel may date to before 500 AD, the critical role that the camel played in Soomaali expansion is not evident until after 500 AD, when Soomaali-iv speakers, particularly the Banaadir-Northern subbranch thereof, progressively trekked northward into drier and/or more soil-poor areas of limited potential for anything but camel raising. Other, Soomaali-iii, groups that benefited from the new adaptation included the Garree, who began at the end of the millennium to settle dry regions of northern Kenya and drier portions of the interriverine regions.

Other than camels the first millennium of the present era saw the spread of two additional domesticated animals – chickens and horses. They may have arrived via long-distance trade which came to the Horn from Southern Arabia and Egypt via the Red Sea and developed Indian Ocean connections, probably as part of wider networks that ran from the Mediterranean into the Indian Ocean. There is documentary evidence of important trading sites along the northern Somali coast, but the linguistic evidence is lacking to carry this indication much further.

With the onset of the present millennium (1000 AD), successive episodes of northern Soomaali migration completed the spread of Soomaali language in the Eastern Horn. In the northwest, whish is an agricultural area typified by Highland crops, we seen an ethnic commingling similar to that which took place in southern Somalia: the Northwestern Soomaali interacted with Hararis and Northern Lowland East Cushites. In the northeast Horn, a drier area where the camel predominated, we see the progress of a relatively unimpeded northern Soomaali out migration, across very lightly uninhabited lands.

A second notable development in the southern Somali region involved the emergence and the expansion of a sub branch of the Jubba group, the Tunni, from the middle Jubba southward to the car lower Shebeele, into territories already inhabited by Jiiddu. This movement dates probably to very early in the second millennium; later movements spread Tunni into areas of Banaadir-Northern speech into the immediate coastal hinterland of southern Somali, between the lower Shebeelle and Baraawa on the coast.

Later in the first half of the second millennium the proto-Maay populations expanded widely across the interriverine areas of southern Somalia, The northwestern sub branch of Maay must have moved into areas often previously settled by Garree and by Jubba speech communities. The Southern Maay migrated into Southern Cushitic, Tunni, Jiiddu and Banaadir regions, and the Northeastern Maay cam to occupy middle Shebeele-Northern tongues.

The ninth and tenth century trade resurgence as well attested to through various kinds of evidence. This trade led to the rise of towns on the Indian Ocean coast and distinctive town cultures and eventually in language from the people of their immediate hinterland. The first three centuries of the present millennium were a period of religious change, when Islam spread along the Banaadir Coast. This process started in the towns through their commercial contacts with the Muslim Middle East world. In the Northern Somalia, Islam also spread, though it was perhaps not tied as directly as in the south to the town, bus was still mediated through trade contacts with the Arabs as the oral traditions indicate.

By the second have of this millennium (1500 AD), Islam had become the religion of most or much of these Somali regions, though not without incorporating aspects of earlier beliefs. Islamization involved adjustment from one worldview into another, and syncretism between the new religion and the earlier Soomaali religious belief. The whole Eastern Horn is likely to have a common pre-Islamic religion since the word "waaq," which survives in toponyms, ethnonyms, personal names and proverbs, is an old Eastern Cushitic word that meant "God."

Prospects For The Future
The work has not touched on local history, leaving to others the analysis of more extensive research of local dialect vocabularies. In these, word-borrowings unique to one dialect or a sec of dialects will reveal past contacts. Specialized vocabularies will contain evidence of economic, material or cultural developments limited to certain

areas. Another dimension to be pursued in future historical study is oral tradition, which must be collected in more detail and depth. The objectives of fleshing out the evidence and discovering the linkages, and the overlaps, and the correlation of this sort of documentation with that provided by linguistic evidence, remains to be done. There are as well vast opportunities for archaeology in Somali which need to be encouraged and pursued with vigor. Somali is a region with exceptionally good preservation of archeological remains of all kinds. And the archaeological correlations, once better knows, can be tied to established linguistic reconstructions.

This history has concentrated on economic aspects, and specifically on domestic food production, but collection of further lexical and comparative ethnographic evidence will allow reconstruction of the cultural practices, beliefs and other elements of material culture for different sub-regions and for more specific periods of time. Topics that remain to be treated include ancient Soomaali age structure practices, residence patterns, and kinship relations, among many others. Only the beginnings have been made here toward uncovering the early eras of history of the Eastern Horn of Africa.

References

Bender, M. Lionel. "The Languages of Ethiopia: A New Lexicostatistic Classification and some Problems of Diffusion." Anthropological Linguistics 13 (1971): 165–288.

Ceruili, Enrico. "Gruppi etnici ne&,ri nella Somalia." Archivio per l'Antropologia e la Etnologia LXIV (1934): 182.

Ceruili, Enrico. Somalia-scriti vari editi ed inediti, 3 vols. Rome: Istituto Poligrafico della Stato, 1957, 1959, 1964.

Ehret, Christopher. "Cushitic Prehistory." In The Non-Semitic Languages of Ethiopia, edited by Lionel Bender, 85–96. East Lansing; Michigan State University, 1976.

Ehret, Christopher and Mohamed All. "Soomaali Classification." Paper presented at the Second International Congress of Somali Studies, Hamburg. 1983. In Preeedings of the Second International Congress of Somali Studies, edited by Thomas Labban, 1:201–69. Hamburg: Helmut Buske Veriag, 1984.

Fleming, Harold C. "Balso and Rendille: Somali Outliers." *Ressagne di Studi Etiopic* 20 (1964):35–59.

Heine, Bemd. "The Sam Languages: A History of Somali, Rendille, and Boni." Afroasiatic Linguistics 99 (1978):1–93.

Lewis, I.M. "The Somali Conquest of the Hom of Africa." *Journal of African History* 1 (1960): 21:1–3 o.

Lewis, I.M., ed. Islam in Tropical Africa. London: International African Institute at the Oxford University Press, 1966.

Turton, ER. "Bantu, Galla and Somali Migrations in the Horn of Africa: A Reassessment of the Juba/Tana Area." *Journal of African History* XVI (1975):519–37.

Sasse, Hans-Juergen. "The Consonant Phonemes of Proto-East Cushitic (PEC): a First Approximation." *Afroasiatic Linguistics* 8 (1979): 1–67.

Appendix

TABLE 2
SOOMAALI LEXICOSTATISTICAL ANALYSIS:*

```
Bayso
54  Jiiddu
40  40  Rendille
43  48  52  Garree
41  55  49  65  Tunni
45  51  67  72  76  Baardheere
47  50  52  64  68  79  Daafeed
47  52  54  65  70  79  84  Luuq
43  48  53  62  67  79  85  87  Bay
44  48  55  67  70  80  82  84  87  Dhiinsoor
48  52  55  67  70  81  82  86  84  88  Baydhaba
45  49  54  61  65  76  81  85  82  81  87  Afgooy
40  51  58  63  72  78  79  78  74  81  76  72  Baraawe
44  46  54  65  68  69  70  72  66  71  73  72  77  Jamaame
42  47  51  64  62  64  63  69  62  64  68  64  73  81  Xamar
40  43  50  58  63  63  65  64  62  68  66  65  69  79  75  Cadale
43  39  51  58  57  61  60  65  60  65  68  63  69  72  65  78  Hargeysa
40  41  55  60  62  63  61  62  64  65  68  62  69  74  68  79  88  Qardho
```

*From Ehret and Ali, 1983.

TABLE 3
BANAADIR-NORTHERN LEXICOSTATISTICAL ANALYSIS:*

```
Harar
83  Jabuuti
83  91  Dirldhabe
80  84  84  Zeylac
83  87  87  91  Jigjiga
82  85  83  87  92  Gabiley
85  86  91  90  91  89  Boorama
83  87  84  85  84  88  86  Baabli
82  89  85  84  86  86  89  91  Hargeysa
82  85  82  82  84  88  91  88  91  Ceerigaabo
80  82  82  82  66  87  90  89  90  93  Burco
87  83  84  82  83  86  89  88  68  90  92  Laas Caanood
83  80  83  79  82  79  81  83  85  81  82  89  Kismaayo
79  85  82  80  82  84  87  86  68  86  86  89  88  Qardho
82  82  84  82  83  82  87  87  88  88  88  86  85  92  Gaalkacyo
61  85  83  82  82  84  86  88  88  87  86  89  86  88  92  Hobiyo
85  80  82  82  84  83  84  68  87  85  85  83  82  86  88  Wardheer
85  85  84  81  85  84  88  85  85  83  82  87  84  86  89  68  Qallaafo
86  77  80  76  77  78  78  84  85  81  80  82  87  83  81  83  78  85  Baali
86  75  80  76  80  80  74  84  79  77  77  78  82  79  83  84  83  87  86  Digoodi
83  73  75  74  77  74  77  82  78  77  76  78  81  79  80  79  77  86  80  84  Buuloburti
77  69  74  72  72  72  72  77  76  74  71  76  80  76  78  75  76  79  78  79  80  Buur Hakaba
75  72  78  79  78  77  77  82  78  79  78  79  81  79  82  81  78  82  78  81  77  81  Cadale
73  66  65  63  66  67  66  70  69  67  68  66  76  73  73  73  68  76  73  76  79  76  75  Jowhar
65  64  69  62  67  64  69  68  68  66  67  68  70  68  68  70  67  73  68  75  69  71  75  72  Xamar
72  71  77  64  72  69  71  74  73  71  72  72  78  78  77  79  75  80  81  83  76  76  76  76  80  Merka
74  71  75  67  74  69  72  75  71  69  71  71  78  74  77  79  75  81  71  79  79  76  79  79  81  88  Jamaame
72  63  69  68  66  64  68  73  69  64  65  67  73  69  71  72  69  76  71  80  74  76  69  67  73  75  77  Baraawe
```

*From Ehret and Ali, 1983.

28

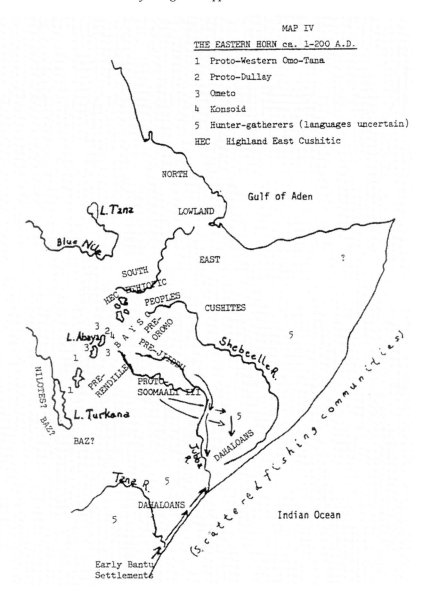

MAP IV

THE EASTERN HORN ca. 1-200 A.D.

1   Proto-Western Omo-Tana

2   Proto-Dullay

3   Ometo

4   Konsoid

5   Hunter-gatherers (languages uncertain)

HEC   Highland East Cushitic

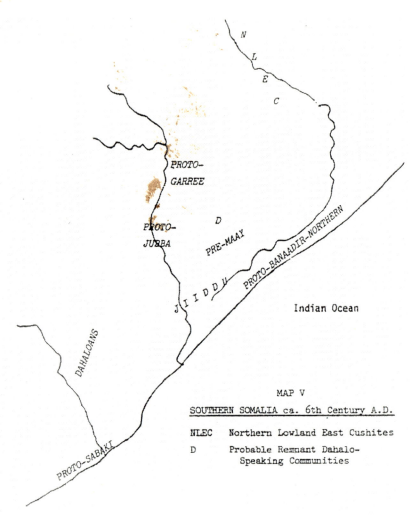

MAP V

SOUTHERN SOMALIA ca. 6th Century A.D.

NLEC   Northern Lowland East Cushites

D   Probable Remnant Dahalo-
        Speaking Communities

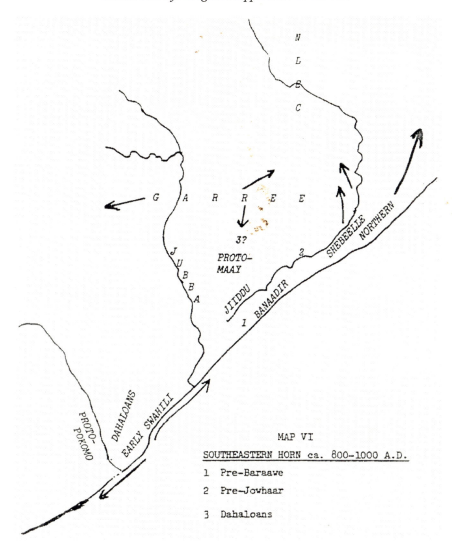

MAP VI

SOUTHEASTERN HORN ca. 800–1000 A.D.

1 Pre-Baraawe

2 Pre-Jowhaar

3 Dahaloans

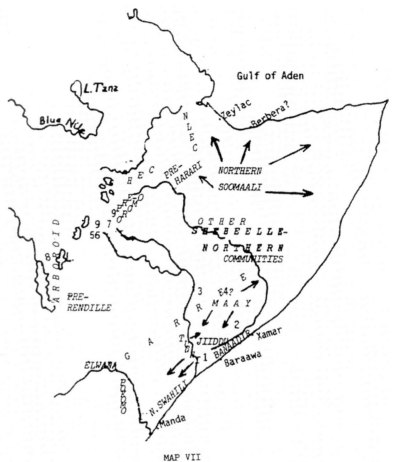

MAP VII

EASTERN HORN ca. 11th - 13th Centuries

1	Banaadir Communities	7	Bayso
2	Pre-Jowhaar	8	Pre-Dasenech
3	Pre-Baardheere	9	Ometo
4	Dahaloans	HEC	Highland East Cushites
5	Dullay	NLEC	North Lowland East Cushites
6	Konso		

Chapter Three

The Somali Political Economy in Eastern Ethiopia, Circa 1941–1948.[1]

Cedric Barnes,
British Academy Post Doctoral Fellow,
SOAS, University of London.

THE HISTORY of the British Military Administration (BMA hereafter) and the return to pre-1936 territorial arrangements and divisions of the Somali lands has been presented either as the triumph of Ethiopian independence[2]; or the betrayal of the hopes for Somali unification and the repartition of the Somali nation by the very same forces of imperialism.[3] Most authors have focused on high politics while overlooking the political and economic circumstances of the local populations concerned.[4] This is unfortunate since these politics were complex, had deep historical roots, and not as clearly divided as nationalist historians and their sympathizers have depicted.[5]

The purpose of this chapter is not so much about the activities of the British Military Administration, nor about that of the Ethiopian government, but rather about the changing political economy of the region and how that in turn affected the every day politics of the people and their reactions to the restoration of Ethiopian rule in the region. The empirical evidence presented in this chapter[6] suggests that the idea of *a priori* Somali nationhood was not enough to convince the majority of Somalis in the Jigjiga and Reserved Areas to resist the restoration of Ethiopian rule after a period of British Military Administration following the defeat of the Italian Empire in Ethiopia. While it is true that Somali nationalism in the form of the Somali Youth Club and League prompted significant political awakening in the Jigjiga region of eastern Ethiopia, nationalist politics only unified local Somalis as long as it served their political and economic interests to do so. When the tide turned and the return to Ethiopian rule looked certain, the Somali population was quick to realign themselves within the Ethiopian political structures. To be sure nationalist sentiment did not go away, and most likely went underground, however it remains the case that nationalism, as a political force, was somewhat ephemeral and quickly subsumed under the imperatives of the local political economy of Jigjiga. Local politics involved a great deal of shifting and crosscutting alliances and enmities. Unlikely alliances were made and old understandings broken. For the Somali populations who lived through this period, local society and economy was far more relevant than abstract concepts of national citizenship and nationalism. However, the latter was of increasing interest to some, and the following decade saw a greater participation in heated debates surrounding the future of the Somali lands and modern Somali nationality.

War and Post-war Economy in the 'Ethiopian' Somali-lands

Ethiopia's occupation by Italy (*circa* 1936–41) and the British Military Administration (*circa* 1941–48) of Ethiopia and the Somali lands considerably altered the political horizons and expectations of Somalis. For the mainly non-Christian groups incorporated into the Ethiopian empire in the late nineteenth century, the Italian occupation of Ethiopia and uniquely in the Somali case, the continued British Military Administration of their region, had been a liberating experience. This period marked a watershed for the region's history, and this was especially true for Somalis in the east of the Ethiopian Empire. Indeed the historical aftermath of the end of the Italian East African Empire in Northeast Africa is particularly important since it marks a turning point in the region's political history and the start of the decolonisation process.[7]

By the mid-forties Ethiopia, Eritrea and the colonial Somali lands had been involved in large-scale modern war for the first time in their history. The impact widened as the war gathered momentum in the early forties. In Ethiopia, it is difficult to discern the impact of Italian rule[8] from that of the Second World War. However, the Italian period had left some important legacies, not least of which was the determination to modernise Ethiopia's economy and infrastructure. The increased demands for imports and the Italian government's efforts to articulate Ethiopia with its two coastal colonies saw the slow improvement of roads, particularly in the east where Italian Somalia was joined to Eastern Ethiopia. The roads between Harar and Dire Dawa, Harar and Jigjiga, Jigjiga and the border with British Somaliland, and Jigjiga towards Mogadishu, were much improved.[9]

During the Italian occupation a transit-trade agreement was concluded with the British Somaliland Protectorate to transport goods from the Protectorate port of Berbera via Harar since the volume of trade was too much for Djibouti and the Italian Somaliland ports were too distant. The British were accommodating towards transit trade hoping that the Italian government would be co-operative with regard to grazing and water rights for Somali clans from the Protectorate who crossed the border into the then Italian controlled eastern Ethiopian borderlands – the areas known as the Hawd and Ogaden.[10]

The roads and trade agreements suddenly improved communication between Somali speakers previously divided by clan politics and colonial boundaries that separated them. Furthermore, for many Somalis, the increase in transit trade carried by motor lorries through their lands represented a considerable opportunity for economic gain through participation in expanded trade. For example the up-country settlement of Hargeisa in the British Protectorate benefited considerably from the increased trade with Italian controlled eastern Ethiopia, and profits made by local Somali there were invested in urban property and permanent stone buildings. In the British Protectorate in 1933, there were 6 private cars and 49 commercial vehicles. By 1937, there were 51 private cars and 316 commercial vehicles, at least 150 of which were owned by Somalis.[11] The British Somaliland Annual Report for 1936 noted that 'many who have never thought of trading previously are taking caravans over the border and doing very well'.[12] Inter-territorial connections through war, administration, trade, and transport significantly altered Somali politics and this new form of politics was especially apparent in the growing urban centers. The new political economy quickly spread to the urban areas of the Ethiopian Somali lands among the Somali populations of Jigjiga, Harar and Dire Dawa.

For the first year after the Italian defeat in 1941, the former Ethiopian Empire was administered as Occupied Enemy Territory since the Italian conquest had been legally recognised by the British in 1938. After the remaining Italian forces have been defeated and cleared from the country the political relationship between the returned Ethiopian Emperor and the British were revised and changed. The result was the 1942 Anglo-Ethiopian agreement[13] that handed back a certain amount of administrative control to the Emperor. However, under the agreement the BMA retained control over the railway line to Addis Ababa, the municipality of Dire Dawa, and the borderlands with French Somaliland (later Djibouti) and British Somaliland and the growing town of Jigjiga. This area became known as the Reserved Areas (RA hereafter), which included the farmed plains around Jigjiga and the important wet season grazing lands of the Hawd. The Ogaden, formerly part of the Ethiopian Empire, which the Italians had invaded and absorbed into the Italian Somaliland administration, was also retained by the BMA for strategic purposes.

The Ogaden was administered as part of ex-Italian Somaliland, but the RA had its own administration. Although the British did not deny Ethiopian sovereignty of the RA and the Ogaden, by virtue of its continuing separate administration from Ethiopia, their future became implicitly bound up with the disposal of ex-Italian Somaliland to be decided at the end of the war.[14]

On his restoration, Hayla-Sellasse soon resumed his halted attempts to transform Ethiopia into a modern centralised, bureaucratic, and above all 'national' state. Territorial integration and political centralisation was high on his agenda. Furthermore, the arrangements which the British created for the Emperor's return to power promoted a national spirit, partly due to continued foreign 'occupation' and partly encouraged by the national infrastructure wrought by the Italians and the peculiar economic boom that fed off the Second World War. Domestically, the post-war situation in Ethiopia encouraged the already strong 'nationalist' resentment that Hayla-Sellasse and his Ministers felt under the terms of the Anglo-Ethiopian agreement.[15]

In 1944, the 1942 Anglo-Ethiopian agreement was terminated and replaced by a treaty that reduced British involvement in the internal government of Ethiopia, though the Ethiopian government did not secure the return of the RA and Ogaden.[16] Because of the 1944, agreement the Ethiopian government took more control over its revenues and territorial administration. Despite this fiscal control, the outlook on the internal taxation and budgetary front in Ethiopia was gloomy. However unexpectedly high earnings from cereal exports (and to a lesser extent, coffee) due to wartime conditions, helped augment the Ethiopian government's meagre coffers.[17]

The 1942 export trade figures, the bulk of which was made up of cereals, had quadrupled by 1943.[18] In early 1943, the purchase of cereals (mainly for British and American customers) was centralised in the hands of the joint allies' civil and military Purchasing Commission in Addis Ababa, to which the Ethiopian Government initially agreed to grant a monopoly. However, seeing an opportunity for increased government revenues, the Ethiopian government began to take the view that this arrangement was earning large profits for foreign agencies at Ethiopia's expense. After the British Government had released $3 million for the purchase of cereals during 1943 and 1944, the Ethiopian government announced that its own Ministry of Agriculture would assume the monopoly of purchasing cereals and would sell to the British and American buyers (such as the United Kingdom Commercial Corporation) at the railhead instead. The system meant that the Ethiopian government could fix prices for wheat, maize and sorghum at much higher levels than previously realised.[19] During 1944, the price of grain had increased threefold,[20] which exacerbated the already general effects of the world food crisis.[21] In 1947 the price of wheat was still climbing and stood at 200 percent above the already inflated

1946 figure, but in spite of this the volume of cereals exported continued at high levels, which even the imposition of an export tax did little to reduce.[22]

The Italian occupation and Second World War had changed the character of the Ethiopian economy. Money wages had become widespread, as had the production of crops for cash. Italian rule, despite its own economic problems had made cheap consumer goods more widely available, and the demand for luxury goods increased with exposure to the Italian way of life. Before the Italian invasion, the level of trade and production in the old Ethiopian Empire was at an extremely low level (in part due to the world-wide depression). Although the Italian government poured vast amounts of money into the country, the export trade was not developed. However, imports, crucially, escalated to thirty times their previous levels. Italian road building – even though it amounted to only a third of what had been planned, and half of those completed roads were damaged by the war – made a considerable difference to the ease of trade, as did the amount of motor lorries left behind by the Italians. After its restoration, the Ethiopian government, while apparently ill equipped to restore territory-wide government, was, with British concerns for supply routes, able to reopen communications and commerce. In a matter of months, trade and commerce reached far higher levels than pertained before the occupation. Moreover the unprecedented level of demand for Ethiopian grain from the Allied military forces created a lucrative market for cereals which had not been exported in any significant quantities before then.[23]

In view of the economic conditions prevailing during the forties, especially the sudden value of cereals, the continued separation of the Reserved Areas around Jigjiga was particularly galling for the restoration government in Addis Ababa. By the 1940s Jigjiga had become an important grain-basket for the eastern region following the expansion of agriculture into the plains below the Harar plateau and the conversion of Somali pastoralists to farming. The grain price boom had thus made farming in the Jigjiga region extremely profitable since it was close to export markets in Berbera on the British Protectorate coast. However, the area was out of the reach of the 'nationalist' government monopolists in Addis Ababa. Instead, Somali farmers and traders were able to realise profits from high grain prices denied to their neighbours and kinsmen who had been returned to Ethiopian rule and who were subject to the Government monopoly. In Jigjiga, these unique economic circumstances set the Somali inhabitants and the Ethiopian government on a collision course that increasingly took on the aspect of competing 'nationalism'. However, contrary to nationalist historiography Somali society was by no means united.[24] On top of the usual clan divisions, the economic and political circumstances of the Jigjiga and the Reserved Areas made local Somalis keenly aware of internal inequalities. Clannish calculations were compounded by advantages of alliances with external power and the possibilities of self-government.

Farms, trade and chiefs – Jigjiga and the Reserved Areas

Farming in Jigjiga was intimately linked with the history of Ethiopian rule in the western Somali-lands. From the late nineteen-tens Jigjiga and its environs had been subjected to more direct rule and stringent tax collection by the Ethiopian government. The Ethiopian government appointed a number of Somali chiefs to facilitate rule and revenue collection – revenue that was vital for the Ethiopian centralist project.[25] These factors demanded an increase in farming in traditionally pastoral areas, since grain was initially used to pay Ethiopian 'taxes'. Increased grain supplies encouraged settlement and attracted Somalis to the Jigjiga markets, leading in some ways to an 'Ethiopianisation' of Somali life. However, it also resulted in the greater Somalisation of the town of Jigjiga.[26] Oral informants report that even before the Italian occupation the early thirties had seen a notable increase in farming and sedentarisation of the Somali population.[27] Indeed, before the Italian invasion, there had also been an increase and improvement in the ease of trade by virtue of the new and improved road connections and faster motor transport that had stimulated the market for grain, especially from the British Protectorate.[28] These local developments were continued and expanded upon during the Italian occupation after 1936 and during the British period for most of the 'forties.

During the 'thirties the Ethiopian government had claimed large areas of land in and around Jigjiga and further out on the fertile Marar plain (northeast of the town).[29] The first Ethiopian actions towards land and leadership dated back to the governorships of Takla-Hawaryat (1917/8–20/21?) and Gadla-Giyorgis (1921–27/28?).[30] Although it is difficult to discern the exact nature of land policy in Jigjiga from the available records and oral interviews,[31] it appears that Takla-Hawaryat had established a taxpayer system, which recognised taxable units and local leadership by grouping together a few farmers and the land that supported them.[32] The main purpose of the system was a form of indirect rule primarily to get the Somali to pay taxes to the state and help maintain the local garrison. The Jigjiga district was different from much of highland Harar, since most of these Somali taxpayers and their Somali office-holding 'chiefs' were directly accountable to the local governor and were not subordinated to soldier-settler estates, the system that operated in the highlands.[33] However, from the 1920s, (during Gadla-Giyorgis' governorship) Takla-Hawaryat's system was gradually replaced and land was 'measured' by *qalad*. The primary object of measurement was to maximise the number of taxpayers.[34] As a local informant had it, 'when the Somalis first started to farm grain was given to soldiers as *hirto* (tithe), then after we began farming properly we paid *geber* (monetary tax)'.[35] Another informant put it, 'the Amhara were colonisers – what they wanted was taxation'.[36]

Land measurement began initially near the garrison centres and only later was it applied to areas further a field. For example land measurement and registration only affected the more distant lands east from Jigjiga in the 'thirties. Indeed it was not until the 'thirties that the Yaberre clan who inhabited these areas turned to farming, a shift that they put down to livestock losses after the bad drought of 1928. The Ethiopian government measured and registered land into units known as *garad*, consisting of about six families, each of who were *gabbar* (tax-payers). Each unit put forward one of its number as a *garad* (a kind of 'headman'). The *garad* were responsible to *damina* or *akiil* ('agents') who oversaw a large amount of *garad* units and collected their taxes for the *suldaan*, who was ultimately responsible for his clan's taxation and representation to the Ethiopian government (in the person of the Deputy-Governor of Jigjiga).[37]

Land measurement was targeted most in the good agricultural lands near to Ethiopian garrisons centres e.g., around Jigjiga and Qochar to the northeast. Each resident Somali taxpayer had a piece of land, but office holders were apportioned extra land according to their status as government functionaries. After land had been apportioned to the Somali tax-payers and office holders, the remainder was held by the government, which it might redistribute, sell, or retain[38] Some of this 'excess' land was sold or granted to 'outsiders' and was registered as *qalad* (as opposed to *garad*). *Qalad* was sometimes carved out of existing *garad* units, and was equal to half a *garad*.[39] *Qalad* owners are remembered as 'Amhara', which probably designates their external origins and religious beliefs rather than ethnicity. However, since few 'outsiders' wished to farm the areas themselves – often because they feared to farm among hostile Somali – they brought in tenants, most often local Somali or Oromo.[40] Much government land remained unsold and continued to be used as grazing by local Somalis in return for a nominal fee.[41]

Before the Italian occupation *qalad* ownership and tenancy, which was by no means widespread, was most common in the better agricultural regions, in particular the Gerri-Jaarso regions in the foothills of the highlands to the northeast of Jigjiga.[42] During the Italian period, however, all the land reverted to Somali ownership and there were no direct taxes, a situation that continued under the BMA. For the agricultural areas around Jigjiga that made up the RA the return to Ethiopian government threatened the restoration of *qalad* ownership and reintroduction of tax.[43]

Sorghum was the main crop produced in the RA and was the staple grain food for the majority of the population. The tree-less Jigjiga plain, inhospitable to grain-eating birds, was favourable to the cultivation of sorghum. The soil in depressions formed by the undulations of the plains was very fertile and, if rainfall was sufficient, yielded well. The Jigjiga district was self-supporting in sorghum through much of the forties, and surplus was exported to British Somaliland.[44] In the good growing conditions of the forties, encouraged by the healthy market for grain and the tax-free status of the RA,[45] large quantities of grain were produced and brought to the market at Jigjiga and exported to British Somaliland and beyond.

The restored Ethiopian government protested against this unrestricted export of grain, much of which emanated from the Harar area under Ethiopian control, presumably to avoid the government monopoly.[46] There was also a healthy export trade in pastoral products of cattle, hides, skins and ghee. In addition to buying local grain, the British Army, which maintained a significant presence in the region, was a good customer for slaughter cattle. Along with grain sales, ghee, hides and skins were useful ways of acquiring cash and had the highest export value.[47] This healthy export market represented a considerable loss of potential revenue to the Ethiopian government.

However, despite the free market conditions, the economic boom was not without problems for the relations between the local Somali clans. It was soon obvious that in what had once been a relatively complimentary economy of agro-pastoralism, the two parts of the economy began to rival each other in the heightened market conditions. From as early as 1942, conflicts are recorded between clans over land rights, and between farmers and pastoralists and the various groups of traders. The focal point of the trade was Jigjiga, and it was often in the market that tensions spilled over. One of the foremost tensions was between the local Darood 'Jidwak' (primarily Bartirre and Yaberre) clans of the district and the Isxaaq clans from the Protectorate whose presence had increased during the war thanks to the British administration of all the Somali lands and increased trade with the Protectorate.[48] In the seasonal river valley of the area, Darood (Bartirre) cultivators were at loggerheads with Isxaaq (Habr Awal) herdsmen who objected to the restrictions laid on the grazing of their sheep and camels by the spread of Bartirre cultivation in Jigjiga,[49] and around wells along the great stock routes from the British Protectorate.[50] The murder of Xaashi Cilmi, an important Isxaaq (Habr Awal) trader and land-owner in late 1942, allegedly by a Darood 'Jidwak' directed assassin, was put down to jealousy over the Isxaaq dominance in trade – although the most immediate cause was revenge for a road accident involving a member of a Darood 'Jidwak' clan killed by an Isxaaq lorry driver along the now very busy road from Jigjiga to Hargeisa in the Protectorate.[51] The market place in Jigjiga was the scene of several other violent incidents of intra-clan rivalry, sometimes with a hand-grenade lobbed in for good measure.[52]

Concomitant with agricultural (and economic) expansion was a growth in clan identity with certain areas, and disputes in land became more common.[53] The upheavals of the last decade brought about splits, even within clans and sub-clans themselves, as alliances crumbled in the face of new uncertainties. One example was the Oromo element of the mixed Oromo-Somali (Gerri-Jaarso) clans who tried to break free of their Somali (Gerri) association. Earlier, when the Ethiopian government reoccupied the Hararge province to the limit of the Reserved Areas in 1942/3, the imposition of taxation on those excluded from the Reserved Area occasioned dispute and led to the arrest of clan-leaders (who were of Gerri 'Somali lineages'). The removal of Gerri leadership gave Jaarso elements (of Oromo lineages) the chance to break free of their subservient role to Gerri.[54] Such fissiparous tendencies were present among the large Isxaaq Habr Awal clan also. When the clan *suldaan* of the Ethiopian sections died in Jigjiga his son succeeded him. But the appointment of the new *suldaan* was seized upon by a powerful lineage of the Habr Awal clan, the Jibril Abokir, themselves primarily agriculturists, who saw it as an opportunity to secede from the overall Habr Awal clan leadership, which was still mainly concerned with pastoral politics.[55]

The agricultural boom also encouraged the Yaberre – one of the Darood 'Jidwak' confederation of clans – to emerge from the traditional dominance of their kin of the Bartirre clan. Bartirre and Yaberre were generally thought to be of the same clan since their villages usually contained persons of both tribes. However, as cultivation increased division beset their confederational relationship. By the mid-forties, in areas that in 1941 had little or no cultivation, Yaberre disputed land rights with Bartirre and with the agricultural Jibril Abokir section of the Isxaaq Habr Awal clan. The British noted that this assertive Yaberre claim to exclusive land ownership was attributable to their revered clan leader, *Sheekh* Xasan. British reports note that *Sheekh* Xasan was particularly alert to the importance of bureaucratic proof and could produce any number of documents (of Ethiopian, or Italian origin and some of his own manufacture) that laid claim to the disputed lands. *Sheekh* Xasan had also imported Oromo farmers, most probably from the Harar highlands – areas that had, by then, been handed back to Ethiopian rule. These Oromo farmers, described as industrious and skilled, were able to augment the clan numbers, and increase land under cultivation claimed by the Yaberre. They were probably rewarded with light tenancy agreements and acted as a buttress to the Isxaaq and other rival clans, including the Yaberre's close kin, the Bartirre. A British officer in the RA reported that although *Sheekh* Xasan was unpopular with other clan leaders, who complained against his 'malpractices', it was found that the Yaberre clan he led 'were prosperous and industrious, well-behaved and likeable, and that they respected and admired their leader'.[56]

Another clan to emerge with locally defined presence and identity during the thirties and forties, and which owed much to the process of sedentarisation through agriculture and changing administrations, was the Akiishu. According to oral informants, the Akiishu were Oromo clans and lineages that had been subsumed by Somali clans after Oromo lost ground in the region in the eighteenth and nineteenth centuries. Most of the Oromo lineages that eventually coalesced into an Akiishu identity were scattered among primarily Isxaaq (Habr Awal) clans in the Protectorate, but other Oromo clans were present in Somali clans all over the western Somali lands.[57]

Oral tradition claims that the originator of the Akiishu 'unification', *Sheekh* Cumar, came from one of these subsumed Oromo lineages. The *sheekh* was originally a member of a *tariiqa*, most likely a *jamaaca* settlement (a Muslim religious community), which cultivated the land in one of the river valleys descending from the Harar highlands into the Jigjiga plains. He was reportedly a good farmer and a noted Islamic scholar. When the region was incorporated into the Ethiopian empire earlier in the century, Amhara' destroyed the *jamaaca* and *Sheekh* Cumar left the area.[58] During the late twenties, *Sheekh* Cumar settled in the border area with the British Protectorate. This was about the same time that Isxaaq clans there were taking up cultivation. This process often provoked dispute and division within clans. It is claimed that *Sheekh* Cumar became involved in mediating one such dispute that arose in a local Habr Awal clan that contained subsumed Oromo lineages. Oral testimony recounts that the more senior 'Somali' lineages of the Habr Awal had attempted to make a junior 'Oromo' lineage of the clan pay a blood money claim for which they denied responsibility. *Sheekh* Cumar challenged the Habr Awal's own *sheekh* and succeeded (by close reference to the Qur'an and Sharia) in showing the Habr Awal *sheekh's* decision to be flawed. Embarrassed by this failure, the Habr Awal clan decided to let *Sheekh* Cumar and the Oromo lineage live separately from the clan in land west of Hargeisa in Gebele.[59]

When the Italians took over the area in the mid-thirties, they registered all the clans present in the district. This process was used by the exiled Oromo 'Akiishu' lineage[60] to claim complete independence from the Habr Awal, who as British subjects, could not register with the Italian authorities. Over time and during the agricultural boom of the forties Akiishu identity grew and members claimed exclusive rights to land and attracted other subsumed Oromo lineages from surrounding Somali clans. Akiishu informants remember that BMA officials recognised their claim and demarcated Akishu land between the lands of Darood 'Jidwak' clans of Yaberre and Bartirre. Furthermore, some of the Oromos whom *Sheekh* Xasan had attracted to Yaberre land wanted to join the Akiishu, but *Sheekh* Xasan would not allow it. Finally, the British decided that the Yaberre chiefs had too many 'Oromo'. These Oromo later allied themselves with the Akiishu.[61]

The agricultural expansion continued throughout the forties. The quantities of sorghum arriving in Jigjiga were higher than at anytime in a generation, so much so that there was insufficient storage in the town. Most parts of Gerri and Yaberre land to the northeast of Jigjiga had been turned over to agriculture, and large tracts of Bartirre land had been enclosed for agriculture. Even the Abasguul, traditionally the least agricultural of all the Darood 'Jidwak' confederation, were enclosing land. At the border with the British Protectorate, the Jibril Abokir sub-clan of the Habr Awal (Isxaaq) clan extended their cultivation westward to land they had previously used for grazing. British policy deemed it necessary to demarcate 'tribal' cultivation areas with boundaries that intended to allow for ample expansion in agriculture. However this plan was frustrated by the fact that the Protectorate clans took up cultivation only at the periphery of their clan areas, suggesting that sometimes cultivation was purely for political and territorial reasons.[62]

During the nineteen-forties agriculture was playing an ever more important role in the lives of Somali living in the Reserved Areas. The majority of the local clans (Gerri-Jarso, Yaberre and Bartirre) lived in permanent villages and farms. Others were at a transitional stage, but all the major clans had cleared considerable areas for cultivation. By the mid'forties, about five hundred square miles was under the plough and was increasing every year. Many Somalis had already sold or disposed of their camels, and the bulk of their other livestock, to make room for crops. By 1946 of the 300,000 population present in the RA, half were thought to be completely dependant on agriculture. British officials expressed worries about the long-term sustainability of cultivation, which was neither directed, nor did they think, prudently undertaken.[63]

During 1944, there was much nervousness among the Somali population who thought that the end to the 1942 Anglo-Ethiopian Agreement would result in the handing back of the RA to the Ethiopians, making all Somalis subject to taxation, as sections of the Gerri-Jarso clan had been in 1942–43. However, the arrangements for continued British administration of RA were kept under the 1944 agreement. Nevertheless, it seemed likely that Ethiopian rule would eventually return. This uncertainty helps to explain the ill-tempered jostling among the local clans to farm and stake a claim on land whilst the grain price boom and freedom from taxation lasted. Furthermore, the Somali chiefs and their clans were conscious that their political positions might not last when the Ethiopians returned, especially those who had benefited during Italian and British rule such as the emergent Yaberre and Akiishu clans. Moreover, the Ethiopian government, despite being denied control of the RA, had made sure of a quasi-governmental presence in Jigjiga soon after the restoration of Hayla Sellasse. Even under the BMA, 'outsiders/Amhara' who formerly owned *qalad* land in Jigjiga and who were dispossessed by the Italians, were beginning to return to the Reserved Areas. Indeed, soon after the establishment of the BMA, an Ethiopian Vice-Governor was installed in the town and an Ethiopian court functioned, much to the annoyance of the British. Despite the presence of the British administration, the Ethiopian Vice-Governor undertook the sale and exchange of land and registration of properties in the RA, and issued eviction orders against the Somali occupants of *qalad*, land that had been abandoned or confiscated during the Italian occupation. Former landowners' claims were recognised, as were the positions of those Somali clan leaders appointed before the Italian invasion.[64]

The Somalis in the RA were in the difficult position of having to keep in with both the Ethiopian and British authorities. Prudently, and no doubt profitably, some of the local Somali clan notables were often in the pay of both the Ethiopian government *and* the BMA.[65] The Ethiopian government in Harar kept up its contact with important Somalis, and the marriage of the Emperor's son, the Duke of Harar, brought an opportunity for Somali notables (64 from Jigjiga and 76 from the Ogaden) to be entertained and awarded presents and honours.[66] It was a peculiar situation in which Ethiopia moved to exert its authority and succeeded in creating a dual authority. This had been summed up very early on by an Ethiopian policeman who, on attempting to arrest a Somali in Jigjiga with the words 'By Haile Sellasie, I arrest you', received the reply 'By King George, I will not be arrested'.[67]

The Somali Youth League in Jigjiga

During 1946, the BMA withdrew from Dire Dawa, leaving only the Jigjiga district and the Hawd still in the so-called RA. The Ogaden continued to be ruled under the BMA of ex-Italian Somaliland. However, within the stipulations of the 1944 agreement the Ethiopian government could give the BMA notice to quit the RA, and in theory the Ogaden, within three months. The Ethiopian government did not do so for another two years, but in this period, Somali uncertainty began to express itself in more formal, political ways.[68] By the mid-forties, tension arose between elements of Somali society in the RA and the Ogaden, and Ethiopian administration in waiting. The return of the RA to Ethiopian rule became a highly politicised issue. Some Somalis, such as the Yaberre chief, *Sheekh* Xasan, who had flourished under British and Italian rule, viewed the return to Ethiopian rule with considerable suspicion. Even before the arrival of an organised Somali political body in Jigjiga, the Yaberre leader, *Sheekh* Xasan, was overtly anti-Ethiopian and seen as a great protagonist of Somali unity.[69] He later became a leading member of the Somali Youth Club (later League) in Jigjiga.[70]

The Somali Youth Club – locally known as *kulub* – was founded in Mogadishu on 15th May 1943, primarily as an urban self-help organisation, and to begin with, a large percentage of its membership was drawn from Mogadishu. From Mogadishu and other urban centres in ex-Italian Somaliland, Club branches extended into the small garrison, market and well centres in the Ogaden – then still administered from Mogadishu, but also to Jigjiga in the Reserved Areas, and to Dire Dawa and Harar in Ethiopia. As its name suggested, most of the members were aged between 18 and 32 and were exclusively Somali. Membership was drawn from what a British report described as the newly emerged 'middle class' of Somali, in particular private traders and those from monthly salaried groups such as government clerks, servants of Europeans, medical dressers, and members of the Somalia *Gendarmerie* (approximately seventy-five percent of the Somalia *Gendarmerie* stationed in Mogadishu were members of the Club). By 1947, certain headmen and notables had also joined.[71]

The aims and objectives of the club were summed up in a British report as 'fraternity, liberty and progress', and in the expression 'Somalia for the Somalis'. The Club encompassed a very wide range of opinion and motives, but its primary objective was the furtherance of the interests of the Somali people by breaking down clan barriers, ending tribal disputes, and by providing educational and social facilities for its members. Its earliest role was as a social welfare club, against a background of high prices in wartime Mogadishu and other urban centres.[72] In order that none of its members did anything that would bring the Club's name into disrepute with the British authorities, the Club even appointed its own internal 'police' whose duty it was to bring to account members of the Club found breaking the law.[73] The Club did much to aid the young, inexperienced BMA that had been so hastily established after the unexpectedly rapid collapse of the Italian armies in the Somali lands in 1941.[74] This accounts for the unusually cordial and close relations between the 'nationalist' Club and the British administration of the ex-Italian and Ethiopian Somali lands. Many of its members came from the *Gendarmerie* established under the BMA and the BMA did as much as it could to afford assistance to the Club without being seen as partisan by non-Club Somalis.[75]

In early 1946, the Club's benign and modest aims shifted as the future of the ex-Italian colonies began to be discussed in an international forum by the Peace Conference powers, to which the British Foreign Secretary Bevin proposed the idea of a Greater Somalia. By early 1947, its membership increased from approximately 1,000, mainly in Mogadishu, to around 25,000 members throughout Somali-speaking lands.[76] Although Bevin's idea of a Greater Somalia – the unification of all the Somali territories under one administration, preferably British, under United Nations Trusteeship – was almost immediately opposed by the USA and USSR,[77] the idea continued to have adherents among British administrators on the ground and was quickly picked up by the Somali Youth Club.

The implicit inclusion of the Ethiopian Somali lands in Greater Somalia was particularly contentious, not least because the 1942 and 1944 British agreements with Ethiopia explicitly recognised Ethiopia's sovereignty over the Ogaden and Reserved Areas. Moreover, the Four Power Commission, appointed in April 1946 to decide the future of the ex-Italian colonies, would not directly consider the Greater Somalia idea, but only the future of ex-Italian Somaliland. Yet, despite the overwhelming odds against the United Somalia idea, the Club continued to hold on to the hope of its attainment, a belief that the British did little to dispel, and probably discreetly encouraged for the sake of political expedience. Against this background of international politics and hopes for unification of the Somali lands, the Somali Youth Club changed its name to the Somali Youth League (SYL).[78]

Until early 1947, the League was not anti-Ethiopian. Abdulqadir Saqawa Din, the first President of the then Somali Youth Club, had even gone to Addis Ababa in August 1946 for an interview with Emperor Hayla-Sellasse. An interview was granted and the Emperor professed himself in sympathy with the Club and offered them any assistance in his power, adding ambitiously that the flag of Ethiopia was the banner of all Africans.[79] Later in the same year, a petition had been presented to the Chief Military Administrator in Mogadishu requesting union with Ethiopia.[80] However, by May 1947 the cordial attitude towards Ethiopia had changed markedly. One oral informant from Jigjiga claims that it was opinion from there, at one of the furthest outposts of the Club that helped change the agenda of Somali political activity. The informant, a member of the Club, remembers that the Jigjiga SYL were horrified at the Mogadishu Committee's petition to join with Ethiopia and wrote letters to Mogadishu exclaiming: 'the Ethiopians are colonisers, they are stronger than us, they are barbarous and arrogant, they will consume you, they want to cheat you, to take the land – never allow them [to do this]'.[81]

On 17 May 1947 during a 'tea party' in Jigjiga to celebrate its fourth anniversary, a religious and nationalistic speech was made by one of the SYL members. The speech made clear that the League was against the return to Ethiopian rule, although an 'inspector' visiting from the SYL headquarters in Mogadishu assured the British that nothing would be done to embarrass them.[82] In June, a deputation of local SYL supporters went to the British Senior Civil Affairs Officer in Jigjiga and reminded him that the European powers that had administered the neighbouring territories had done so by treaty, but that the Ethiopians occupied the RA and Ogaden by force and against the will of the tribesmen. The delegation also claimed that the Ethiopian government had never made any real attempt to administer the territory and was not at present capable of doing so.[83] This call for greater administration and, in effect, 'development', was not voiced before the war. In earlier times light administration and little interference had suited many Somali clans.

According to British sources, the SYL membership in Jigjiga drew support largely from those who had benefited from the Italian occupation, the war and the continuing British occupation. Whilst they were drawn from different clans, the majority were Darood. Many were increasingly urban-based and dependent on wage labour and were employed as policemen, soldiers, drivers, clerks, and servants. There was also a preponderance of traders. The commodity boom and price rises brought together traders and wage earners, who found that they had common interest against the traditional dominance of trade by Arabs, Indians (and also Somali traders of the Habr Awal clan from the Protectorate). The other important area of support was the agricultural entrepreneur *Sheekh* Xasan, 'headman' of the 'junior' Yaberre clan (described 'as the brains behind the SYL'), who had done well from the bumper harvests, high grain prices and tax-free conditions.[84]

All of these interests were, to varying degrees, threatened by the return to Ethiopian rule. This threat helped coalesce the interests of the new urban wage earning sector with the more conservative agriculturist Somali, who were not natural supporters of the SYL's aims but who feared claims by former landlords and backdated taxation. A list of prominent SYL individuals in the RA compiled by the British authorities reveals those most at risk from a return to Ethiopian rule, both politically and economically. These included the Yaberre chief *Sheekh* Xasan; Hussein Liban, an Akiishu trader and a relative of the Akiishu *Suldaan*, whose livelihood and identity had flourished since the Ethiopian defeat; and Osman Ali Garad, who was the acting *garaad* of the Gerri, whose brother had been arrested in the local disturbances in the area during 1942 and whose clan land was threatened by returnee *qalad* owners. Less inherently threatened by a return to Ethiopian rule, but of great influence in the Ogaden was the President of the Harar SYL branch, *Garaad* – sometimes *Suldaan* – Makhtal Dahiir, an Ogaadeen chief who had been sporadically loyal to the Ethiopian government and who was notoriously anti-British.[85]

The spread of the SYL to Harar and Dire Dawa (outside the RA and Ogaden) was most alarming from the Ethiopian point of view. They were towns which were now under full Ethiopian control, but which were of considerable historical, political and strategic significance to the Ethiopian centralists. Towards the end of 1947, the anti-Ethiopian feeling in Harar and Dire Dawa had stiffened. This was in part a religious revival directly linked with the demotion of Amhara 'Christian' political dominance and the end to the stranglehold over trade that the foreign merchants had enjoyed in Harar, during the Italian occupation. The Italian regime had given Harari townsmen employment in government albeit in a minor capacity. Furthermore, the departure of foreign 'British' Arab and Indian trading concerns enabled Harari to increase their involvement in trade. In the same way, local Somalis in Jigjiga had in the years during and since the Italian occupation, gained salaried employment and a foothold in trade. Nevertheless, after three years since the British restoration of Harar to Ethiopia, Harari townsmen saw that they had lost social and economic gains made under the Italians. They lost opportunities in government, in salaries paid to Muslim functionaries, and in terms of education. Where the Italians had promoted Arabic as a language of administration that many educated Muslim Harari regarded positively, the restoration Ethiopians promoted Amharic, a language intrinsically linked with Christian Amhara rule. Partly because of these grievances a Harari association was founded sometime in 1945 or 1946, which is remembered with two Arabic titles, the *jam'iya al-wataniya* or *jam'iya hurriya al harar/iya*, translated respectively as 'the nationalist society' or 'the society for Harari freedom'.[86]

Garaad Makhtal Daahir (who also held the Ethiopian title *Balambaras*) established the Somali Youth Club in Harar sometime in 1946 and soon after the Harari; societies allied themselves and merged with the Club. When Makhtal first arrived in Harar he was well received by the Ethiopian government, which saw him as an important historical ally in the Ogaden. British sources report that while he was in Harar the Ethiopian government paid him a healthy monthly allowance.[87] Indeed, Makhtal's first visit to Harar after the Italian defeat was to complain *against* the British Military Administration and its disarmament campaign in the Ogaden during 1943–44.[88] At that time, the Ogaden clans were anti-British because the disarmament campaigns left them vulnerable to raids by Isxaaq clansmen from the British Protectorate, and unable to defend water and grazing rights in the Hawd. By the second half of 1947 however, Makhtal was a leading campaigner against return to Ethiopian rule and for the unification of the administration of the Ogaden and RA with ex-Italian Somaliland under United Nations trusteeship – apparently against the wishes of some of his clansmen. A British source suggests his change in attitude happened when he asked for an audience with the Emperor to bargain for conditions for his support for a return to Ethiopian rule. Makhtal was sent to Addis Ababa and kept waiting for a month without gaining an audience.[89] However, during his stay in Addis Ababa, Makhtal met several Eritrean Muslims who influenced his attitude to the restoration of Ethiopian rule.[90] He then returned to Harar and went back to the Ogaden to encourage the League to claim full independence.[91] However there are several conflicting accounts of Makhtal's activities – his own included[92] – and it does seem that Makhtal and other Somalis vacillated between sides.

The Ethiopian government was quick to react to the radicalisation of the League within territory restored to rule from Addis Ababa. In June 1947, several prominent Somalis from Jigjiga and the Ogaden were called to Harar, where pressure was put on them to dissociate from the SYL. Some, if not all of them, signed documents in which they agreed to resign from the SYL.[93] As 1947 progressed the Ethiopian government's line towards the SYL hardened because the SYL activity in Harar was too direct a threat to Ethiopia's sovereignty. Moreover, the religious side to the SYL had latterly become more pronounced. Placards calling on Moslems to unite against their enemies were posted on Ethiopian government buildings in Dire Dawa. In response, the Ethiopian police in Jigjiga arrested the Qadi (Islamic judge) of the Somalis (illegally since the RA was still under British administration) during August 1947.[94]

In Harar, the Ethiopian authorities forbade open meetings of the SYL. The Ethiopian Vice-Governor *Blatta* Ayelle Gabre, whose record of collaboration with the Italians made him suspect in the eyes of many Ethiopian nationalists, took an extremely unyielding attitude towards the League.[95] In early September, after Makhtal had returned to the Ogaden, the Ethiopian authorities in Jigjiga attempted to arrest the Vice-President of the Harar branch of the SYL, Haji Kalile Ahmed, but large numbers of SYL members prevented him being taken to Harar.[96] Later in the same month, Jigjiga was visited by the then President of the Mogadishu branch of the SYL, Haji Mohamed Hussein, who had travelled by car from Mogadishu with the SYL flag flying on the bonnet.[97]

In a bold move signalling the Ethiopian sovereignty of the Ogaden, the American Sinclair Oil Company gained a concession from the Ethiopian government to prospect for oil in the Ogaden, but without the consultation of local Somali clans.[98] It caught the British off-guard and underlined the fact that the 1944 agreement had run its course and the return of the Reserved Areas could be requested by the Ethiopian government at any time. Furthermore, in the face of an increasingly belligerent SYL and in anticipation of regaining control of the RA, the Ethiopians appointed a more vigorous Ethiopian representative in Jigjiga, Major Demeke Retta, whom the British officials described as 'a senior official of strong anti-British persuasion to check the growth of the SYL in Jigjiga'.[99]

Makhtal Daahir meanwhile continued to play a double game, but other important Ogaadeen chiefs (*Suldaan* Bihi and *Ugaas* Mahomed), although still in the pay of the BMA, made it known that they were in favour of the reoccupation of the Ogaden by Ethiopia.[100] There followed several attempts in December 1947 to woo Makhtal back into the Ethiopian fold and he visited Jigjiga (as a British protected person) where he had interviews with the Ethiopian Governor of Jigjiga, and Director General of the Harar Province. Meanwhile, a SYL 'Inspector' from Mogadishu arrived in Jigjiga with the intention of taking representatives of all the RA clans to meet the Four Power Commission in Mogadishu in January. However, only the chiefs of Yaberre and Gadabuursi attended – the chiefs of the Gerri, Bartirre and Abasguul decided it was inadvisable to compromise themselves so deeply in their support for the now anti-Ethiopian SYL at this stage. For their part the Ethiopians dispatched their old Somali ally, *Balambaras* Abdullahi Farah 'Cagoole' to Dhagaxbuur in the Ogaden, liberally provided with funds to propitiate Ogaadeen support.[101] One informant remembers that at this time Somalis were pro-Ethiopian during meetings with the Ethiopian representatives in the day, whereas at evening meetings with the British officers they were pro-British and pro-League.[102]

By late 1947, it was clear to the British and Ethiopian governments that it no longer served a useful purpose for British to hold on to the Reserved Areas and the Ogaden.[103] Moreover, the failure of the BMA to effectively restrain the Ogaadeen clans from harassing representatives of the Sinclair Oil Company present in the area brought the general efficacy of the BMA as the guarantor of Ethiopian sovereignty of the Ogaden into question.[104] In anticipation of their resumption of government in the RA and Ogaden, the Ethiopian government moved first to put an end to opposition in Harar, arrested and imprisoned all suspected SYL members and others besides – many of whom escaped capture by fleeing to Jigjiga.[105] In February, the local SYL delegation to the United Nations 'Four Power' Commission on the future of the Italian colonies in Mogadishu returned after having failed to get even a hearing. Nevertheless, on their return a SYL flag was paraded about Jigjiga and the BMA quickly received complaints from the Ethiopian authorities.[106] After the move against Harari opposition in January, in March 1948 meetings were held between senior Ethiopian officials and, by now, the far more compliant Somali notables including Makhtal (who unlike many of his Harari SYL supporters remained free). These Somali notables were taken to Harar for interviews with the Vice-Governor and to Addis Ababa to meet with the Emperor.[107]

On 18 March, leading Somalis were informed of the early withdrawal of the British from the RA. On 20 March, the flying of any flags other than those of Great Britain and Ethiopia was forbidden. The official SYL activists removed their flag and substituted it with a Union Jack but this too was taken down on advice from the BMA. However, on the 23 March a party of 'young' Somalis newly arrived from the Ogaden, took possession of the SYL offices and illegally hoisted the SYL flag contrary to the League's official wishes. The young radical SYL men threatened British officials and a party of senior moderate League activists who attempted to lower the flag in compliance with the British authority's orders. Finally, the police supported by an armoured car proceeded to the League's offices and removed the flag, which the young Ogaden group resisted. A grenade was thrown, killing one of the RA policemen; and fighting ensued and over 20 Somalis were estimated killed, along with two Police and several more Somalis wounded.[108] This was the only violent incident directly linked to the return of the Reserved Areas to the Ethiopian Government, and when the Ogaden was returned later that September there were only isolated problems. Only Makhtal Dahiir rejected outright the Ethiopian government and led a small *shifta* band for two years after the hand-over, but his activities were not widely supported.[109] Many of the Ethiopian Somali (mainly Darood) clans valued their pre-war *de facto* autonomy under Ethiopia. Indeed life under the British who used the Ethiopian Darood clan's chief rivals the Isxaaq as their local auxiliaries had often proved humiliating. As many Ethiopian Somali saw it the return to weak Ethiopian rule was better than unification under the British who they saw as strong rulers – 'if you give your stick to a blind man you will be able to take it back later'.[110]

Conclusion

Ultimately the SYL in eastern Ethiopia struggled to maintain a united front. There were too many divisions and differences between clans, and clan leaders, between the agricultural and pastoral Darood, traditional leaders and the young radical townsmen influenced by the Mogadishu SYL. Moreover, the British alliance with the acquisitive Isxaaq of the British Protectorate made the prospect of continued British rule unpalatable to the majority Darood in the Ethiopian Somali lands.

There was therefore no stomach for the continued resistance to restored Ethiopian rule, particularly after the repression in Harar in January 1948. As before the occupation, the Ethiopians were now able to dilute Somali solidarity through the manipulation of older networks of power in Jigjiga and the Ogaden.

Indeed, once it was clear that the gains made by certain individuals and clans would not be jeopardised by the return to Ethiopian rule – at least not in the short term – former firebrands like *Sheekh* Xasan were gradually co-opted by the Ethiopian government. The Akiishu became an important prop to Ethiopian rule in Jigjiga and the surrounding areas;[111] their *suldaan* Odoowa is remembered as particularly close to Hayla-Sellasse despite the SYL connections of his brother, Xasan Gerri.[112] The Bartirre clan leader Dool Xirsi, who had also benefited from Italian rule, was quick realign himself with Ethiopian rule, continuing the tradition of Bartirre dominance in Jigjiga supported by Ethiopian patronage.[113]

Notes

1. This paper is drawn from Cedric Barnes, 'The Ethiopian state and its Somali periphery, *c. 1888–1948* (Ph.D. dissertation, University of Cambridge, 2000). The research benefited from grants from the AHRB, Trinity College, the Smuts, Prince Consort and Thirlwall, and Worts Funds. I would like to thank my research assistants Bashiir Xaaji and Bashiir Abdullahi for their help in interviews and translation in Jigjiga. Tim Carmichael also afforded me a great deal of assistance in Ethiopia, and has continued to give me help and encouragement. The interviews cited were conducted by the author in Jigjiga, Region 5, Ethiopia in 1998.

2. See for example the accounts in Bahru Zewde, *A History of Modern Ethiopia* (London, 1991), pp. 178–182; and a fuller account in Harold G. Marcus, *Ethiopia, Great Britain and the United States, 1941–1974* (Berkeley, 1983), pp. 8–78.

3. I.M. Lewis, *A Modern History of The Somali* (London, 2002), Pp. 129–131; John Drysdale, *The Somali Dispute* (London, 1964), pp. 65–73

4. Two studies that do concentrate on local circumstances but which are somewhat partisan are Tibebe Eshete, 'A history of Jigjiga town: 1891–1974' (Unpub. MA thesis, Addis Ababa University, 1988) which has a distinct 'Ethiopian' bias; and Charles L. Geshekter, 'Anti-colonialism and class formation: the eastern Horn of Africa, 1920–1950', *International Journal of African Historical Studies* (Vol. 18) No. 1, 1985, pp. 1–32, who is sympathetic to the Somali nationalist version.

5. Two accounts which look deeper into the background are Saadia Touval, *Somali Nationalism, International Politics and the Drive for Unity in the Horn of Africa* (Cambridge, Mass., 1963), who is sensitive to the complexities of local politics; and Tim Carmichael, 'Political Culture in Ethiopia's Provincial Administration: Haile Sellasie, Blate Ayele Gebre, and the Harari Kulub Movement', in M. Page *et al, Personality and Political Culture in Modern Africa: Studies Presented to Professor H.G. Marcus* (Boston, 1998) whose work concentrates on the interaction of Harari and Somali politics.

6. The following abbreviations will be used below: BDFA – *British Documents on Foreign Affairs: Reports and Papers from the Foreign Office Confidential Print*, General Editors, Kenneth Bourne, D. Cameron Watt, and Michael Partridge, (University Publications

of America, 1997); BMA – British Military Administration; BSP – British Somaliland Protectorate; FO – Foreign Office; PRO – Public Records Office, UK; RA – Reserved Areas; {S}CAO – {Senior} Civil Affairs Officer; WO – War Office.

7. See Saul Kelly, 'Britain, the United States, and the end of the Italian Empire, 1940–52', *Journal of Imperial and Commonwealth History*, Vol. XXVII, No. 3 (2000), p. 51.

8. The Italian period itself is not well served by published material. Alberto Sbacchi has sketched out the main events in his *Ethiopia Under Mussolini* (London, 1985), and *Legacy of Bitterness: Ethiopia & Fascist Italy, 1935–41* (Lawrenceville, 1997) – both studies concerned with the political problems of the Italian adventure at various levels in Ethiopia, Italy and the wider world. Haile Mariam Larebo's *The Building of an Empire-Italian Land Policy and Practice in Ethiopia 1935–1941* (Oxford, 1994), is grounded in the specific economic difficulties of the Italian regime in Ethiopia and the gap between the grand plans and their actual implementation in Ethiopia. The accounts suffer from the incomplete documentary record that has much to do with the brevity of the Italian occupation and its quick demise at the hands of an invading army.

9. 'Memorandum – Road Making in Harar District', Eldon Ellison to Consul Gen. Addis Ababa, Harar, 2 November 1937, PRO: FO 371/20929/J5028.

10. Hargeisa District Quarterly Intelligence Report, Hargeisa [BSP], 30 June 1937, PRO: FO 371/20925/J3819.

11. Cited by Geshekter, 'Anti-Colonialism and Class Formation', p. 24.

12. Cited by Patrick Kakwenzire, 'Colonial rule in the British Somaliland Protectorate, 1905–39', (Unpub. Ph.D., London, 1976), p. 530

13. For an overview see Harold Marcus, Ethiopia, Gt. Britain and the United States, pp.10–12, and for details see Lord Rennel of Rodd, British Military Administration of Occupied Enemy Territories in Africa, 1941–47 (London, 1948), pp. 88–92.

14. Rodd, *British Military Administration.*, pp. 74, 201, also see Drysdale, *The Somali Dispute*, p. 69. For an admirable summary on the complex diplomatic situation see again Kelly, 'Britain, the United States, and the end of the Italian Empire'.

15. 'Enclosure in No. 57 – Ethiopia: Political Review for 1943', Foreign Office, 13 June 1944, (J1864/1/1), *BDFA*, Part III, Series G, Vol. 4, pp. 243–255.

16. For an overview of the negotiations and content of this agreement see Harold Marcus, *Ethiopia, Great Britain and the United States*, pp. 33–39.

17. Rodd, British Military Administration, pp. 82–92

18. Cook to Eden, Addis Ababa, 17 May 1944, (J1915/6/1), *BDFA*, Part III, Series G, Vol. 4, p. 236.

19. 'Enclosure in No. 57 – Ethiopia: Political Review for 1943', Foreign Office, 13 June 1944, (J1864/1/1), *BDFA*, Part III, Series G, Vol. 4, pp. 243–255.

20. 'Enclosure in No. 21 – Commerce in Ethiopia, A.D. Bethell, Advisor to Ministry of Commerce, Addis Ababa, 18 July 1944', Howe to Eden, 2 September 1944, (J3238/2/1), *BDFA*, Part III, Series G, Vol. 4, pp. 464–499.

21. 'Enclosure in No. 44, Economic Report (A)', Cook to Bevin, Addis Ababa, 10 April 1946, PRO: FO 371/403/469.

22. 'Ethiopia, Annual Report for 1947', Weld-Forester to Bevin, Addis Ababa, 4 June 1948, PRO: FO 401/40.

23. 'Enclosure in No. 21 – Commerce in Ethiopia, A.D. Bethell, Advisor to Ministry of

Commerce, Addis Ababa, 18 July 1944', Howe to Eden, 2 September 1944, (J3238/2/1), BDFA, Part III, Series G, Vol. 4, pp. 464–499.

24. I believe, for example, that I.M. Lewis overstates the case when he wrote, "Nevertheless, the general character of opposition to Ethiopian control was indisputable", in Lewis, *A Modern History of the Somali;* and in general see Charles L. Geshekter, 'Anti-colonialism and class formation: the eastern Horn of Africa, 1920–1950'.

25. 'Memorandum of General Information on Harar Province', Dodds to Thesiger, Harar, 27 June 1917, PRO:FO 371/2854/159303; and oral informant, Dool Ableele, Interview 5, Jigjiga, 19/6/98; and generally Barnes, 'The Ethiopian State and its Somali Periphery', pp. 93–126.

26. Oral informants, Xaaji Faarax Cumar Celi, Interview 17, Jigjiga, 2/7/98; Ustaad Axmad Maxamad Boore, Interview 10, Jigjiga, 21/6/98; Dool Ableele, Interview 5, Jigjiga, 19/6/98; Maxamad Cabdullahi Farah, Interview 6, Jigjiga, 27/6/98.

27. Oral informant, Dool Ableele, Interview 5, Jigjiga, 19/6/98.

28. Barton to Henderson, Addis Ababa, 26 March 1930, PRO: FO 371/14593/J1386, and Barton to Simon, Addis Ababa, 18 January 1932, PRO: FO 371/16098/J734.

29. SCAO R.H. Smith, BMA, RA, Ethiopia, 6 August 1947', PRO: FO 1015/41; for Harar province as a whole see Ezekiel Gebissa, 'Consumption, Contraband, and Commodification – A History of Khat in Hararge, Ethiopia, c. 1930–1991, (Unpub. Ph.D. Thesis, Michigan State University, 1997).

30. See Barnes, 'The Ethiopian State and its Somali Periphery', pp.100–113; also see Tibebe Eshete, 'A history of Jigjiga town: 1891–1974' (Unpub. MA thesis, Addis Ababa University, 1988), pp.45–62.

31. I was unable to consult Italian archives, which I presume would have the most detail on the subject, although probably subject to bias and omission. But see sketchy information on Jigjiga in Enrico Brotto *Il regime delle terre nel Governo del Harar* (Harar, Governo del Harar, 1939), pp. 50–51, 55–56.

32. See Tibebe, 'A History of Jigjiga Town: 1891–1974, pp. 49–60; also see NJ Cossins, J.C. Bille, and K.E. Flattery, 'Land use study of the Jigjiga area, Ethiopia', (Joint ILCA/RDP Ethiopian Pastoral Systems Programme, Addis Ababa, 1984) p. 6

33. For comparison see Ezekiel Gebissa, 'Consumption, contraband, and commodification', pp. 59–64; and see Enrico Brotto *Il regime,* pp. 55–56.

34. See Tibebe, 'A History of Jigjiga Town: 1891–1974, pp. 49–60; also see Cossins, Bille, Flattery, 'Land use study of the Jigjiga area, Ethiopia', p. 6; and Enrico Brotto *Il regime,* pp. 55–56

35. Oral informant, Suldaan Nimcaan Sheekh Xasan Sheekh Ismaaciil, Interview 8, Jigjiga, 13/6/98

36. Oral informant, Xaaji Faarax Cumar Celi, Interview 17, Jigjiga, 2/7/98.

37. Oral informant, Xaaji Faarax Cumar Celi, Interview 17, Jigjiga, 2/7/98.

38. See Tibebe, 'A History of Jigjiga Town: 1891–1974, pp. 49–60; also see Cossins, Bille, Flattery, 'Land use study of the Jigjiga area, Ethiopia', p. 6; and Enrico Brotto *Il regime,* pp. 50–51.

39. Oral informant, Xaaji Faarax Cumar Celi, Interview 17, Jigjiga, 2/7/98.

40. Oral informant, Suldan Xasan Cabdi Cumar, Interview 9, Jigjiga, 17/6/98.

41. See Tibebe, 'A History of Jigjiga Town: 1891–1974, pp. 49–60; also see Cossins, Bille, Flattery, 'Land use study of the Jigjiga area, Ethiopia', p. 6.

42. Oral informant, Maxamad Cali Xuseen, Interview 7, Jigjiga, 15/6/98.
43. Oral informant, Xaaji Faarax Cumar Celi, Interview 17, Jigjiga, 2/7/98.
44. 'BMA-RA, Annual Report by the CAO for the year ended 31 December 1944', PRO: FO 1015/41/3A.
45. 'BMA-RA, Annual Report by the CAO for the year ended 31 December 1943', PRO: FO 1015/41/2A.
46. 'BMA-RA, Annual Report by the CAO for the year ended 31 December 1944', PRO: FO 1015/41/3A.
47. Ibid.
48. 'BMA-RA, Annual Report by the CAO for the year ended 31 December 1943', PRO: FO 1015/41/2A.
49. 'BMA-RA, Annual Report by the CAO for the year ended 31 December 1944', PRO: FO 1015/41/3A.
50. Report by Capt. Flower Acting CAO, Jigjiga, RA, 20 April 1945, PRO: WO 230/63.
51. Oral informant Xassan Xaashi Cilmi, Interview 11, Jigjiga, 25/6/98.
52. Report by Capt. Flower Acting CAO, Jigjiga, RA, 20 April 1945, PRO: WO 230/63
53. 'BMA-RA, Annual Report by the CAO for the year ended 31 December 1943', PRO: FO 1015/41/2A.
54. Ibid.; oral Informants, Adam Hasan, Mangistu Dilnassaw, and Kasahun Charkose, (Group) Interview 20, Gersum/Funyanbira, 1/6/98.
55. Report by Capt. Flower, Acting CAO, Jigjiga, RA, 20 April 1945, PRO: WO 230/63
56. Ibid.; oral informants Xaaji Faarax Cumar Celi, Interview 17, Jigjiga, 2/7/98, Farah Dhamel Daahir Husen, Interview 16, Jigjiga, 4/7/98; and Jirde Ismaaciil Aadau, Interview 18, Jigjiga, 26/6/98.
57. See Tibebe, 'A history of Jigjiga town: 1891–74', pp. 8–10; and also on the pre-Somali populations of this area see I.M. Lewis, 'The Galla in northern Somaliland', Rassegna di Studi Etiopici, 15 (1959), pp. 21–38, and oral informant Jirde Ismaaciil Aadau, Interview 19, Jigjiga, 26/6/98.
58. Oral Informants, Xasan Cabdi Raxmaan Sheekh Muxamad [Descendant of Sheekh Cumar], Interview 3, Jigjiga, 1/7/98, and Jirde Ismaaciil Aadau, Interview 18, Jigjiga, 26/6/98.
59. Ibid., (oral informants); Gebele was one of the first agricultural areas in the Protectorate on the border with Ethiopian territory.
60. By now led by a Suldaan Oodowa who had been nominated by Sheekh Cumar before his death and to whom the Sheekh's son, Muxamed acted as a spiritual guide, Ibid.
61. Ibid., (oral informants); and also see 'BMA-RA Monthly Notes for September 1947', SCAO, Jigjiga, 7 October 1947, PRO: FO 1015/41; and 'BMA-RA, Annual Report by the CAO for the year ending 31 December 1947', PRO: FO 1015/49.
62. Ibid.
63. 'BMA-RA, Annual Report by the CAO for the year ended 31 December 1946', PRO: FO 1015/90/2A.
64. SCAO Smith, BMA, RA, Ethiopia, 6 August 1947', PRO: FO 1015/41; Report by Capt. Flower Acting CAO, Jigjiga, RA, 20 April 1945, PRO: WO 230/63.
65. 'BMA-RA, Annual Report by the CAO for the year ended 31 December 1944', PRO: FO 1015/41/3A.
66. 'BMA-RA, Annual Report by the CAO for the year ended 31 December 1946', PRO: FO 1015/90/2A.

67. 'BMA-RA, Annual Report by the CAO for the year ended 31 December 1943', PRO: FO 1015/41/2A.

68. 'BMA-RA, Annual Report by the CAO for the year ended 31 December 1946', PRO: FO 1015/90/2A.

69. 'BMA-RA, Annual Report by the CAO for the year ended 31 December 1944', PRO: FO 1015/41/3A.

70. 'BMA-RA, Annual Report by the CAO for the year ended 31 December 1946', PRO: FO 1015/90/2A.

71. 'Memorandum on Native Clubs in Somalia', [n.d. probably late 1946], PRO: FO 1015/51/8B.

72. Oral informant, Yassin Mussa Ahmed, Interview 12, Jigjiga, 28/6/98

73. 'Memorandum on Native Clubs in Somalia', [n.d. probably late 1946], PRO: FO 1015/51/8B.

74. For evocative accounts of the makeshift and shoestring British military administration of the ex-Italian Somali lands Gerald Hanley's novel *A Consul at Sunset* (London, 1951), and his *Warriors* (London, 1993) – the reprint of the half of his book *Warriors and Strangers* (1971) which dealt with Somali lands – are particularly good reading.

75. 'Extract from Brigadier Stafford's Fortnightly Report No. 2, 26 November 1946', PRO: FO 1015/51.

76. 'Memorandum on Native Clubs in Somalia', [n.d. probably late 1946], PRO: FO 1015/51/8B

77. For details see Kelly, 'Britain, the United States, and the end of the Italian Empire'

78. [?] Nairobi, 7 March 1947, PRO: FO 1015/51/2A, and also HQ East African Command, Monthly Intelligence Review, April 1947, PRO: FO 1015/51.

79. 'Memorandum on Native Clubs in Somalia', [n.d. probably late 1946], PRO: FO 1015/51/8B.

80. Periodical Intelligence Report No. 1, HQ East Africa Command, 1 January 1947, PRO: FO 1015/51/2A.

81. Oral informant, Dool Ableele, Interview 5, Jigjiga, 19/6/98.

82. Smith to CAO Middle East Land Forces, Jigjiga, 17 May 1947, PRO: FO 1015/51.

83. 'BMA: RA, Monthly Notes for June 1947', SCAO, Jigjiga, 6 July 1947, PRO: FO 1015/41; BMA – Annual Report by the CAO on the Administration for the year ended 31 December 1947', PRO: FO 1015/49.

84. Smith SCAO, BMA, RA, Ethiopia, 6 August 1947', PRO: FO 1015/41; and Smith SCAO, to HQ, Middle East Land Forces, RA, Ethiopia, 19 June 1947, PRO: FO 1015/51.

85. *Ibid. Balambaras* (an Ethiopian title) Makhtal Daahir of the rer Haroun rer Delal Ogaadeen sub-clan was a *Garaad* and had considerable power in the Ogaadeen around Dhagaxbuur. His name is mentioned in the reports concerning the Dhagaxbuur agreement in 1928 and in those of the Boundary Commission. The British thought him 'an appalling liar', and who was notoriously anti-Isxaaq despite being married to a sister of one Abdi Warsama, a Habr Awal Isxaaq and 'leading citizen of Hargeisa'. From a notable Ogaadeen family with large camel herd, Makhtal's family were 'like a government with its own army', and he inherited the title *Garaad* from his brother at the age of 13. It seems that he was first recognised by the Ethiopian authorities during Lij Iyyasu's time who gave him guns and horses in return for his collaboration and tribute of livestock. He was a long term although expedient collaborator with Ethiopian government and helped to found Dhagaxbuur in the interest of 'getting

guns' and trade in general. He was obstructive whenever the British tried to get grazing rights enforced for the Isxaaq in the Hawd and Ogaden, in particular during the Anglo-Ethiopian Boundary Commission hearings. He alleges that the British offered him a salary if he would support British claims to the Hawd and Ogaadeen, which he thought poor recompense for the territorial concessions to the Isxaaq that the British had requested. [Somaliland] Fortnightly Intelligence Report, Lt. Col. Bennet, Burao [BSP], 30 September 1935, PRO: FO 371/19156/J7003; and oral informants Cali Adan Maxamad, Interview 15, Jigjiga, 6/7/98; Farah Dhamel Daahir Husen, Interview No. 16, Jigjiga, 4/7/98; and Makhtal Daahir, Interview 14, Addis Ababa, 13/7/98.

86. This account is taken from Tim Carmichael, 'Political Culture in Ethiopia's Provincial Administration', p. 201.

87. British Legation to Foreign Office, Addis Ababa, 27 September 1947, PRO: FO 1015/51. Makhtal was thought of as something of an Ethiopian patriot and had resisted Italian rule for a time. On the Ethiopian collapse he tried to escape via the British Protectorate, but the authorities there were not well disposed to him because he had been so obstructive in the 1930s border demarcation. Not wanting to offend the new neighbouring Italian colonial regime in Ethiopia, the British handed Makhtal over to the Italians. The Italians took him to Mogadishu where he was imprisoned for three months after which a court there sentenced him to death, but then transferred him to Harar where he was imprisoned but released eight months later. He spent the rest of the war 'quietly' near Dhagaxbuur. See oral informants: Cali Adan Maxamad, Interview 15, Jigjiga, 6/7/98; Farah Dhamel Husen, Interview 16, Jigjiga, 4/7/98, and Makhtal Daahir, Interview 14, Addis Ababa, 13/7/98.

88. Oral informant, Farah Dhamel Husen, Interview 16, Jigjiga, 4/7/98.

89. British Legation to Foreign Office, Addis Ababa, 27 September 1947, PRO: FO 1015/51.

90. Telegram – British Legation to Foreign Office, Addis Ababa, 25 October 1947, PRO: FO 1015/51.

91. British Legation to Foreign Office, Addis Ababa, 27 September 1947, PRO: FO 1015/51.

92. Oral informants: Cali Adan Maxamad, Interview 15, Jigjiga, 6/7/98; Farah Dhamel Husen, Interview 16, Jigjiga, 4/7/98, and Makhtal Daahir, Interview 14, Addis Ababa, 13/7/98.

93. 'BMA-RA, Monthly Notes for June 1947', SCAO, Jigjiga, 6 July 1947, PRO: FO 1015/41.

94. BMA-RA, Monthly Notes for August, 1947', Senior Civil Affairs Officer, Jigjiga, 4 September 1947, PRO: FO 1015/41.

95. HM Consul to HM Minister, Addis Ababa, 27 August 1947, PRO: FO 1015/51, and see Carmichael, 'Political Culture in Ethiopia's Provincial Administration'.

96. BMA-RA, Monthly Notes for September, 1947', SCAO, Jigjiga, 7 October 1947, PRO: FO 1015/41.

97. *Ibid.*

98. BMA-RA, Monthly Notes for August 1947 SCAO, Jigjiga, 4 September 1947, PRO: FO 1015/41, and see BMA-RA, Annual Report by the CAO for the year ended 31 December 1947', PRO: FO 1015/49.

99. BMA-RA Monthly notes for October 1947', SCAO, Jigjiga, 1 November 1947, PRO: FO 1015/41.

100. *Ibid.*

101. 'BMA-RA Monthly notes for December 1947', SCAO, Jigjiga, 2 January 1948, PRO: FO 1015/41. 'Cagoole' Cabdullahi Farah of the rer Ali Ogaadeen clan spoke both Amharic (unusual for an Ogaadeen clansman) and Arabic, and the British considered him 'dangerous schemer who is always making trouble'. He was disabled from birth and could only move about on his hands and knees. Oral informants remember that although from an Ogaadeen clan he was brought up in the Harar highlands around the *katama* of Gersum where he attended Quranic school – perhaps on account of his disability, Here he may have come to the notice of Ethiopian officials since Gersum was one of the garrison centres for the Ogaden. The nickname 'Cagoole' referred to his disability which had great significance for Somalis who feared the great 'spiritual' power they believed disabled people to possess, and consequently treated such individuals with great respect. See [Somaliland] Fortnightly Intelligence Report, Lt. Col. Bennet, Burao [BSP], 30 September 1935, PRO: FO 371/19156/J7003; and oral informants Maxamad Cabdullahi Farah (Cagoole's son), Jigjiga, Interview 6, 27/6/98; Yassin Mussa Ahmed, Interview 12, Jigjiga 28/6/98; Xassan Xaashi Cilmi, Interview No. 11, Jigjiga, 25/6/98.

102. Oral informant, Xassan Xaashi Cilmi, Interview 11, Jigjiga, 25/6/98.

103. 'Ethiopia, Annual Report for 1947', Weld-Forester to Bevin, Addis Ababa, 20 July 1948, PRO: FO 401/40.

104. 'Ethiopia, Annual Review for 1948', Lascelles to Bevin, Addis Ababa, 9 February 1949, PRO: FO 401/41.

105. *Ibid.*, and 'BMA-RA, Monthly Report for January 1948', SCAO, Jigjiga, 1 February 1948, PRO: FO 1015/41, for the story in Harar which was far more dramatic than events in Jigjiga see Tim Carmichael, 'Political Culture in Ethiopia's Provincial Administration'.

106. 'BMA-RA Monthly Report for February 1948', SCAO, Jigjiga, 10 March 1948, PRO: FO 1015/41.

107. 'BMA-RA Monthly Report for March 1948', SCAO, Jigjiga, 10 April 1948, PRO: FO 1015/41.

108. *Ibid.*

109. Oral informants: Cali Adan Maxamad, Interview 15, Jigjiga, 6/7/98; Farah Dhamel Husen, Interview 16, Jigjiga, 4/7/98, and Makhtal Daahir, Interview 14, Addis Ababa, 13/7/98.

110. Oral informant, Cali Adan Maxamad, Interview 15, Jigjiga, 6/7/98.

111. Oral informants: *Ustaad* Axmad Maxamad Boore, Interview 10, Jigjiga, 21/6/98.

112. Oral informant, Jirde Ismaaciil Aadau, Interview 18, Jigjiga, 26/6/98.

113. Oral informants: Dool Ableele, Interview 5, Jigjiga, 19/6/98; Maxamed Cali Xuseen, Interview 7, Jigjiga 15/6/98. Interestingly, Dool Xirsi was not considered the rightful *garaad* of the Bartirre, but had kept his position with Ethiopian support and his own patronage network. Oral informant, Yassin Mussa Ahmed, Interview 12, Jigjiga, 28/6/98.

Chapter Four

Pithless Nationalism: The Somali Case

Hassan Mahaddala
Southern University

> A nation's existence is, if you will pardon the metaphor, a daily plebiscite,
> just as an individual's existence is a perpetual affirmation of life.
>
> – Ernest Renan

Obviously people do not change their nationality as often as they do their voting behavior. Renan's central thesis is that a nation – a collectivity over and above the tribe – is a subjective phenomenon. According to the French publicist, nationality is a voluntary association subject to one's perception of incentives or disincentives.[1] This being the case, the whole literary arsenal that lend credence to "natural nation" – i.e., history, anthropology, politics, philology, etc. – must also be subjective. To the extent that these are so, the task of the researcher is not only to investigate the accuracies of these "meta-narratives," to borrow Lyotard's term, but explain how they inspire national formation or spark nationalism.[2]

In this study, we will examine the existing literature on Somali nationalism under a new light. Although we will not concern ourselves with the correctness of the literature, we will dispute some of its findings. In particular, we will question the validity of the dominant ethnicist perspective and challenge the foundational myth on which Somali nationalism was constructed. In order to do so, we will closely scrutinize those "natural features" – i.e., race, language, history, religion, common habitat, etc. – that are often cited in the literature as the "legitimating elements" of the Somali nation. As we shall demonstrate, although Somalis possess many of these objective characteristics in common, they do not owe their national formation or sentiment to them. As a traditional society, Somalis did not develop or cultivate these "national" peculiarities enough to emit those transcendental values that cause people to coalesce and gel together as a nation. To this day, they exist in the mind of the average Somali as empty shells devoid of contents and meaning. Hence, our apt use of the term pithless nationalism in their regard.

Literature Review

The literature on Somali nationalism is limited both in volume and in scope. Most studies on the subject are written from a single perspective: an historical one. Accordingly, they present the Somali nation as an historical community with an age-old feeling of "oneness". Somali nationalism, the historians maintain, springs from this ancient sentiment. In this section, we will examine how these historical expositions led to the "ethnicization" of Somali nationalism.

To arrive at an ethnicist conception of Somali nationalism, the historians focus on three areas of monumental implications for national formations:

- The migration of ethnic Somalis from the Arabian Peninsula;
- Their conversion to Islam about the first century of the faith;
- Their endless feuds with their regional protagonists, the Christian Abyssin- ians.

Mass migrations, profession of common faith, and inter-ethnic wars constitute some the most potent factors that can cause "an alignment of values" among peoples. After an extensive examination of these events, the historians offer a chronological and spatial account of the Somali people's history. Aided by an accident of nature that bestowed on Somalis a number of common natural traits, the historians postulate an ethno-cultural nationalism.[3]

Typical of these studies is I.M. Lewis's work entitled *A Modern History of Somalia: Nation and State in the Horn of Africa.* In this book, the author aims "to provide a sociologically and anthropologically informed history of the Somali people." To this end, he delves deeply into the description of the physical and social environment, which, as he sees it, had over the centuries molded and hemmed the Somali people together as one nation. To him, Somali nationalism springs from this ancient natural environment. He remarks:

> Somali cultural nationalism is a centuries old phenomenon and not something which has been recently drummed up to give credence to political claims. It is the source rather than the product of nationalist aspirations.[4]

The dictating logic behind Lewis' proposition seems to be this: an objective environment can only produce an objective nation. Probably this is why the author and his fellow historians are magnetically attracted to the physical and social settings of the Somalis. Elsewhere, after discussing these features, the prolific author observes:

> Although the Somali did not traditionally form a unitary state, it is this heritage of cultural nationalism which, strengthened by Islam, lies behind Somali nationalism today.[5]

Saadia Touval, author of *Somali Nationalism: International Politics and Drive For Unity in the Horn of Africa*, takes a similar approach as Lewis'. Like the latter, he first discusses the history of the Somali people, adds an entire catalogue of primordial qualities shared by Somalis, and from this extrapolates an ethnicist sentiment. As he put it:

> Somali nationalism stems from a feeling of national consciousness in the sense of "we" as opposed to "they" which has existed among the Somali for many centuries. It was nurtured by tribal genealogies and traditions, by the Islamic ties and by conflicts with foreign peoples.[6]

In another study, Touval repeats these assertions. In his words: "There are strong cohesive ties – tradition of common ancestry, common language and cultural heritage, and Islamic religion – which bind Somalis, and form the basis of their national consciousness.[7]

Another author who defines Somali nationalism in similar terms is Rupert Emerson. Writing a foreword note for Touval's book, the eminent professor stated:

> One of the distinctive attributes of the Somalis…is that they possess a good measure of the elements, derived from the example of the classic Western European prototypes, which have in the past been assumed to be the essential ingredients of the nation.[8]

After making this assertion, Emerson cited the "essential ingredients" of the Somali nation as common language, religion, descent, and territory. In his opinion, these constituted the sources of Somali nationalism.[9]

Likewise, E.A. Bayne, editor of the *Northeast Africa Series*, views Somali nationalism in ethnicist terms. According to him, unlike other Sub-Saharan Africans, Somalis share "a deeply felt sense of nationhood." This sense of nationhood, as he sees it, is not limited to an elite class of people nor instilled by them. Rather, it is a sentiment that pervades the whole collectivity and derives from "an emotional, cultural, and historical experience shared by all Somalis.[10]

Without arguing with the obvious fact that Somalis constitute an objectively definable community, one may question, however, the validity of the proposition that equates their nationalism with cultural nationalism. As we will see in the following section, the literary and the artistic materials that are required for the development of such a "romantic" enterprise were not available to Somalis.

Ethno-Cultural Nationalism and The Genesis of Somali Nationalism

As an offspring of Romanticism, cultural nationalism, in order to take effect, requires a certain degree of cultural development and political sophistication, which the Somalis of the pre-World War II era did not possess.[11] It is built on the literary and artistic materials produced by cultural nationalists, such as the "L'Illuminati" of Europe, who not only praised the uniqueness and special characteristics of their nations – i.e., race, language, literature, territory, history, religion, etc. – but portrayed them as living organisms, which, if left unprotected or continually nurtured, were capable of dying. Cultural nationalism exalts all the natural features of the nation.[12]

Before embarking on their nationalist campaigns, most political nationalists study these works and frame the ideological charter of their movements around them. Thus, after the idea of an organic nation took hold in the psyche of the European masses, ethnic nationalism developed.[13] Now let us see whether a similar trend existed in the Somalian environment before the twentieth century, when Somali nationalism began.

Race and The Development of Somali Nationalism

The role of race in the development or vigor of Somali nationalism is extremely limited. Although Somali nationalists occasionally spoke of their nation in ethnicist terms and, at times, demanded independence on the basis of that, unlike their European counterparts, especially the Germans, they never made any reference to their people's ethnic purity or stressed the need for protecting it from adulteration.[14] Unlike their European counterparts, who preferred smaller and ethnically homogeneous states over the polyglot empires of their era, the post-War Somali leaders were rarely concerned with race. Apparently, they lacked the literary and artistic treasures from which to construct such a racialist conception to inspire and mobilize the masses.

Moreover, prior to the twentieth century, when Somalis first began to coalesce as a nation, they were divided into antagonistic clans who raided and pillaged one another,[15] in the same way that Stalin stated the Georgians treated one another before their absorption into the Russian Empire.[16] Given these facts, one may conclude that racial affinity and ethnic considerations did not inspire the development of Somali nationalism or sustained it, for that matter. This is why Somali political leaders rarely employed them as reasons for separate political existence.

The Role of Somali Language in Somali Nationalism
Another factor that comes to mind when dealing with cultural nationalism is the issue of philology. For most cultural nationalists, the national language holds a certain aura of beauty (as in the case of the French) or possesses a certain level of purity (as in the case of the Germans), which requires protection and continuous nurturing. In the Somali case, however, the available evidence suggests that the Somali language, although nation-wide, never acquired the aura of the French language; and, since it is heavily indebted to Arabic, unlike the German language, it could not have been considered a candidate for protection from adulteration.[17]

Additionally, the majority of the Somali nationalists were proficient in Arabic, and revered the language of the Koran more than the "vernacular" Somali; and this is why they pressed the colonial governments to institute Arabic as the official language of the country.[18] By the same token, this is why the Arabic alphabets became the first try of those who were trying to develop a script for the Somali language in the nineteen-fifties.[19]

Furthermore, the Somali language was not written until 1972, twelve years after independence, and, therefore, could not have inspired among the Somalis the kind of sentiment that, for instance, printed Spanish instilled among the Spanish-speaking peoples of the Americas and Europe, as Benedict Anderson had elegantly elaborated.[20] For all these reasons, one may be led to believe that the Somali language did nothing to inspire the development of Somali nationalism.

Language is also important to cultural nationalists for another reason, namely as a medium by which national literature is composed and dispensed. Here, the main interest lies in the national literature itself, which is revered for at least three reasons. First, the national literature is the best artistic tool to record and communicate national glories and failures for posterity. Second, it praises the nation and paints a vision of national grandeur for all its members. And third, being an artistic accomplishment itself, a national literature is a source of national pride, which can attract and gel diverse communities together. In these ways, the national literature can hold a nation together when other transcendental values are either weak or non-existent.[21]

Now let us turn to Somali literature and see if it performs these functional uses for the Somali people. Although Somali literature is vast and captures most of the national experience, this experience was, before the Second World War, parochial at best and divisive at worst. It was an experience that was shaped by clan rivalries and inflated clan ego; and Somali poetry, which is the single most important category of literary and artistic works in the country, catered to these sectarian (as opposed to national) interests. Accordingly, it celebrated and exalted local symbols and figures, who often made their name at the expense of other rival Somali clans.[22]

For these reasons, before the Somali independence movement began in the nineteen-forties, there was no pre-existing repository of "national literature" that the political nationalists could use to rally the nation. In other words, the Somali literature did not have a transcendental value and therefore did not hold the nation together in the same way that, for instance, national literatures held the Italian and German principalities together before their final merger in the nineteenth century.[23] Due to this fact, Somali literature contributed little or nothing to the development of Somali nationalism.

The Effect of Common Territory on Somali Nationalism

Another objective factor which is often touted by students of Somali affairs is the Somali people's possession of a common territory. Both John Drysdale's and Louis Fitzgibbon's books, cited above, place particular importance on the territorial aspect of Somali nationalism. However, for most Somalis of the early twentieth century, this territory was devoid of sentimental (as opposed to economic) value that could inspire a cultural movement. As Lewis had observed, for most Somalis "land has no mystical or ritual value" and "political ascendancy is not conferred by or symbolized in mystical ties to the earth but derives from superior fighting potential.[24] It is for these reasons that Somali nationalists did not develop a territorial concept comparable to the German Lebensraum;[25] and, throughout their career, never spoke of their country in such glowing terms as, for instance, the Germans spoke of the Black Forest or the Italians of their side of the Alps.[26]

Most of all, for the Somalis of the nineteenth century, this territory was vague and undefined. As a matter of fact, the Somali chiefs, like the Sultans of Morocco, did not rule over territorially defined tribes but rather ethnically defined ones.[27] "The barren terrain in which nomadic pastoralism is the prevailing economy does little to foster, and indeed actively militates against the formation of stable territorial groups"[28] and, one may add, territorial sentiment.

Perhaps this is why in their protection treaties with the British government in the eighteen-eighties, the Somali elders were satisfied with the extension of British protection to the people and did not press for equal protection for the land. In fact, according to Judge D.J. Latham Brown, who studied the subject, when the Somalo-British protection treaties were being devised, the Somali leadership did not bother to define the confines of their country; and, in his opinion, this is why London was legally justified in ceding Western Somaliland to the Abyssinian Empire in 1897.[29]

In this sense, Somali nationalism was not motivated by a territorial sentiment.

As a matter of fact, as late as 1957, at the height of Somali nationalist fervor, the Provincial Assembly in Southern Somalia expressed its willingness to accept "any borderline" with Ethiopia, "regardless of its location," as long as that arrangement would take into account the security of the emerging state and the socio-economic interest of the Somali people.[30] For all these reasons, one may conclude that Somali nationalism was not inspired either by the beauty of the "national land" or the loss of it to foreigners.

The Concept of Common History and Somali Nationalism

Another feature of a nation that is often expressed in connection with cultural nationalism is the possession of "common history." Cultural nationalists always claim that their nation was molded by common historical events and institutions; and that it once enjoyed political unity and led an independent life. For these intellectuals, therefore, nationalism is a mere re-arising of a historic nation and a legitimate undertaking to regain its past unity and political independence. It is along this line of thought that students of Somali nationalism often discuss the life and times of the Awdal Sultanate (1528–1543) and its leader, the Imam Ahmed Ibrahim Al-Ghazi (1506–43).[31]

Did Somalis really possess a common history before colonialism? Or, to put it in another way, was Somali nationalism a mere re-awakening of the Somali nation? The answer to these questions is simply no. For one thing, the Awdal Sultanate was founded on postulates of religion not of nationality.[32] Although the bulk of the population of the Sultanate was ethnic Somalis, the Sultan and his ministers appear to have been non-Somalis. Even the army of the state was multi-national and included Somalis, Oromos, Afars, and even Turks. Second, the Sultanate was too territorially limited and ephemeral to leave any lasting memory in the collective mind of the Somali people. Finally, the Somali, being independent-minded and anti-authority, could not have looked back at an autocracy with admiration and could not have been inspired by it almost five centuries later.

Besides, there is always the difficult of deciding when a common history becomes common. According to Professor Karl Deutsch, a common history is not always perceived common to all. People who are affected by the same historical processes and events do not always share these experiences. Instead each community would accentuate that part of history that fits its particular aspirations. Take, for instance, the Czechs and Germans of Bohemia. These peoples had long inhabited the same territory and were exposed to the same historical events and incidents. Yet, these experiences, instead of molding them into a single nation, made them bitter enemies.[33] The same may be said of the Somali people. As Lewis and Andrzejewski had observed:

> In the past the Somali have never formed a single political entity and have existed as a loose cultural grouping of various distinct and often opposed political units. Each of these clans and lineage groupings – often bitterly opposed to others by feud – has its own particular history.[34]

In light of these facts, one might contend that Somali nationalism was not aimed at recapturing a past history; and, in my opinion, this is why Somali nationalists did not demand independence on the basis of a common history.

Religion and Somali Nationalism

The role of religion (Islam) in the development of Somali nationalism must not be over-emphasized, either. Even in countries (such as England and France), where religious ideals contributed to the development of nationalism, the latter was derived mainly from socio-political factors that over the centuries slowly seeped into the national faith. Take, for instance, the medieval concept of "corpus Christi mysticum," which envisioned a Christian nation, whose members were equal before God. When in the eighteenth century, the state apparati were secularized, the religious concept was also supplanted by the latent concept of "popular sovereignty," which envisioned a nation, whose members were equal before the law and entitled to political rights. It was only after this juncture that the mobilization of the whole "nation" along religious lines became possible, and the political nationalists in these countries were able to "nationalize" religion.[35]

In the Somali case, however, a similar fusion of religion and culture is not discernible. Although Somali religious leaders, beginning with the Imam Ahmed Al-Ghazi, made considerable use of Islam for mass mobilization, their religious sermons were devoid of any aesthetic cultural values; and to this day, the Somali saints are "venerated for their own personal piety and religious efficacy rather than for sociological reasons."[36] Furthermore, the teachings of Somali clerics did not include nationalist principles – which, for instance, would have proclaimed the equality of the Somali people or extended political rights to the individual – that could inspire cultural nationalism.

For all these reasons, the contribution of Islam to Somali nationalism should not be exaggerated. Both Somalia's colonial leaders and intellectuals are guilty of doing that. Perhaps they were misled by the fact that the origin of the entire Somali nation is traceable to a few Muslim saints – a phenomenon to which Lewis had aptly referred to as "cult of the saints."[37] In reality, though, the contribution of religion to Somali nationalism was limited to adding certain veracity to the nationalist message and conferring added credibility on the messenger himself. Accordingly, one may conclude that Islam may had reinforced the political nationalism of the Somalis, but did not cause or define it, as Lewis and Samatar would have us believe.[38]

The Sources and Nature of Somali Nationalism

In terms of source and inspiration, Somali nationalism stemmed from two main "isms," namely traditionalism[39] and anti-colonialism.[40] Although they originated from two separate sources, both phenomena were stimulated by the peculiarities of the "colonial situation" of the nineteenth and twentieth centuries.[41] Consequently, both were opposed to the colonial system and therefore posed alternative socio-political formations to the prevailing state of affairs. In this regard, Somali nationalism owes its origin, and its strength as an *idee-force*, to the two phenomena we conveniently call traditionalism and anti-colonialism.

In general, traditionalism – or traditional nationalism, as it developed later – was a "counter" movement. When it rose in Europe, in the eighteenth century, it appeared as an anti-Jacobin enterprise. Its advocates – i.e., Edmund Burke, Vicomte de Bonald, and Friedrich von Schlegel – feared and detested the excesses of the French Revolution and its rationalist philosophy. In reaction to these, they propounded and publicized conceptions that reverenced traditional political institutions, cultures, religion, and even languages. They argued that these were divinely ordained and enjoined the Jacobins not to violate them.[42]

In the colonial areas of Africa and Asia, traditional nationalism was also a "counter" philosophy. It rose in reaction to the destructive effect of European colonialism. In their attempts to institute imperial regimes, the colonialists trampled on native political institutions, culture, and religions, and, as a consequence, aroused popular interests in these matters. It was in this regard that B.G. Tilak, an Indian traditional nationalist, sought to popularize the past greatness of the Mahratta Empire and revived its most prominent religious symbol, the elephant-headed goddess Ganesh; and Edward Blyden, a black nationalist from the West Indies, studied the ancient civilization of the Negro, and exhorted blacks outside Africa "to betake themselves to their ancestral home, and assist in constructing a Christian African Empire."[43]

The purpose of these traditional nationalists, said Elie Kedourie, "is to transform the 'heap of loose sand,' which is the traditional society battered and pulverized by Europe, into something solid and powerful, into a battering ram...."[44] The efficacy of "cultural gospel" in this regard was obvious. The colonial peoples needed only to be reminded of the cultural achievements of their ancestors – i.e., the gargantuan empires they found, the majestic temples they erected, and the divine scriptures they left behind – to stimulate their consciousness and spur them to action.

Like its counterparts in Asia and other parts of Africa, Somali traditional nationalism was a popular reaction to the pulverizing effect of European colonialism. At its incipient stage, it consisted of a welter of ideas and sentiments that reverenced local institutions. However, during the colonial imposition – a period of inordinate pressure and intensified collective action – the constitutive ideas of Somali traditionalism took shape and gave rise to a new popular attitude that reverenced the shared ideals.

This observation can be explained with two examples. Take Islam, for instance. Before the colonial onslaught, Somalis viewed Islam in spiritual terms only, and therefore imputed no socio-political value to it. Also Somali religious figures were venerated for their personal piety and possessed little or no extra-religious status in society. With the onset of colonialism, these matters changed. Islam became one of the defining characteristics of the Somali nation; and Somali religious authorities, hitherto uninterested in worldly affairs, assumed the task of defending this Islamic/Somali nation.

The existence of a common religion and a conscious Muslim leadership who vowed to defend it did not guarantee the success of traditional nationalism. It required the existence of a popular language with which to express the new conceptualization of Islam. This function fell, of course, on the Somali language. Having served this purpose well, the latter soon gained a new socio-political significance for the Somali people. It became the language with which they expressed their world views and political aspirations.[45] It was in this regard, it seems, that the Somali language acquired a "sentimental value" for the Somali people and became the linchpin of national solidarity in the nineteenth century.

In sum, traditional nationalism sparked interest "in all things Somali." By late nineteenth century, most Somalis became conscious of their common national features and soon imparted "a congregational character" to them, to use a borrowed phrase. Thenceforth, it became possible for the foes of colonialism to mobilize Somalis along socio-cultural lines. It was in this regard that the great Sheikhs, the Sheikh Hassan Barsane and the Sayyid Mohammed Abdulla Hassan, conceived the existence of a "Somali nation" and resolved to liberate it from colonial rule during their sojourn in Hijaz (Saudi Arabia) in the late nineteenth century.[46]

In addition to traditionalism, Somali nationalism was also inspired by the difficulties of the colonial situation. The colonial regimes, as soon as they established themselves, employed the power of the state to deprive their subjects of liberty, property, and even life. The disruption and violence attendant on these activities aroused a common feeling of deprivation and degradation among Somalis. This popular resentment gave rise to an anti-colonial feeling among Somalis who soon coalesced as a community under this common condition of oppression.

Although it benefited from the national conception of traditionalism, Somali anti-colonial nationalism was not built on the objective characteristics of the Somali nation. Rather, like its counterparts in other colonial areas of the world, it was built primarily on concrete grievances against the colonial regimes, and was, as such, expressed in anti-colonial terms. In this regard, this aspect of Somali nationalism, although indebted to the ethno-cultural characteristics of the Somali nation, was not akin to an "organic" nationalist conception. Rather, it was, in large measure, an anti-colonial phenomenon, whose ultimate aim was to overthrow an unjust system of government.

Conclusion

We have shown that Somali nationalism was not an ethno-cultural enterprise. In order to be regarded as such, a nationalist conception must conform to at least four requirements. First, its tenets must be derived from the primordial characteristics of the nation. In Africa, where the traditional state consisted of a conglomeration of tribes and ethnic groups espousing a collage of belief system and ways of life, this was not readily achievable. The African ruler, as one Abdul Said put it, "sought to form and maintain functional relationships with groups which could provide arms, men, money, and goods. In return, he served as their spiritual authority and protector from alien tribes in times of war."[47]

Second, it must be expressed in "organic" terms. In countries where organic nationalism took hold, the ensuing rhetoric equated the nation with a living organism that needed, not only nurturing and protection, but with one that could not thrive under foreign rule. Third, it must praise the nation or paint a vision of national grandeur in the mind of the average member of the nation. Fourth, demands for political independence must be made on the basis of the objective characteristics of the nation.

As I have demonstrated above, this was not the case with Somali nationalism. There are three main reasons for this. First, the literary and cultural materials required for the construction of cultural nationalism were not at the disposal of the Somali leadership before the colonial era. Somali nationalists were not intellectually sophisticated people, who were able to construct such a romantic enterprise as cultural nationalism. Second, given the international atmosphere of the post-war period, propagating such a discredited ideology as cultural nationalism would have been political suicide, and the Somali leaders seem to have understood that.

Finally, nationalism is an illusive subject. Because it straddles several areas of studies – i.e., history, politics, sociology, psychology, philology, economics, etc. – it defies all boundaries of research design. Studies which begin in one field of study often end up in another. This inherent fluidity of the subject is most pronounced in the new countries of Africa and Asia, especially those possessing a certain measure of ethnic and cultural homogeneity as the Somalis. This is why all historical studies of Somali nationalism became entangled with the ethnography of the nation and hypothesized an ethno-cultural nationalism.

This study has attempted to steer away from these pitfalls. Instead of using the common qualities of the Somali people as an indication of nationhood, we have used them as veritable subjects of our examination. By scrutinizing them, we have exposed their ineffectual role in the development of the Somali nationalism and the baselessness of the ethnicist perspective. By starting with the erroneous premise that Somalis are "not of Africa," the proponents of this view have arrived at an equally erroneous conclusion. Contrary to their stance, we hold that Somalis are "of Africa" and that their nationalism is akin to the continental variety.[48]

Nationalism in the Continent lacks the ingredients that say, European nationalism contains. Ibrahim Abu-Lughod had convincingly demonstrated the "emptiness" of African nationalism. According to the eminent professor, African nationalism managed to grow without religious, linguistic, historical, territorial or ethnic contents.[49] In their stead, it derived its vigor and contents from the dictates of the map, a shared label of Africanness, colonial legacy and a common cause of political independence."[50]

With the exit of the colonial powers, Somali nationalism lost its twin pillars of anti-colonialism and traditionalism. Somalis, who did not live under "white oppression" anymore, could not fathom "external differentiation" except in relation to other Somalis. This had the effect of reversing the orientation of Somali nationalism – i.e., from outward – to inward-looking. Inward-looking nationalism magnified political and social relations among Somalis. The outcome was the "retribalization" of national politics.[51]

The retribalization of politics had another negative effect on Somali nationalism. It had conditioned what Herbert Spiro had referred to as the "primacy of politics." In less developed societies like the African nations, there is no distinction among the many different aspects of politics. "Hence they pour everything into the pot of politics."[52] This is why in Somalia, as in the rest of Africa, every social good and value became contestable. Kwame Nkrumah's oft quoted aphorism, "seek first the political kingdom, for all else would be added unto it," acquired an internal application. In post-colonial Africa, if power was to be wrested, it was to be wrested, not from foreign rulers, but from other Africans.

As every ethnic and tribal community sought the "political kingdom," traditional nationalism in Africa had also suffered. In post-colonial Somalia, where some clans had long appropriated national values (at the exclusion of others) and others feigned disclaim of them, traditional nationalism lost both its national significance and political luster. With the demise of Somali traditionalism, the politicization of local culture and symbols began in earnest. The ensuing social agitation had exposed many hidden social contradiction and spawned new ones. In due course, the outlook of every community reverted back to its pre-colonial position. Soon, what constituted national tradition became highly disputed. Thus began the end of Somali traditional nationalism.

Notes

1. Ernest B. Hass, "What is Nationalism and Why Should We Study It?," *International Organization*, vol. 40, no. 3 (Summer, 1986), p. 713.
2. Jean-Francoise Lyotard, *The Post Modern Condition* (Minneapolis: University of Minnesota Press, 1984), pp. XXIII–IV.
3. See, for instance, I.M. Lewis, A Modern History of Somalia: Nation and State in the Horn of Africa(Boulder, Colorado: Westview Press, 1988); Saadia Touval, Somali Nationalism: International Politics and Drive For Unity in the Horn of Africa (Cambridge, Massachusetts: Harvard University Press, 1963); David D. Laitin and Said S. Samatar, Somalia: Nation in Search of a State (Boulder, Colorado: Westview Press, 1987); John Drysdale, The Somali Dispute (New York and London: Fredrick A. Praeger, 1964); and Louis Fitzgibbon, The Betrayal of Somalis (London: Rex Collings, 1982).
4. I.M. Lewis, "Introduction," in I.M. Lewis, ed., *Nationalism and Self-Determination in the Horn of Africa* (London: Ithaca Press, 1983), p. 9.
5. Ibid., pp. 16–17.
6. Touval, *Somali Nationalism*, p. 84.
7. Saadia Touval, "The Somali Republic," *Current History* (March, 1964), p. 156.
8. Rupert Emerson, "Foreword," in Touval, *Somali Nationalism*, p. v.
9. *Ibid.*, p. vi. Here the author discusses Somali nationalism in connection with the irredentist goals of the Somali Republic.
10. E.A. Bayne, "The Somali Political System," In Christian P. Potholm, ed., *Four African Political Systems* (Englewood Cliffs: Prentice-Hall, 1970), p. 190.
11. According to Hans Kohn, cultural nationalism was inspired by romantic ideas that praised and fancied folk culture, language and environment. It was a reaction against the ethnically heterogeneous empires of the era. Its adage was "small is beautiful." See Hans Kohn, *Nationalism: Its Meaning and History* (Princeton: D. Van Nostrand Company, 1955), pp. 29–37.
12. Cultural nationalists are high-level intellectuals, who study the history, language, art, literature, geography, and even the genetic makeup of their nations. In their works, they fancy and exalt the objective characteristics of their nations, and insist that, in order to preserve these "natural qualities," they need a state of their own. See, for instance, John Hutchinson, "Moral Innovators and the Politics of Regeneration: The Distinctive Role of Cultural Nationalists in Nation-Building," *International Journal of Comparative Sociology* 33, no. 1 & 2 (1992), pp. 101–107.
13. Political nationalists are high-level politicians and technocrats, who study, and are inspired by, the works of cultural nationalists. With the exception of few, who, for one reason or another, may drop out of the movement, they are the ones who rally the masses and lead their countries to independence. For the activities of these nationalists, see L.B. Namier, *1848: The Revolutions of the Intellectuals* (London: Oxford University Press, 1944).
14. See, for instance, the Somali Youth League's statement on the ethnic homogeneity of the Somali nation in *The Report of the Four Power Commission* (London, 1949), pp. 10–11. The Four Power Commission *consisted* of the representatives of the United States, Britain, France, and the Soviet Union, which took over the colonies of the defeated powers.
15. I.M. Lewis, A Pastoral Democracy: A Study of Pastoralism and Politics Among the

Northern Somali of the Horn of Africa (London: Oxford University Press, 1961), chapter 8.

16. Joseph Stalin, *Marxism and National Question* (New York: International Publishers, 1942), p. 11.

17. For the influence of the Somali language on political thought, see David D. Laitin, *Politics, Language, and Thought: The Somali Experience* (Chicago: The University of Chicago Press, 1977), p. 25; and Hussein Adam, "Language, National Consciousness and Identity – The Somali Experience," in Lewis, ed., *Nationalism and Self-Determination in the Horn of Africa*, pp. 31–42.

18. Petitions concerning the subject are numerous. For a sample of these, see UN Doc. T/PET. 11/617, p.4 ; UN Doc. T/COM. 11/L. 77, p. 3; UN Doc. T/COM. 11/L. 81, p. 1; UN Doc. T/PET. 11/86, p. 2; and UN Doc. T/PET. 11/171, p. 2.

19. Jeanne Contini, "Somali Republic: A Nation of Poets in Search of an Alphabet," *Africa Report* (December, 1963), p. 17. According to Contini, since the turn of this century, some thirty-three scripts which have been devised for the Somali language were in Arabic alphabets. See also Denis Herbstein, "The Alphabet War," *Africa Report* (May–June, 1991), p. 68.

20. Benedict Anderson, Imagined Communities: Reflections on the Origins and Spread of Nationalism (New York: Verso, 1983), chapter 4.

21. W.B. Pillsbury, *The Psychology of Nationality and Internationalism* (New York: D. Appleton and Company, 1919), p. 237.

22. See, for instance, see B.W. Andrzejewski and Muse Galaal, "A Somali Poetic Combat," *Journal of African Languages*, Vol. 2, Part 1 (1963), pp. 15–28. Those who are interested in Somali literature may consult the following works: B.W. Andrzejewski and I.M. Lewis, *Somali Poetry: An Introduction* (London: Oxford University Press, 1964); B.W. Andrzejewski, "The literary Culture of the Somali people," in Katherine S. Loughram et al., ed., *Somalia in Word and Image* (Washington DC.: The Foundation for Cross Cultural Understanding, 1986), pp. 3566; and Said Sheikh Samatar, "Somali Verbal and Material Arts," in Loughram et al., ed., *Somalia in Word and Image*, pp. 27–33.

23. Pillsbury, The Psychology of Nationality and Internationalism, p. 236.

24. Lewis, *A Pastoral Democracy*, pp. 2–3.

25. *Lebensraum* is a German territorial concept which holds that a great nation requires a great space (land) to fulfill its world destiny.

26. This author is aware of Mohammed Warsame's (Hadrawe) poem which praises and exalts the beauty of the Somali country, but this was written long after independence.

27. Herbert A. Gibbons, *Nationalism and Internationalism* (New York: Fredrick A. Stokes Company, 1930), p. 3.

28. Lewis, A Pastoral Democracy, p. 2.

29. D.J. Latham Brown, "The Ethiopian-Somali Frontier Dispute," *International and Comparative Law Quarterly* (London), vol. 5, part 2 (1956), p. 248. The lands in question include the Haud and the Reserved Area, both now part of Ethiopia.

30. See UN Doc. T/1344, p. 30.

31. See, for instance, Harold D. Nelson, *Somalia: A Country Study* (Washington, DC: The American University Press, 1981), pp. 10–12; Touval, *Somali Nationalism; Lewis, A Pastoral Democracy*, p. 17.

32. Awdal was a theocratic state and cared little about nationality. Besides, nationalism is

a modern phenomenon, appearing more than two centuries after the collapse of the Sultanate.

33. Karl Deutsch, *Nationalism and Social Communication* (Cambridge, Mass.: MIT Press, 1966), p. 19.

34. Lewis and Andrzejewski, *Somali Poetry*, p. 7.

35. See Jurgen Gebhardt, "Religion and National Identity," paper presented at the Conference for the Study of Political Thought, sponsored by Tulane University's Murphy Institute of Political Economy and Department of Political Science (March 25–27, 1994), pp. 7–10.

36. Lewis, "Islam in Somalia," in Loughram et al., ed., *Somali in Word and Image*, p. 140.

37. Lewis, *A Pastoral Democracy*, p. 129.

38. For the role of Islam in Somali Nationalism, see Lewis, "Islam in Somalia," in Loughram et al., ed., *Somalia in Word and Image*, pp. 139–167; Laitin and Samatar, *Somalia: Nation in Search of a State*, pp. 44–47.

39. By traditionalism we mean popular attachment to ancient institutions and cultural ideals, whose perpetuation people feel necessary for their survival. In the colonial areas of Africa and Asia, traditionalism consisted of three main parts: a general admiration of ancient institutions and way of life, a belief in the possibility of recapturing these ideals in the future, and militant activities designed to achieve that end.

40. Anti-colonial nationalism refers to a popular reaction (military or political) to the destructive effects of colonialism – i.e., political oppression, economic exploitation, and cultural domination. For the anti-colonial perspective of Somali Nationalism, see Hassan Omar Mahadallah, "The Origin and Essence of Somali Nationalism" (Ph.D. diss., Tulane University, 1997).

41. The term was coined by Georges Blandier. It refers to the novel setting – i.e., social, economic, and political – which developed as a result of European conquest of Africa and Asia in the nineteenth century. This colonial setting was sustained by rules and regulations which were invented and enforced by the colonial powers at the expense and over the objections of the indigenous peoples. Nationalism in these areas was, therefore, one of the many consequences of this situation.

42. Carlton Hayes, *The Historical Evolution of Modern Nationalism* (New York: Richard R. Smith, 1931), pp. 84–119.

43. As quoted in Kedourie, *Nationalism in Asia and Africa*, p. 54.

44. Ibid., p. 66.

45. See Douglas Jardine, *The Mad Mullah of Somaliland* (New York: Negro University Press, 1969), p. 33. This book was first published in 1923 by Herbert Jenkins, Ltd., London.

46. This point was shared with me by Sheikh Mohammed Haji Abdullahi Sheikh Hassan Barsane, a grandson of Sheikh Hassan Barsane. According to Sheikh Mohammed, although his grandfather and the Sayyid agreed to cooperate in their struggle against the colonialists during their stay in Hijaz, they soon parted ways after the Sayyid began killing Muslim Somalis, who had fallen out of favor with him.

47. Abdul A. Said, *The African Phenomenon* (Allyn and Bacon Inc., 1968), p. 31.

48. For the African origin of the Somalis, consult Richard Leakey, Herbert Lewis, Mohamed Noah and Abdi Kusow. Although the literature is significant in volume it did not expand into related areas of Somali studies. As a result, it escapes the view of many scholars.

49. Ibrahim Abu-Lughod, "Nationalism in a New Perspective: The African Case," in

Herbert J. Spiro, ed., *Patterns of African Development: Five Comparisons* (Englewood Cliffs, NJ: Prentice Hall, 1967), pp. 38–61.

50.   Ali Mazrui, "On the Concept of 'We Are All Africans'," *American Political Science Review*, vol. 57, no. 1 (March, 1963), pp. 88–91.

51.   The term is Ali Mazrui's. See his article, "Violent Contiguity and the Politics of Retribalization in Africa," *Journal of International Affairs*, vol. 23, no. 1 (1969), p. 89. He defines it as "the resurgence of ethnic loyalties in situations of rivalry in the arena of resource allocation and domestic power politics."

52.   Herbert J. Spiro, ed., *Africa: The Primacy of Politics* (New York: Random House, 1966), p. 8.

Chapter Five

Somali Responsese to Colonial Occupation (The Inter-Riverine Case)

Mohamed Haji Mukhtar
Savannah State University

ONE OF THE WAYS in which the national master narratives have constructed and characterized Somali historiography is nowhere clearer than in studies of colonial resistance and nationalism. These narratives uncritically equate the history of colonial resistance, and therefore Somali nationalism with the *Darwiish* movement, and ignore the contributions of the largely peasant, and urban populations, particularly, the population of the Inter-riverine regions in the forging of the modern Somali nation. There are a number of reasons for the existence of such lopsided historiography. First, this narrative depicts the Somali people as primarily, though falsely, as a country of nomads, and both the agricultural and urban cultures of the region as marginal to the perceived majority of nomadic-pastoralists.[1] Second, Touval, and other influential scholars, ignore totally the possible involvement of the Inter-Riverine region in the forging of the modern Somali nation.[2] Third, the Inter-Riverine clans and sub-clans did not proportionally participate in the political administration of the country, from the colonial occupation to the present, and, thus, they were not properly documented historically.[3] Fourth, post-Independence Somali scholarship neglected Italian, French and Arabic sources. Indeed, in the colonial era, Italian was paramount, because southern Somalia was colonized by Italy, and primarily Italian scholars conducted research in that region.[4] Finally, in 1972, the *Far Somali* script adopted for the national language was based on *Af-Mahaa*, the language of the pastoralists-nomads. This, of course, led to greater scholarly focus on the literary and poetic traditions of the north, leaving the south in general and the Inter-Riverine region in particular as a secondary field for the study of Somali language, history and traditions.[5]

In this chapter, I propose to explore some of the hitherto hidden and ignored accounts and resistance movements of the people in the Gosha, Banadir, and in general the Inter-riverine regions of Southern Somalia. I specifically intend to provide a more inclusive picture of the different ant-colonial movements and, therefore, a more global understanding of Somali history, culture, and of the making of the modern Somali nation.

Colonial Occupation of The Inter-Riverine Region

The Anglo-Italian agreements of March 24, 1891 and April 15 of the same year, gave Italy the triangle of land, known as the Horn of Africa, as part of her colonial "Sphere of Influence."[6] Italy's attempts to build a colonial empire failed, however. All attempts, both military and political, to consolidate control over the Horn, were in vain, partly because of Italy's inept colonial administration but, mostly, because of active resistance from Somalis in the south and Ethiopians in the north.[7]

The Gosha Rebellion 1890–1907

The Inter-Riverine region of Somalia is unique because of its non-ethnic revolts against European colonialism, rather unlike what one finds elsewhere in Africa. From the late 19th century onwards, the region was the center of *jama'a* uprisings against colonial suppression of certain traditional religious, cultural, and economic institutions. The Gosha Rebellion[8] led by Nassib Buunto[9] was a non-sectarian struggle against slavery. Nassib Buunto was successful in establishing one of the most powerful confederations in Goshaland, incorporating Somalis of Bantu origin as well as others. His diplomatic skills engaged both European and African powers in the region to sign peace treaties that recognized as the sole ruling authority in the Gosha region. Thus, Zanzibar, Egypt, Germany, Italy, and Great Britain recognized him as the Sultan for all Gosha. By 1892, Nassib Buunto was declared as the sole authority over 46 villages of the Gosha on both banks of the Juba River, extending from Yoontoy at the mouth of the river in the south to Mfudu in the north.

In addition to his diplomatic skills, Nassib Buunto was also a charismatic military leader. He recruited the bulk of his fighters from freed slaves who fled from Italian, Zanzibari, and Somali *Abans* or masters. Colonial reports estimated that from twenty to forty thousand organized militias were under his command. He possessed up to 1,000 guns, and most of his troops were armed with bows and poisonous arrows and spears.

He established what was later called the Nassib Buuto Center for freed slaves which offered the escaped slaves not only refuge and freedom but a better way of life by promoting and developing communal ways of farming and cattle herding and training them in new skills for building houses and for manufacturing necessary tools and weapons.[10] It was in this center that the army of Nassau Bunt fought against the Italians and delayed their penetration into the fertile hinterlands of the region for decades. Nassau Bunt was celebrated as the African Sparta us, for his fight for the freedom of slaves. In 1931, Umber to Bargain published a book entitled, *Nell Terra did Nassau Bunt, lo Spar taco Della Somalia Italian* (In the land of Nassau Bunt, the Sparta us of Italian Somaliland).

The Banadir Resistance 1888–1924

The "Bandar Resistance,"[11] though religious in origin, was also based on economics as the Bandar ports played a significant role in the region's internal and external trade, supplying the hinterland with imported commodities as well as providing markets for livestock and major local products. Moreover, it was only in these coastal towns where significant commercial life existed and cottage industries like the production of Banadiri cloth and the manufacture of utensils and other indispensable tools flourished. It was, therefore, essential to defend these vital economic resources.

The Banadiri traders of the interior were also concerned that foreign occupation of the ports would not only mean they would be put out of business as independent agents, but indeed that internal trade would be completely dislocated because inevitably farms and grazing lands whose coastal pastures and wells the nomads used during the dry season would also be occupied. The Banadiris ambushed the Italians at Lafoole, in 1896, when the Wa'dan clan attacked the first Italian expedition on the Shabelle River led by Antonio Cecchi, the Italian general consul in Zanzibar. Cecchi and all, but three members of his expedition were killed: The Italian media dubbed it *La Strage di Lafole*, Massacre at Lafoole! For Banadiris, Lafoole was as glorious a victory as the Ethiopian triumph over the Italians at Adowa in the same year. Banadiris call 1896 *Ahad Shekki*, the Sunday year of Cecchi. The Italian colonial advance was halted for the next ten years.[12]

In the early 1890s, another Banadiri group, the Biamal, joined the resistance. Italy occupied Marka, the center of Biamal culture, but in 1904, the Markans assassinated the first Italian resident of the city, Giacomo Trevis. This action triggered the Italian occupation of another port town, Jazira, about 30 miles south of Mogadishu. Biamal leaders called for a *shir*, "clan assembly," mobilizing the Banadiri clans, mainly Biamal, the Wa'dan, the Hintire and other clans of the Geledi confederacy, against the Italian advance and decided to isolate the ports from trade with the interior.[13] The *ma'allims* "Qur'anic school teachers" and *imams* "religious leaders" of Marka led the war of resistance to colonial occupation of the interior, but they and their followers paid dearly. A local *lashin* poet who attacked those who refused to take up arms said: *Reer Janna waa jid galeen, Reer Jahima iska jooga*: "those who resist are heaven bound. Those who submit can stay home in Hell where they belong." Italian garrisons in both Marka and Jazira were under siege and barely survived. Though Italy sent support troops, they suffered considerable losses. In February 1907, at Turunley, also known as Dhanane, north of Marka, some 2,000 Banadiri warriors, led by Sheikh Abdi Abiikar Gaafle[14] fought 1000 Italian troops, assisted by some 1,500 Arab, Eritrean, and Somali mercenaries led by Lieutenant Gustavo Pesenti. The attack started after midnight, February 9, 1907 and lasted to the noon of the 10th. The Banadiri warriors retreated, leaving behind several hundred dead and as many wounded. Although the Italians had high casualties, they considered Turunley a major military victory, one which Lieutenant Pesenti, the commander of the regiment, celebrated in an eyewitness account, *Danane* (Dhanane).[15] Turunley marked the end of the of the mighty Banadir resistance. On July 1908, at Finlow, the Biamal avenged Turunley defeating some 500 Italian troops. However, by 1908, major centers such as Afgoy capitulated to the Italians. However, the Italian conquest was not complete, and from 1910 to the 1920s, under the leadership of Sheikh Abdi Abikar Gaafle, the Banadiri coalition remained the leading opponent of Italian rule in the Riverine region.[16]

The Fascist Era and The Policy of Disarmament

The Fascist administration began in December 5, 1923, with the appointment of Cesare Mario De Vecchi di val Cismon as governor of Somalia. Only the Banadir coast was under direct Italian control, but with the elimination of the Banadiri in 1908 and the dervishes in 1922, Italian colonial dreams were sure to be fulfilled.

De Vecchi, flushed with military ardor, sought to eliminate all who stood against what Fascist propaganda called *la Grande Somalia* "Greater Somalia." De Vecchi knew that after the fall of the dervishes, Britain would no longer support Italian colonial interests in the Horn. Meanwhile, Somalis were heavily armed and well trained for combat in the Great War. An estimated 16,000 rifles were in Somali hands, more than what was available for the Italian colonial forces. Thus, after the war, the governor's first task was to disarm and confiscate arms and ammunition from all Somalis, but particularly from the clans in the Inter-Riverine region. To this end the governor, reconstituted the old Somali police corps, known as the *Corpo Zaptie*, and trained them to act as an effective force for carrying out the new colonial policies. Fresh cadres were recruited, and the older and less effective elements were suspended. New barracks were built. Young Italian officers from the *Carabinieri* trained and supervised the new forces.[17] In early March 1924, De Vecchi ordered leaders of the Upper Shabelle[18] clans and *Jama'a*[19] Sheikhs to hand over all arms and ammunitions to the *Corpo Zaptie* within forty days.[20]

In mid-March 1924, Sheikh Hassan Barsane, the leader of Jiliale *Jama'a*[21] condemned the new Italian colonial policies. Barsane invoked a *shir*, where the participants, inflamed with millenarian zeal, denounced the Governor's order: "In the name of Allah, most Gracious, most Merciful... I have received your letter and understood its contents, but must advise that we cannot your orders and join with you in a covenant... Your government has its laws, and we have ours. We accept no law other than ours. Our law is the law of Allah and his prophet... We are not like other people, none of us has ever enrolled in the *Zaptie* (colonial force), never. Not even one...[22] and if you come to our land to fight against us, we will fight you with all possible means, just as we fought the dervishes and the Ethiopians. Allah said: "Few can defeat many with Allah's will" (Sura 2, verse 249)... The world is very close to its end, only 58 years remain. ...[23] We do not want to stay in this world. It is better to die while defending our Muslim laws. All Muslims are one.[24]

As a continuation of Riverine resistance, the Jiliale Jihads resisted and defeated early Fascist attacks along the north and middle of the Shabelle Valley, defending the north and central Banadir region. Unfortunately, however, Barsane fell into the hands of the Italians and was imprisoned and died in a Mogadishu jail in 1928, causing a major setback. From 1925, the *Jama'a* suffered from a shortage of ammunition. Finally, the *Jama'a* was forced to surrender and hand over its guns to the colonial forces.

De Vecchi's problems, however, were not over. Further resistance emerged from the Qadiriyya settlements, a Sufi order. In 1922, Sheikh Faraj, known also as Sufi Baraki, launched a campaign against Italian colonial activities on the Banadir. He united several *Jama'a* settlements: Buulo Marerto, Golwiing, Muki Dumis and others scattered in the Lower Shabelle region, and set up his headquarters in Barawa, the birthplace of Sheikh Uways Ibn Muhammad al-Barawi,[25] the founder of the movement. Sheikh Faraj's *akhwaan* "brotherhood" were trained religiously as well as militarily to protect the farmlands from the Italians penetrating the fertile Lower Shabelle region. In 1923, the above centers were attacked and mostly destroyed by Italian colonial forces. Sheikh Faraj traveled to Tiyeglow town in Upper Juba to coordinate with another movement that emerged there, the Tiyeglow Jama'a led by Sharif Alyow Issaq al-Sarmani.[26] Tiyeglow, where earlier the dervishes had suffered a serious defeat was the headquarters of the movement, for it resisted early waves of Italian occupation. The town was also located in between the two holiest places in the Reewin territory, Sarmaan (the headquarters of Asharaf) and Bioley (the headquarters of Uwaysiyya and where the shrine of Sheikh Uways is located).

To consolidate the power of the movement resisting the "infidel" Italians, the two leaders agreed to put more emphasis on defending the port towns of the Banadir and the farmlands of the Lower Shabelle. Therefore, forces from the Tiyeglow *akhwaan* led by Sharif Alyow went with Sheikh Faraj to support the *akhwaan* in

Buulo Marerto and other Lower Shabelle centers. The movement sought internal unification and reform, to counter divisive clanism and those officials, salaried chefs and qadi's it labeled hypocrites, actually collaborators in the pay of the Italians. The movement constructed defenses in preparations for the resistance.

Fulfilling the new strategies of the movement, the construction of two secure fortresses was finished in early 1924 in Dhai-Dhai, later known as Jama'a Dhai-Dhai, and in Qorile, later known as Buulo Asharaf, after Sharif Alyow. The Italian authority was troubled by these developments. De Vecchi warned Sheikh Faraj to give up what he called "unhealthy activities."[27] The two fortified camps dispatched delegations throughout the Inter-Riverine region to recruit more supporters. They also contacted Sheikh Murjan, a prominent Qadiri holy man in the Lower Juba, who not only blessed the movement, but also supported it materially. The colonial authorities felt endangered and, as a preemptive measure sought to negotiate with the leaders of the movement to prevent a rebellion. This move failed and a Zaptie force was sent to strike against Sheikh Faraj and his allies, but defeated.

On October 20, 1924, more Zaptie forces attacked Dhai-Dhai Center. The *akhwaan* defended their camp and forced the colonial troops to retreat and leave behind some of their dead and injured. Sheikh Faraj considered these victories a miracle and it reinvigorated his jihadic movement. In early November, more colonial troops attacked the strongholds of the movement; many centers were burned and the *akhwaan* fought bravely, but were overwhelmed by superior troops and weaponry. After many losses, they retreated towards the north and northwest. Sheikh Faraj and a small number of the *akhwaan* remained in the Lower Shabelle region, introducing guerilla tactics to fight the enemy. On May 31, 1925, colonial troops surprised Sheikh Faraj in his hiding place and defeated his *akhwaan*. He was wounded, captured and sent to Barawa, where he died from his injuries soon after.[28] Meanwhile, Sharif Alyow, having survived death or capture by colonial troops, was able to retreat to Tiyeglow, his hometown and continued the struggle there. The defeat of Jama'a movements and the death of both Sheikh Faraj and Sheikh Hassan Barsane and the retreat of Sharif Alyow al-Sarmani cleared the way for the Italian dream of establishing the *Impero Coloniale Fascita* (Fascist colonial empire) in 1936.

Characteristics of The Inter-Riverine Resistances

In dealing with Somali resistance towards European colonial powers, much attention has been given to the Northern Somali resistance, particularly the movement that was launched by Sayyid Muhammad Abdulle Hassan known as "the Dervish Movement".[29] Southern Somali resistance is not often discussed in the Somali scholarship. There were a number of reasons for this. Perhaps the most important was the fact that Somalia's history, culture or otherwise has been seen mainly through the eyes of what some scholars call the "Orientalist scholarship,"[30] which classified southern Somalis as Bantu, culturally inferior to the northern more Arabic oriented nomads. In addition, Somalia's post-independent historiography and its obsession of pastoral monolithic culture contributed a great deal of generalization that diverted scholars from examining other important themes of Somalia's past.[31]

Current scholarship however, is pointing out the significance of anti-colonial resistances in southern part of the country, particularly the Inter-Riverine region. It is necessary to point out scholars whose interest and attention in the field has vigorously renewed. This list include among many others, Lee Cassanelli,[32] Virginia Luling,[33] Bernhard Helander,[34] Herbert Lewis,[35] Catherine Besteman,[36] Kenneth Menkhaus,[37] and Abdi Kusow,[38] and myself[39]. The list of scholars, Somalis and non-Somalis who contributed to this endeavor could go on and on, but I would like to mention those who contributed to Ali Jimale[40] and Catherine Besteman's edited volumes: *The Invention of Somalia* (1995), and *The Struggle for Land in Southern Somalia: The War Behind the War* (1996). All contributors have been engaging their studies in aspects of the Inter-Riverine region of Somalia from late 1960s.

What I have highlighted above is a brief outline of some of the Inter-Riverine resistances towards the colonial administration. It needs thorough study. My intention is to sketch out as many movements emerged in the region and lay out the ground for further research leading to offer broader picture of the Somali anti-colonial resistance. Nevertheless, I would like to offer several characteristics that Southern movements might differ from the Northern ones.

PAN-CLANAL

The Inter-Riverine society, unlike its northern counterpart was more diversified. During the advent of colonial powers, it was divided not only along clan lines, but also on Sufi order affiliations. They were divided between pastoralists and agriculturalists. Moreover, the region absorbed people from the neighboring countries, Arabs, Persians, Polynesians, Oromos, and Bantus.

One would wander how a society of this complex could forge a meaningful resistance against colonialism. Nevertheless, the region produced successful movements that transcended from defending particular clan interests but fighting for the protection of broader regional political and economic interests. The economic sectors of the region were interdependent, where any threat to one sector will undermine the other. In fact, the early Italian blockade of the Banadir ports was a threat to not only a particular clan or trader, but it damaged the sophisticated network of the hinterland with the coast. The caravan routes started to fade, and the value of goods dropped sharply. The oral tradition of the time indicates sufferings from the inflation caused by the blockade.[41] Indeed, this triggered the emergence of the early inter-riverine resistances that involved numerous clans of the coast such as the Biamal, the Tunni, the Geledi, the Wa'dan, the Abgal, the Shikhal and others. A coalition of these forces prevented the Italian penetration to the hinterlands of the Inter-river region for over two decades 1886–1925.

ANTI-COLONIAL WORK ETHICS

From 1893 to 1905 when the Italian government assumed direct administration of the southern portion of the Inter-Riverine region, the two succeeding companies: Filonardi Company 1893–1896, and Benadir Company 1896–1905 introduced new laws on customs and tariff regulations which were alien to the Inter-Riverine society. Most of the early responses were provoked by these measures. Italian colonial records of the time indicated a great deal of the Inter-Riverine discontent towards the new ordinances.[42] With the introduction of forced labor during the penetration of the interior and the toleration of slavery in the newly established plantations, the Inter-Riverine resistance took a new dimension. The Nassib Buunto movement represents a good example of resistance against slavery and forced labor. The effects of forced labor on the consciousness of the Inter-Riverine people during this period, as well as, the Fascist era was indeed the seeds of southern Somali resistances and the foundation of the their modern political parties in the 1940s. Stories of the anguish and bitter memories of the period can still be found in the oral tradition of the Inter-Riverine people. Terms like *cologno* (corvee labor) and *teen* (shift labor) are reminders of a tragic period of the Inter-Riverine history. During these eras, the Inter-Riverine people were forced to work on plantations, roads, canals and other construction projects. Workers in the plantations were treated harshly, and many died from overexertion and disease. Many whom I interviewed in 1976–1979 still recalled the tragedies involved in the shift working conditions, what they call locally "beed."[43] The tragedy of Keli Asayle "The Canal of Mourning" is well remembered in the Dhooboi villages.[44]

RELIGIO-POLITICAL

Islamic belief normally included metaphysics, a cosmology and a moral and political theory. It is understandable that, in the conditions of late 19th century Somalia, the sense of oppression by colonial authority, and the moral crisis accompanying the disruption of the Inter-Riverine society should lead to the emergence of movements of Islamic basis. The *Jama'a* movements played a leading role in raising the political consciousness of their communities. The sheikhs who led them were considered as the educated elite in the middle of the high proportion of illiterate people. Most of the Jama'a centers were located in the agricultural area of the region where the colonial plantations were also developed. Thus, the *Jama'a* centers became very threatening to colonial activities.

The *Jama'a* centers became safe heavens for runaway slaves and others of low social status, giving them a fresh start and helping integrate them into the religious and economic life of the region. The centers were also, the means by which many individuals who had lost land and livestock in the early years of the penetration could require land and earn a living while also practicing their faith. Moreover, the *Jama'a* centers were actually a means by which the Somalis could avoid serving the colonial forced labor regime. Thus, the *Jama'a* communities played a tremendous social and economic role and led most of the southern resistance of the time.

As we have seen, the *Jama'a* were scattered throughout the entire Inter-Riverine region, and the colonial authorities failed to suppress their activities decisively. Italian frustration is clearly manifested in their reports to Rome. Governor Riveri (1920–1923) noted in 1921, that the multiplication and extension of *Jama'a* communities might be a cause for concern, since they were acquiring more land and more political adherents along the Shabelle Valley. "By substituting the universal ties of religion for strictly ethnic ones," Riveri added the *Jama'a* communities "could constitute, sometime in the future, a real danger to the political tranquility of the colony."[45]

As the examples cited above of Sheikh Faraj and Sharif Alyow, reveal, Riveri's warning was prophetic. The *Jama'a* communities were playing a central role not only in organizing the Inter-Riverine agricultural production but also in uniting Inter-Riverine people socially and politically.

No wonder that during the Fascist era the Italian policy toward the *Jama'a* communities had moved full circle. Although, by 1926, the most powerful *Jama'a* resistances were defeated and their leadership were either killed or detained, the Fascist administration remained suffering from constant sporadic disturbances and severe sabotages from the *akhwaan* "followers of martyred Sheikhs." In a secret report, Governor Rava (1931–1935) instructed his District Commissioners not to authorize the establishment of any new *Jama'a* and to direct all petitions to him for a "case by case review." Then he articulated the new policy, one which would have tremendous significance in the years to come: the colonial government should avoid encouraging a unitary Islamic solidarity but should instead work toward a new concept of "positive unity: All Somalis under the Italian government." Thus, the idea of *La Grande Somalia* had been put in motion.[46]

MILLENARIAN

It is evident that the oppressive laws imposed by the Italian colonial administrations and the forms of exploitations followed the implementation of colonial policies forged the emergence of the Inter-Riverine movements. It is also clear that millenarianism is reflected greatly on the directions and attitudes of these movements towards both in opposition to the colonialists and to rally their followers.

Barsane's letter to the Fascist Governor cited above and his foretelling the end of the world within 58 years is a clear illustration. The statement that "we are living in a time of unparalleled woes," provides an empirical basis for most 19th and 20th century's African anti-colonial movements. It is principally, the millenary aspects of the doctrine, and its implications, that tend to produce a clash between the prophetic power and the colonial power.

The early followers of Sheikh Uways al-Barawi also believed that he would be murdered by the Dervishes of the north, and that would be one of the signs of the end of the world. Sheikh Ibdille Issaq, another millenarian, from Bardera predicted, "When we are close to the end of the world, captains and commissioners will conquer our country."[47]

From this attitude springs the refusal to cooperate with the infidel colonial authorities. Similar movements inspired by messianic or millenarian doctrine sprung all over Africa during the colonial time, such as Kimbangu in the Congo who believed that the world would end on October 21, 1921,[48] and Adamawa in Northern Cameroons who believed that the Mahdi "the God-guided one" era has already lapsed, and it was now the epoch of the Dajjal "anti-Christ." The necessary preliminaries for the end of the world are already taking place, and it would in fact come about 1400 years of the death of the Prophet Muhammad.[49] Thus, the believers Muslim and Christians alike had nothing to loose in this just struggle. If they die for the cause, they become martyrs, and if they win, they are heroes. Nassib Buunto, the leader of the Somali anti-slavery movement was hanged in 1907. Sheikh Uways al-Barawi was also murdered in 1907. Sheikh Hassan Barsane, who was sentenced to death in 1924, had his sentence commuted to life imprisonment and died in jail in 1929, while Sheikh Faraj was killed in 1925.

This, indeed, was the fate of many messianic leaders in other parts of the continent. Mwana Lesa (meaning "son of God") was hanged in Rhodesia in 1926. Simon Kimbangu was sentenced to life imprisonment and died in detention in Elizabethville in 1950. Mulomozi wa Yezu of the Belgian Congo was also hanged in 1944. There were hundreds of political prisoners during the Italian colonial administration in Somalia, of whom many were declared "dangerous" by the colonial authorities. Ideas of martyrdom and resurrection found strong ground in the Inter-Riverine anti-colonial movements.

Conclusion

What I have tried to do in this paper is to briefly introduce one of the themes neglected in the modern scholarship of Somali studies. The historical experience of this region offers some instructive lessons for historians accustomed to the standard image of Somalia as an intolerant, nomadic culture, whereas, indeed, the whole of the southern mostly agrarian region is and was remarkable for its tradition of incorporating and assimilating diverse people and cultures. The Inter-Riverine people felt the burden of colonial oppression as much if not more than their northern counterparts did through their experience of forced labor during the Fascist regime. In this struggle, many cross-clan resistance and religious movements emerged to further the cause of Somali unity. The region's history may also offer a tradition of tolerance for cultural and social diversity no less patriotic than a tradition of proud exclusiveness. It was in this region that the founding fathers of modern Somali nationalism were born: Abdulkadir Sakhawuddin, the founder of the Somali Youth League (SYL); Haji Mohamed Hussein, the founder of the Somali Democratic Union (SDU); Sheikh Ali Jimale, the founder of the Somali National Congress (SNC); and Sheik Abdullahi Boghodi, the founder of the Hizbiya Dastur Mustaqil al-Sumal (HDMS) (the Somali Independent Constitutional Party).

Notes

1. Leading studies in this aspect, see Lewis, I.M., *A Pastoral Democracy* (Oxford: Oxford University Press, 1961), Burton, Richard, *First Footsteps in East Africa* (2 Vols., London: Tylson and Edwards, 1894), Samatar, Said S., *Oral Poetry and Somali Nationalism: The Case of Sayyid Mahammad 'Abdille Hassan* (Cambridge: Cambridge University Press, 1982).

2. These scholars thought that the Inter-Riverine region had been far less important than the dramatic events led by Ahmed Gurey and Muhammad Abdulle Hassan, which forged the modern Somali nation. See Touval, Saadia, *Somali Nationalism: International Politics and the Drive for Unity in the Horn of Africa* (Cambridge, MA: Harvard University Press, 1963), Lewis, I.M., "The Somali Conquest of the Horn of Africa," Journal of African History, vol. 1, no. 2, 1960 and Trimingham, J.S., *Islam in Ethiopia*, (London: Franc Cass, 1952).

3. Colonial administrations employed more nomadic Somalis in their colonial forces, such as *Corpo Zaptie* in the South and the Camel Corps in the North. Similarly, in the civil services, the majority of the *turjuman* "translators," *Karani* "clarks," and even *wardie* "watchman," were preferably selected from the non-Riverine communities. This preference is clearly reflected in the formation of the early national armed and police forces. From 1956 to 1991, there were 26 Somali governments all led by the Darood, Hawiye and Issaq clans. For further details on clan and sub-clan representation in the Somali governments, civil servants and police and armed forces, see Haji, Aves Osman and Abdiwahid Osman Haji, *Clan, Sub-clan and Regional Representation in the Somali Government Organization 1960–1990: Statistical data and Findings*. Washington, DC: 1998.

4. Colonial archives are essential in this regard. For Italian colonial records, see Archivio Storico del Ex-Ministero dell' Africa Italiana (ASMAI), for French, see the Centre des Archives d'Outre-Mer, just to mention two important Italian and French sources. In Arabic, the best archival collections are kept in Dar al-Kutub al-Misriyyah. For bibliographical details, see, Carboni, Fabio, *Bibliografia Somala*. Studi Somali, no. 4. (Rome: Il Bagatto, 1983), and Mukhtar, Mohamed Haji, *Historical Dictionary of Somalia, New Edition*. (Lanham: Scarecrow Press, 2003).

5. Prior to 1972, no *Af-Somali* "Somali language" was as dominant as *Af-Mahaa*, because it became the language of the media and instruction in schools and was called *Afka Hooyo* "the mother tongue" much offending those whose mothers did not speak it, thus marginalizing the use of other Somali languages such as *Af-Maay* the lingua franca of the Riverine peoples. The culturally alienated non *Af-Mahaa* speakers particularly the *Af-Maay* speakers opposed the 1972 script and developed their own script known as *Alif-Maay* "Maay Script" adopted since 1994. See Mukhtar, *Historical Dictionary*, Ibid. pp. 30, 31, 84, 142.

6. This triangle is located in the east of a line of demarcation in eastern Africa between the "Spheres of Influence" reserved to Great Britain and Italy, which follow from the sea, up the midchannel (halfway) of the river Juba to a latitude 6 degrees North. Thus, Kismayu, with its territory on the south bank of the river, was left to England. The line then follows the 6th parallel of north latitude up to Meridian 35 degrees east of Greenwich, following up to the Blue Nile. See: Hertslet, E., *The Map of Africa by Treaty*, 3rd edition, vol. II, (London: HMSO), p. 918. According to this agreement, most of the Somali territories were included in the Italian "sphere," with the exception of Jubaland and the Northern Frontier District, NFD, which remained part of British East Africa.

7. In 1896 Somalis at Lafoole defeated Italy in the south and Ethiopians at Adowa in the North. For details about the Lafoole defeat, see Mukhtar, Mohamed H. "Taariikh al-Isti'mar al Itali fi al-Sumal Hatta 1908," (M.A. Thesis, Al-Azhar University, Cairo, 1973), pp. 91–93, and for Adowa, see Del Boca, Angelo, *Gli Italiani in Africa Orientale dall' Unita al Marcio su Roma*, (Rome: Editori Laterza, 1976), pp. 649–741.

8. Gosha is the thickly forested territory of the middle and lower Juba river valley.

9. Makanjira Che Zamani is the real name of Nassib Buunto. It is believed that he came to Gosha leading reinforcement forces from Che Mataka, Sultan of Kulijenda, in East Africa to support Gosha's struggle against the Werday and Ogaden clans. According to Sheikh Mukhtar Sheikh Yusuf Nassib, a grandson of Nassib Buunto, it was the people of Gosha who requested the support of Che Mataka. (Interview with Sheikh Mukhtar, Mogadishu, 1976.) For interesting information about the life and rise of Nassib Buunto, see Bargoni, Umberto, *Nella Terra di Nassib Bunto, Lo Spartaco della Somalia Italiana*. (Livorno: Edizione Marzocco, 1931).

10. Sheikh Mukhtar, Interviews in Nassib Buunto Village 1977.

11. Italian sources very often refer to this resistance as the "Biamal Revolt," as the Biamal clan was the major element in the resistance. See: Gherardo Pantano, *Nel Benadir: La Citta di Merca e la Regione Bimal*, (Leghorn: S. Belforta, 1910). pp. 41–77. Some scholars tend to limit the area which the revolt covered and call it the "Merca Revolt" since Merca was the center of gravity. See: Cassanelli, Lee. V. *The Shaping of Somali Society: Reconstructing the History of a Pastoral People*, 1600–1900, (Philadelphia: University of Pennsylvania Press, 1982), pp. 222–228. For the geographic meaning of Banadir, see, Mukhtar, *Historical Dictionary*, ibid., pp.47–48.

12. For further details about Lafoole, see Del Boca, Angelo, *Gli Italiani in Africa Orientale*, ibid., pp. 741–46; Cassanelli, Lee, V., *The Shaping of Somali Society*, ibid., pp. 204–8, and Mukhtar, M., *Historical Dictionary of Somalia*, ibid., 33, 134.

13. See, Mantegazza, Vico, *Il Benadir*, (Milano: Treves, 1908), pp. 170–1. For information about the Biamals and their role in the resistance against Italian colonialism, see Pantano, Gherardo, *La Citta di Merca*, ibid.

14. A Biamal warrior, ma'allin "teacher-sheikh" negotiated the clan alliances fighting against the Italian colonial occupation. Gaafle was also responsible for allying the Banadir resistance in the south with the dervishes of the north. For details about Gaafle's life, see Mukhtar, *Historical Dictionary*, ibid., p. 199.

15. Pesenti, Gustavo. *Danane nella Somalia Italiana* (Milan: L'Eroica, 1932). As the victorious commander at Turunley, Pesenti could provide an eyewitness account of the tactics and military organization of the Banadiris as well as the weapons they used.

16. For further information about the role of Geledi and Hintire in these resistance, see Cassanelli, Lee V., *The Shaping of Somali Society*, ibid., pp. 208–214, 218–22, and Luling, Virginia, *Somali Sultanate: The Geledi City-State Over 150 Years* (London: HAAN Associates, 2002), pp. 207–19.

17. For further details about the nature of this force, see Vitale, M.A., *L'Opera dell'Esercito 1855–1943, Vol. I, of L'Italia in Africa, Serie Storico-Militare*, (Rome: Istituto Poligrafico dello Stato, 1960), pp. 150–51.

18. The region has a strong economic and strategic importance for the Italians. The Shabelle valley region is the most fertile part of all Somalia, providing rich pasture for livestock. Furthermore, it is on the main road connecting the southern parts of the Italian East African empire, Somalia, with its northern portion, Eritrea.

19. *Jama'a* is an Arabic word for a group of people associating themselves under a given religious order or political association. This institution emerged in Somalia as organized religious farming settlements in the 18th century. The *Jama'a* institution spread widely among the Inter-Riverine people. In 1950, there were over fifty *Jama'a* in Upper Juba region; thirty in Banadir; four in Lower Juba; and eight in Hiran. No *Jama'a* were established in both Mudug and Mijurtinia. See UN Trusteeship Council Report on Religious Settlements in Somalia, 1953. For some of these *Jama'a* that date back to the 18th and early 19th centuries, see Garmaghale (1789), Burgab (1810), and Bardera (1819), see also Castagno, A.A., "Religious Settlements in Somalia," (unpublished collection, 1953).

20. De Vecchi di Val Cismon, Cesare Mario, *Orizzonti d'Impero: Cinque Anni in Somalia*. (Milano: A. Mondadori, 1935), pp. 25–26.

21. Barsane founded this Jama'a in 1890 at Jiliale in the Middle Shabelle Valley. The Sheikh led his followers to oppose the followers of Muhammad Abdulle Hassan, the dervishes and both the Italian and Ethiopian colonial forces during their advance into Somalia. For more about Barsane's life, see De Vecchi, *Orizzonti d'Impero*, ibid. pp. 24–27, and Mukhtar, *Historical Dictionary*, ibid., pp. 209–10.

22. An indication that the riverine people unlike the nomadic clans refused to enlist in the colonial troops and perhaps any colonial job.

23. According to Islam nobody can know, when the Day of Judgment comes, but Allah. "Verily the knowledge of the hour is with Allah (alone)," (Sura 31, verse 34). However, there is a Somali way to calculate the end of the world. They believe time is divided into five major periods. The time of the prophet Muhammad, which they allot for an estimate of 1000 years, then a period of 100 years for each of the four orthodox Caliphs (Abu Bakr, 'Umar, Usman and Ali). Thus, to the Somalis, the year 1400 AH (the Islamic Calendar) represents the end of the world. Since Barsane's revolt emerged in 1342 AH (1924), it was true that only 58 years were left to the Day of Judgment, and according to that calendar, the world ended in 1982. But the Somalis or believers of such calendar made reservations if things were not accurate by saying, "The age of the

world will last until 1400 AH and *wa-shi* "plus" and that *wa-shi* could last for a second, a minute, an hour, a day, a week, a month, a year or even for hundreds, thousands and millions of years."

24. Sheikh Hassan Barsane signs this letter on the 5th of Sha'ban, 1342 of the Islamic Calender (March 12, 1924). For the text and relevant detail of the letter, see: De Vecchi, ibid., pp. 26–27.

25. For more details about the life and deeds of Sheikh Uways, See: Sheikh 'Abd al-Rahman bin Sheikh 'Umar, known as Sheikh 'Abdi'Ili, *Jala'al-'Aynayn fi Manaqib al-Shaykhayn: al-Shaykh al-Waliyyi HajI Aways al-Qadiri wa al-Shaykh al-Kaamil 'Abd al-Rahman al-Zayla'I*, (Cairo: Matba'at al Mashad al -Husayni, 1954). By the same author, *al-Jawhar al-Nafis Fi Khawas al Shaykh Aways al-Qadiri*. (Cairo: Matba'at al-Mashhad al-Husayni. 1964).For substantial information about the spread of Uwaysiyya to East and Central Africa, see: B.G. Martin. Muslim Brotherhoods in 19-Century Africa. (Cambridge University Press. 1976), pp. 160–164. For an interesting account for Uwaysiyya and its anti-colonial activities, see Christine Choi Ahmed, "God, Anti-Colonialism and Drums: Sheikh Uways and the Uwaysiya," (Ufahamu: Vol. XVII, 1989), pp. 96–116, and Mukhtar, *Historical Dictionary*, ibid., pp. 219–20, 257–58.

26. Details about Sharif Alyow's movement see: Cerulli, Enrico, *Somalia: Scritti Vari Editi ed Inediti*, vol. 2, (Rome: Istituto Poligrafico dello Stato, 1959), pp. 166–68.

27. De Vecchi di Val Cismon, Cesare Mario, *Relazione sul Progetto di Bilancio della Somalia Italiana 1925/26*, (Mogadishu: Bettini, 1924), p. 38.

28. De Vecchi, *Orizzonte d'Impero*, ibid., pp. 44–45.

29. Literature on the Dervish movement are numerous in both foreign and Somali languages. See, Jardine, Douglas, *The Mad Mullah of Somaliland*, (London: Herbert Jenkins, 1923); Battersby, H.F. Prevost, *Richard Corfield of Somaliland*, (London: Edward Arnold, 1914); Touval, Saadia, *Somali Nationalism*, (Cambridge: Harvard University Press, 1963): Lewis, I.M., *The Modern History of Somaliland*, (New York: Praeger, 1965): Sheikh Jama' 'Umar 'Isse, *Taariikhdi Daraawiishta*, (Mogadishu: Akadeemiyaha Dhaqanka, 1976) and Samatar, Said, *Oral Poetry and Somali Nationalism*, (London: Cambiridge University Press, 1982).

30. Choi, Christine A., "Finely Etched Chattel: The Invention of a Somali Women," in Ahmed, Ali Jimale, ed., The Invention of Somalia, (Lawrenceville: The Red Sea Press, Inc. 1995), p. 158.

31. Mukhtar, Mohamed H., "Islam in Somali History: Fact and Fiction, "in Ahmed, Ali Jimale, ed. *The Invention of Somalia*, Ibid. pp. 20–21.

32. Lee's works remained the pioneering studies on the pre-colonial history of Somalia. His publications on the area are numerous among which: *The shaping of Somali Society*, (Philadelphia: University of Pennsylvania Press, 1982) and "The End of slavery and the 'Problem' of Farm Labor in Colonial Somalia" in Puglielli, Annarita, (Rome: Proceedings of the Third International Congress of Somali Studies, 1986) currently working on patterns of pre-colonial, trade, politics and population movement in the Eastern Horn.

33. Luling, Virginia, Somali Sultanate: The Geledi City-State Over 150 Years, (London: HAAN, 2002).

34. Helander, Bernhard, "The Slaughtered Camel: Coping with Fictitious Descent Among the Hubeer of Southern Somalia." (Ph.D. Thesis, University of Uppsala, 1988)

35. Lewis, Herbert, "The Origins of the Galla and Somali." in *Journal of African History*, Vol. VII, 1966.

36. Besteman, Catherine, and Cassanelle, Lee, *The Struggle for Land in Southern Somalia: The War behind the War*, (London: HAAN, 1996), and *Unraveling Somalia: Race, Violence, and the Legacy of Slavery*, (Philadelphia: University of Pennsylvania Press, 1999).

37. Menkhaus, Kenneth, "Rural Transformation and the Roots of Underdevelopment in Somalia's Lower Jubba Valley." (Ph.D. dissertation, University of South Carolina, 1986), and "from Feast to Famine: Land and the State in Somalia's Lower Jubba Valley." In Besteman and Cassanelli, ed. *The Struggle for Land*, ibid., pp.133–53.

38. "The Somali Origin: Myth or Reality." In Ahmed, Ali Jimale, ed., The *Invention*, ibid., pp. 81–106.

39. Most of my early studies remained in Arabic or Somali which most of the current Somalists are not benefiting from it. See, Mukhtar, Mohamed H. "Taariikh al-Isti'mar al-Itali fi al-Sumal Hatta 1908," [The History of Italian Colonialism in Somalia until 1908,] M.A. Thesis, University of al-Azhar, 1973; "al-Sumal al-Itali fi Fatrat al-Wisayah Hatta al-Istifqlaal," [Italian Somaliland from Trusteeship to Independence 1950–1960,] Ph.D. Dissertation, University of al-Azhar, 1983. and *Habka Cilmiga ee Baarista Taariikhda Soomalida*," [The Scientific Methodology of Writing Somali History,] Lafoole: 1978).

40. Ahmed, Ali Jimale, "Tradition, anomaly and the wave for the Future: Somali Oral Literature, Nuruddin Farah and Written Somali Prose Fiction." (Ph.D. dissertation, University of California, Los Angeles, 1989), and *Daybreak is Near: Literature, Clans and the Nation State in Somalia*, (Lawrenceville, NJ: Red Sea Press, 1996).

41. Mukhtar, Mohamed H. Fieldnote, 1975.

42. Mukhtàr, Mohamed H. "Taariikh al-Isti'mar al-Italy fi al-Sumal Hatta 1908." Ibid. pp. 137–40. More details about ordinances for the administration of the territory during Filonardi Company, see, Filonardi's report, no. 171, September 16, 1894, ASMAI, pos. 75/1, f. 3.

43. The term "beed" in the Maay language literally means tribute, in this case it is a tribute paid by force to the colonial concessionaries in the form of manpower. During the implementation of the colonial model known as comparticipazione "share," Italian authorities in Somalia required each village or clan to provide a quota of workers to the plantations and construction projects. The negative consequences of these policies to the Inter-Riverine society are well documented in their oral tradition. From my interviews to the elders of Bur Hakaba in 1975, I was told a Weeryr ("type of war poetry") entitled "Beed" which starts as following: *Bariigno liing kooye me Buur beeda yaalle...* ("Oh! Mighty mountain Bur Hakaba village... we won't desert you, we will always be back regardless of our suffering from tributes imposed on you. ....") On recruiting farm labor and its legislation, see also, Cassanelli, Lee V. "The End of Slavery and the 'Problem' of Farm labor in colonial Somalia." In Proceedings of the Third International Congress of Somali Studies, edited by Annarita Puglielli, 275–80. Rome: Il Pensiero Scientifico Editore, 1988.

44. Mukhtar, Mohamed H. Fieldtone, 1975.

45. Riveri, Carlo. Relazione Annuale sulla Situazione Generale dellaa Colonia, 1920–21. Mogadiscio: Ufficio del Governo, 1921, pp. 16–17.

46. Rava, Maurizio. Circolare Governatoriale, no. 160, 21 Aprile, 1932. Mogadiscio: Ufficio

del Governo, 1932. In fact the plan of unifying all territories occupied by Somalis from Bandar Qassim to Kismayu along the Indian Ocean, then towards the hinterland to the Southern frontiers of Ethiopia dates back to 1907. See details of the plan, as it was proposed to the Italian Parliament in, Del Boca, Angelo. *Gli Italiani in Africa Orientale, dall'Unita alla Marcia su Roma,* (Rome: Editori Laterza, 1975), pp. 815–19.

47. Mukhtar, Mohamed H. *Habka Cilmiga ee Baarista Taariikhda.* Ibid., p. 47.
48. Hodgkin, Thomas. *Nationalism in Colonial Africa.* (New York: New York University Press, 1957), p. 108.
49. Hodgkin, ibid. p. 112.

Chapter Six
Men Drink Tea While Women Gossip

Ladan Affi
University of Wisconsin, Madison

DESPITE HISTORICAL INDICATIONS that women have been the backbone of Somali society, their political, cultural, and economic contributions have rarely been acknowledged, and therefore, remain marginalized. They remain absent from most discourses on Somalia. This is due to the fact that it is primarily men who write about the situation in Somalia, viewing male realities as that of the whole society. By writing women out of the history of their society, Somali women have not only been deprived of their rights, but the ramifications extend beyond political and economic rights, instead they encompass all aspects of women's lives. As a result, Somali women, like others before them, are beginning to debunk those views as they claim the right to be heard, to participate and to contest male produced Somali realities. This paper attempts to add to that nascent debate.

By employing the poetry and songs of Somali women, this paper hopes to bring out the many voices and concerns of Somali women. It situates these poems and song in their economic, political and social context. The issues addressed by these poems and songs range from the struggle against the colonizers, to how to deal with old husbands to being overworked. Sometimes, these poems and songs are frank and confrontational, while in others they are indirect and appear in the form of lullabies sung for children but intended for the ears of husbands or others who are oppressing women. That women have been somewhat successful in challenging and altering the master gender narrative can be seen in the fact that some male poets are beginning to recognize and praise the contributions of Somali women. However, women still have a long way to go in having their contributions recognized on its merit. I specifically intend to articulate the narrative ways in which Somali women have been historically oppressed and the counter-narratives they use in order to resist it. The notion of the contested narratives is derived from what Kusow (see, this volume) refers to as national versus empirical narratives. For the purpose of this chapter, national narratives refer to the appropriation and super-imposing of symbols and values that are purely mythical and legendary in nature and, which above all, are selected from the values and norms of the masculine aspects of the society which renders all that is female unappreciated. By empirical narratives, I mean the actual economic and political contributions that Somali women make to the well being of the nation. The contested and gendered ways in which the two narratives define how, when, where, and whose contribution and participation is legitimate create what I refer to as the emergence of gender crisis in Somalia.

Master Gender Narratives

In Somalia, poetry plays a vital role in the society and "interest in it is universal and skill in it is something which everyone covets and many possess. The Somali poetic heritage is a living force intimately connected with the vicissitudes of everyday life" and in fact some scholars have described Somalia as a "nation of bards"[1] Thus, in order to assess the position of women within the Somali master narrative, it is appropriate to employ poetry as well as songs and proverbs about women.

One of the principal narratives that organize gender relations, and therefore, the ultimate subordination of women-folk is derived from the popular Somali proverb *men drink tea while women gossip.*[2] The ways in which this narrative subordinates women is based on the distinction between drinking tea and gossiping. Drinking tea, according to the narrative, is understood as a masculine activity and denotes hardiness, rationality, and pragmatic thinking. Gossiping, on the other hand, is culturally interpreted as softness, emotionality, and lack of pragmatic thinking.

Other narratives liken women to animals, and in the case of the camel, they are less valued than an animal. For example, in the following well-know proverb, a man talks to his camel telling him about the negative consequences if he or the camel died and the positive result if a woman does.

> My death will bring ruin to the family
> Your death, amel, will bring
> Empty vessels and starvation;
> But a women's death brings
> Fresh grooming and remarriage[3]

What is crookedly fascinating about the above poem is that women are not only positioned below camels and men, but in fact her death is a celebrated as a joyous moment and the start of a new beginning. While the effects of the death of the camel result in starvation and empty vessels, while the death of man will bring ruin to the family.

Women are also likened to what some Somalis consider lesser animals – goats and cows. Some proverbs claim, for example, that women and goats fight when they are weak, or a woman who always argues and a cow that always moos, has no advantage in winning a debate. Still other proverbs liken women to children with the assertion that *women are children with big feet* or by pampering women and children, one can get what one wants form them. Taken together, these narratives locate women as lesser human beings, and in some situations, even beneath some animals. In other words, women are mentally lesser than men and need to be dealt with in that manner.[4] The saying that a *man is a man and women are his offspring* clearly demonstrates the inferiority of women to men. Therefore, men assume a paternal role and they can discipline women as well as cajole them to get them to comply with their orders.

Another aspect of the master narrative relates to the assertion that what is considered as moral virtues for men, are in fact, vices for women. This narrative seeks to maintain the status quo by defining what is desirable and what is not. A well-known proverb defines characteristics that are virtues for men as vices for women: *Three that are good in a man are bad in a woman – Bravery, Generosity and Eloquence*. If a woman is brave, she will want to fight with her husband; if she is generous, she will squander her husband's wealth; and if she is eloquent, she will challenge her husband and thus diminish her husband's prestige.[5] Therefore, the master narrative prefers an *obedient woman than one who is intemperate or intelligent or from better family*.[6]

The only proverbs that present women in a slightly positive light are those in which women are of use to men. For example, there are three types of men you will never surpass: *A man with a better horse, you will not catch up to in a day; A man with a better pasture, it will take you a year to accumulate as much wealth; And a man with a better wife, you will never catch up to*. In this case, women have been placed higher than animals and other resources, but women are not valued for themselves but for what they provide to men.

The perpetuation of the master-narrative regarding Somali women was assisted by what Choi-Ahmed characterizes as "colonial anthropology, orientalism, and androcentric Western scholarship."[7] In turn, this has led to the creation of "the myth of the Somali woman as chattel, commodity, and a creature with little power"[8] Despite these scholars' depictions of Somali women as "'commoner,' 'slave,' or low-caste person,'" they are nevertheless forced to confront the real position of women within the society.[9] Contrary to the description of women as a "womb for rent," the reality demonstrates that underneath the façade, women are quite as influential as men and that although Somali women may have a low position in the society they also may have considerable standing within it.[10] However, many of these scholars continue to depict women as powerless and inferior to men preferring to ignore the counter-narratives confronting them.[11]

Counter-Narratives

According to Berger and Luckmann, counter-definitions of reality and identity emerge when individuals "congregate in socially durable groups."[12] As these individuals attempt to neutralize and then amend the national narratives, their "counter-reality and counter-identity may be hidden from the knowledge of the larger community, which still predefines and ongoingly identifies these individuals" in the same manner. Therefore, although patriarchal society prefers an *obedient woman than one who is intemperate or intelligent,* girls are nevertheless raised to be assertive, witty and intelligent.[13]

However, the counter-narratives of women are seldom known nationally and are often passed from grandmother to mother to daughter.[14] In fact, if we examine women's poetry and songs, we will find that far from passively accepting oppression, women "expressed their grievances, hopes and philosophy through poetry handed from generation to generation, from grandmother to mother to daughter, bearers and transmitters of the female cultural heritage."[15]

Additionally, in line with Berger and Luckmann's definition, Somali women created their own socially durable groups in the form of "informal networks, kinship groups, work groups or religious association to strengthen themselves and fight oppression."[16] They used these groups not only to fight oppression but to also provide economic and spiritual support. Women recognize the value of their solidarity networks as demonstrated in the subsequent song where the importance of collaboration among women is highlighted:

Women, join us, join us

Chorus: Here we join, lets aid one another

In war, men cooperate
And become brothers
Shall we aid each other or shall we separate

Chorus: We are ready to join, lets aid one another [17]

WOMEN'S WAYS OF RESISTANCE

In order to counter the lessening of their contributions to their families, women would often sing the following lullaby, which could be interpreted in a variety of ways depending on the listener.

> Oh my daughter, men have wronged us
> For in a dwelling where women are not present
> No camels are milked
> Nor are saddled horses mounted[18]

Outwardly, the lullaby is intended to entertain female children, while simultaneously providing a connection between mother and daughter as women who have been mistreated. The lullaby also addresses those who diminish women's work. In other words, no work gets done – no camels are milked nor are horses saddled – without the presence of women. On another level, the lullaby is intended as a challenge to those who suggest that women do not contribute anything to their birth families. Horses and camels are often the brideprice paid to a woman's birth family by her suitor, and since this wealth is given in her name, a woman clearly indicates her worth.[19] In fact according to Adan, "The bride price is the sole commodity in this society. Through it, the woman asserts herself. After all, an entire economic system depends on her."[20]

The life most Somali women faced was harsh and difficult; nevertheless women protected and valued each other. Mothers, grandmothers, aunts and female relatives looked out for younger women attempting to shield them while simultaneously preparing them for the severity of life. This song, from a mother to a daughter illustrates the protective relationship that exists between women. It also demonstrates that a mother's approval is needed in order for a marriage to take place. Although, it was only men who took part in the formal and contractual aspects of the marriage, it was women who "often created the options on which men acted."[21]

> When you reach marriageable age
> And if God keeps his approval
> A wicked mean and evil man
> A wife-beater and intimidator
> To such a man (I promise) your hand won't go.[22]

The following bridal song by an older woman is intended to remind a young woman getting married that the man that she is marrying is not her relative and that she should be on her guard and her first priority should be to take care of her own needs. In this way, women united against unjust patriarchal institutions and readied younger women for what life would hold for them and how to be prepared for whatever may befall them.

> The man you are marrying
> Is not your father
> He will chase you away tomorrow[23]

Women also support and assist each other in undermining the power that men exercised over their lives. In the following poem, a young woman married to an old man asks her aunt for advice on how to deal with an old demanding husband.

> Oh aunt, how does one deal with an old husband
> Oh niece, you deal with him the way I do
> Oh aunt will you kindly tell me how?
> Say niece – if he asks for milk
> You milk an old goat for him
> When he comments on the plentifulness of it
> You help yourself to half of it
> You supplement the rest with water
> Remember to drink the first mouthful yourself
> Also the unmilked are all yours
> If he ask for meat
> You slaughter a bony old goat for him
> You roast the unskinned shin for him
> When he asks for knife
> Give him a sharpened dagger
> (In the hope that) he cuts off his fingers
> What if he asks for mat and a pillow
> Throw him the Alool-mat
>
> And if he complains about hard it is
> He whose head is large like a python (You fling a hard one at him)
> May God's curse be on him
> You snatch the Alool-mat from him
> You make him lose his composure
> And let the sand sprinkle his grey hair with dirt
> While asleep you place a stick in his nostrils
> And you torturously pull upwards.[24]

In line with the previous poem, an older woman (an aunt in this case) counsels a young woman not to treat her husband well. As well, a woman should lay claim to whatever she is able to – whether it is milk or livestock – perhaps because an old husband is more likely to die than a younger husband. It may also indicate that an old husband will be less likely to take a new wife and thus there is no competition for the young wife. She is therefore free to treat him as she wishes.

In another story from a mother to a daughter, the mother tells her daughter how to treat her husband depending on his age ranging from the twenties to the eighties. The mother tells her daughter that if her husband "is in his eighties, do whatever you want."[25]

Colonialism and The Condition of Women

Cultures are continually transforming themselves as they experience and react to internal tensions as well as external influence and Somali culture is no different. However, colonialism altered the nature of that transformation by speeding up the pace of change due to the intensity of economic exploitation. So, when the British, Italians and French arrived in the late 19th century, Somalia's economic networks and "cohesive ties of a subsistence economy were destroyed and Somalia was integrated into the international mercantile system."[26] In addition to these economic exploitations, women suffered socially and politically under colonialism. As such, the arrival of colonialism in much of Africa including Somalia diminished women's significant contribution to their societies and their sense of independence due to the concepts brought by Christian missionaries and colonial administrators, of women's appropriate place in society.[27] The presence of foreigners in Somalia has often played a part in viewing major economic players as being male and the Somalis who went to the large towns "found that most of the new economic niches were reserved for men. Somali men were expected and encouraged to engage in exchange activities, and the lower rungs of the bureaucratic, political, and military branches of the colonial administration were open [only] to them."[28]

The colonial authorities viewed women as objects and for the most part left them alone to conduct their small businesses or work as laborers rather than integrating them into the economy. In fact, the only time women came under the scrutiny of the colonial state was "if women were loud and troublesome and not clearly under the authority of a man, they might be accused of prostitution and punished."[29] Thus, the colonial state "reinforced kin group and male authority over women without making the men economically responsible for them and without offering women alternative opportunities for economic survival."[30] Even though, the main item utilized by the colonial state – livestock – was for the most part the responsibility of women. The Italians and the British weakened Somali women's power, legitimizing patriarchal control over women and codifying customary and religious law from an orientalist perspective, hence making it more inflexible.[31]

These economic and social restrictions on their lives put women at the forefront in joining the fight against the imperialist threat.[32] Caught between colonial oppression and a patriarchal society, women rallied together to challenge the structures of oppression.[33] They unconditionally took part in the struggle to free Somalia from colonial powers and in the process liberated themselves. In many African countries, it was primarily educated women who joined the fight for liberation, while in Somalia; the majority of women who joined the liberation movements were unable to access the colonial educational system. The outcome of this was that it "prevented the development of any elitist groupings among women."[34] Women from different educational, economic, social and marital positions all became involved in the struggle on an equal basis" and this created an environment of inclusiveness and "increased awareness among women of their power as an identifiable group."[35] In fact, this understanding is clearly confirmed by the following poem by Hawa Jibrell, an activist in the struggle for independence and a well-known poetess:

> We wanted to break away from our seclusion
> We wanted to have the responsibility to express our feelings and our views
> We wanted to show our concerns for our country[36]

Women hoped that independence would provide them with an opportunity "to make a dramatic change in their own situation."[37] They joined the Somali Youth League (SYL) in the late 1940s in large numbers but despite their active participation, many regarded these women as "operating outside of accepted behaviour" and they were reviled. Actually, pro-colonial supporters used this to condemn the SYL characterizing them as a party supported by "women with sharp tongues."[38] As a result, those women who opposed colonial imposition and joined the independence movements such as Hawo Tako, Halima Godane, Barni Warsame and Timiro Ukash "were severely criticized by family, friends and the general public. Some of the married women who joined the liberation movement were divorced as a result. Those who were unmarried at the time had to carry the stigma of being loose women, and some were even disowned by their parents."[39] However, women continued their opposition to colonialism by providing economic support to the independence movement by selling their jewelry, attending demonstrations, composing poetry to encourage Somalis to resist colonialism and even conducting covert activities.

Despite their contribution and the heavy personal price that many of these women were paying, they were not regarded as full members and encountered stiff resistance in their campaign for full membership. It was only when the women threatened to withdraw their support in 1952, that the SYL's Central Committee admitted women as full members.[40] A few years later, when women began to campaign for representation within the committees of the SYL, many male members within the SYL argued that women lacked the requisite "education and did not have the necessary political consciousness" and therefore did not deserve full membership. Ardo Dirir and Hawo Jibril, who were permitted to address the National Congress of the SYL in 1959, responded in this poem on behalf of the women, by comparing the arguments of the men with those of the colonizers.

> Are you not really arguing as the Italians?
> Are you not in fact supporting their contention,
> As expressed in the United Nations, the Somalis are
> Not ready for independence, because they
> Allege that we have not sufficient education or
> Political maturity?[41]

However, it was only when the women threatened to withdraw their support that the SYL recognized women as full members and they began to be represented in the committees.[42] Consequently, women were targeted by the colonial authorities, which responded by imprisoning many of the women. Some like Timiro Ukash "served a number of years in a high security prison in Kismayo. She was pregnant when she was arrested and she was one of several women to give birth in prison."[43]

Despite their targeting by the colonial state and the lack of support from the independence movements and other Somalis, these activist women refused to accept colonialism and continued to encourage defiance. Faduma Hersi Abbane, who was detained several times, composed the following poem to encourage others to be fearless in their resistance to the colonizers by pointing out the positive aspects of imprisonment:

> By God we are not afraid,
> For we are used to jail
> There is a blanket for cover,
> Another to use as a pillow
> Two sets of clothes to wear
> A bath for washing, a big yard for walks
> Plenty of warm tea
> And millet meal to fill one's stomach.[44]

Hawa Tako, like many other women, paid the ultimate price when a Somali man working for the Italians shot her with an arrow while guarding a warehouse used by the independence movement. As the Italians and British prepared to leave Somalia in the late 1950s, they made a half-hearted attempt to give women some rights such as universal suffrage.

The First Post-Colonial State

The newly independent Somali government had to face many socio-economic development problems. Due to modernization and the policies of the colonial government, women became even "more dependent on their husbands, brothers and fathers [especially if] they had no previous skills and opportunities to adjust to modern life." The new Somali government, like other African governments, left the social and political structures of colonialism intact, ensuring that this ideology remained embedded in the socio-political strata, further contributing to the marginalization of women.[45] The unwillingness of the post-colonial government to dismantle discriminatory institutional barriers against women prompted Kaha Ahmed Sar'ad to recite the following poem reminding the government the debt they owed to Somali women and their disillusionment with their performance:

My skin hangs loose on my bones
My eyes are veiled with clouds
Those I have led I now must follow
To go forward without me

Let alone thanks, I have been forgotten

In the new scramble
The people dispersed
Grasping and shouting
Satisfying greed
And I waited

Let alone gifts, I have been ignored

Protested under the shade of our flag
My comrades shamed it
Ignored me, did not receive me
I was sent away from their homes

Let alone rewards, I have been threatened

And I had dreamed
Somalia as one
But no longer is Somalia one home
Now each keeps to his own
I had filled large "Hamo" with dreams
And shouted "do not loosen the ropes"

> Hoping for one great feast
> But I have been cast aside
> So easily thrown over a cliff
>
> Let alone rewards, I have been threatened[46]

In this poem, Kaha Ahmed Sar'ad explicitly denounces the behavior of the post-colonial regime that was engaging in not only clannism but also stealing from the state. She also acknowledges that women who had led the struggle against colonialism were being relegated to the back and their contribution ignored and unrewarded. She also seems to forecast the breaking up of Somalia due to the behavior of male politicians.

Having been left out of receiving the rewards of independence, many women continued to engage in income generating activities such as selling goods in the market. Other opportunities were limited since the government showed a clear preference for dealing with men. A few urbanized women worked as civil servants, but the majority of women participated in the informal sector economy located either in the home, neighborhoods or in the market. However, "women's trade generated little individualism or profit motive and added little to a woman's status or economic power."[47]

The Military Regime and Women

Once Siad Barre came to power in 1969 in a coup d'etat, it appeared that the government was committed to the political, economic and social advancement of women in Somalia, so much so that many Somali men referred to it as the "Somali women's revolution." Barre recognized that Somali women were indispensable to spreading his Marxist-Socialist ideology because of their key role in raising future generations. Therefore, the focus of Barre's government was on the reproductive roles of women rather than their productive capabilities. Barre "declared that the objective of [his] development policy was to create a society based on justice, equality and development. It also aimed to create an atmosphere for greater self-reliance."[48] In turn, women fully embraced Barre's call for reshaping Somali society, as demonstrated by this poem by Hawa Aaje Mohamed:

> If we don't neglect our prosperous land
> If we are not afraid of hard work
> If we join forces
> If the collective farmers compete
> The imported rice would grow
> Onion and garlic will ripen

Potatoes and pumpkin will pile up
The flour we make pasta from will be available
We wouldn't be able to finish the maize from
Bakaraha [a market in Mogadishu]
Then we will compete with half the world
Then we will have our fill of property
That is when we wouldn't need to beg others
The party will assist so hurry up
And the community of socialists must join hands![49]

The poem above is indicative of how occasionally women would align themselves with the patriarchal institutions and ideologies. It also highlights women's political awareness and their desire to see Somalia compete and succeed in the global market.

Under Barre's leadership, "the Somali language was written, and a massive literacy campaign was successfully launched increasing the literacy rate to 55 percent in 1975, from 5 percent prior to the adoption of a national script."[50] Barre's government insisted that girls attend school, particularly beyond the elementary level, leading to some positive changes for women and girls. In the same year, laws were introduced making wage discrimination on the basis of gender illegal and requiring equal pay for equal work.[51] Working woman were also given the right to "14 weeks' maternity leave with half pay if she has worked with the same employer for at least six months and after coming back a woman was entitled to two daily paid breaks of one hour each in order to nurse her child."[52]

In 1975, Barre amended the Family Law Act changing the inheritance laws by giving men and women equal share.[53] Some of the Muslim scholars criticized these legal changes, because they contradicted the Sharia. Barre responded by executing ten of the scholars, with the result that religious groups were silenced.[54] In order to harness women's mobilizing potential, the government also founded the Somali Women's Democratic Organization. The aims of this organization were in "safe-guarding of women's interests, the promotion of their equality and full potential awareness as participants in social, political and economic life."[55] In order to do more effective outreach, it had "branches not only at the national but also at regional, district, town, and village levels."[56] Somali women's membership in the Somali Revolutionary Socialist Party dramatically increased. As demonstrated by the poem below composed by Halimo Ali Kurtin, women explicitly aligned themselves with Barre's militaristic solutions and deferred to his Barre regime by portraying it as a savior.

Then there was lightening and clouds came above us
Our vigilant revolution was born

Siyaad was leading our charismatic army
Women congratulated them and gave motherly salutations
They all sang revolutionary slogans
They did not go home and rest but stood beside the revolution
May the revolution last longer
May the revolution live forever is what they kept singing
Our revolution sorted out the following first:
The backward ones who stalled progress were sorted out
Those who squandered public resources were sorted out
The law that was abused is treated with respect
The mothers who were lost and neglected
They were treated right and were given their inheritance
The heroes of the SRC have corrected it (the law)
They know very well political issues
They manage things through socialism[57]

While Barre appointed several women to vice-minister posts, there were no women given the influential portfolio of full minister, despite their years of political experience and high education.[58] Yet, in the rural areas, women's position changed very little; their involvement was restricted to the informal markets, primarily because "other options for income-generation in this milieu [were] few, especially for the large numbers of women without formal education."[59] Despite Barre's apparent support for women's rights, in the economic sphere, "government gave itself a dominant role and actively restricted the development of the private sector."[60] Even the more lucrative import-export businesses were constrained by the government, which controlled access to hard currency and licenses. Women made up no more than 5% of those who were licensed by the government to take part in the import-export business.[61] Since other avenues were restricted, "women came to dominate retail trade and the open market, where foodstuff and imported consumables were sold, and many retail shops were owned by women."[62] Men on the other hand, having taken over from the European commercial houses after independence controlled large-scale wholesale trade such as frankincense and livestock trade as well as more capital-intensive shops such as construction.[63] Regardless of the government's neglect in promoting women's economic participation, available statistics on Somali women confirmed that that their level of labor force participation was relatively high compared to women in many African countries and that 33.65% of Somali women above the age of ten were in the labour force.[64] However, closer examination of these numbers yields a more accurate picture. Two-thirds of the working women were self-employment, while 15% and 20% were employees and unpaid family helpers respectively."[65] In the end, Barre's regime did not significantly improve majority of women's lives as this poem by a nomadic mother to her daughter indicates. Women continued to shoulder most of the work ensuring the family's survival.

> After a journey so long
> And tiring indeed
> Like a fully laden camel
> Tired as you are under the load
> You at last set a camp
> Beside a hamlet with no blood-ties to you
> Your livestock will need
> To be always kept in sight
> Your beast of burden will need
> To be tied to their tethers
> The newly born baby sheep
> Have to be taken out to graze
> The house will always need
> To be tidy and in shape
> Your children always need
> Your comforting care and love
> Your man will always need
> Your services in different ways
> And may at times scold you
> For services poorly done
> And may at times beat you
> For no apparent reason
> So stop whimpering
> And perform as best you possibly can
> The responsibilities and the duties
> Set out for you to do[66]

Barre's state-sponsored feminism, with its initial commitment to widespread women's advancement led to real change for only very few women. Instead, Barre's vision of a new communal identity resulted in the strengthening of the clan system, further devaluing women's role in society. In response to Barre's increasingly oppressive policies, opposition movements formed and once again, women played a crucial part. Mariam Haji Hassan was a founding member of the Somali Salvation Democratic Front, the first movement to challenge Barre. She went into exile in Kenya, broadcasting her poetry to Somalia, on the opposition movement's radio.[67]

> The committee let us down,
> They eliminated the strong and the intelligent.
> They detain the young as they reach puberty

The process of avenging these wrongs must begin
We must support those preparing to fight[68]

By the 1980s, many women including former members of the Somali Women's Democratic Organization "felt that women were used by the Siad Barre regime just as they were used during the struggle for independence."[69] Others felt that the regime had negative effects on women because, "the changes in the Quranic verses about women by the government resulted in the great misunderstanding of the situation of women. It also provided naturally prejudiced men with the ammunition needed to weaken women's position in development."[70] Once women realized that Barre was not sincere in his promises to them, most women withdrew their support and some even challenged his authority.

The well-known Somali author, Nuruddin Farah wrote of an incident that clearly highlighted women's opposition to Barre's dictatorship when in 1989, in Kismayo:

> A few dozen women, defying the conviction that enjoins female sartorial modesty, bared their breasts in public in front of a crowd of men. Fists raised, voices harsh, they shouted "Rise, Rise!" challenging the men to action, reproaching them for their failure to confront the excesses of the dictatorship. By challenging the men in this manner, the women implied that they would not from then on defer to them as husbands, fathers, or figures of authority.[71]

The security police responded by briefly detaining the women and their male relatives. The women were let go as soon as the crowd dispersed, while the man were held in jail and physically humiliated because the security police believed women to be incapable of being defiant without the knowledge and support of their male relatives.

By the late 1980s, "total development assistance constituted a stunning 57% of Somalia's GNP."[72] As the end of the Cold War approached, Somalia's relevance as a strategic area was reduced and international aid was lessened or completely withdrawn by Western countries. The justification given by the donors was the Barre regime's atrocious human rights record. The real explanation was the conclusion of the Cold War and the decreasing importance of Somalia as a strategic location for the US. The US reportedly told the Somali government that US bilateral assistance would be suspended unless the government improved its respect for human rights.[73] Meanwhile, Somalia's economic, political and social deterioration accelerated. By 1990, Barre lost power over most of Somalia and was sarcastically nicknamed 'the mayor of Mogadishu'. Barre fortified the presidential palace, and lost complete contact with the people. A group of elders, called the Manifesto Group, composed of businessmen, intellectuals, and political leaders called on Barre to agree to a peaceful power transition and a departure from politics. Barre refused and is rumored to have said, if forced out, he would destroy Somalia in the process.

The Civil War and Women

On January 1st 1991, armed opposition groups drove Barre out of Mogadishu and although he attempted a return in the following months, it was never successful.

> As soon as the detested center collapsed, a new vicious jostling for individual and clanistic power commenced [and] an orgy of looting (partly by Barre's fleeing troops) of public and private property erupted, which culminated in anarchy and chaos in most major urban centers. For many thousands of inhabitants of Mogadishu and other areas in Southern Somalia, living became a nightmare as more and more of them were terrorized by armed gangs.[74]

Instead of bringing relief, the fall of Barre only brought more hardships. The Somali state and its institutions disappeared and the traditional social institutions, undermined by decades of dictatorship and misrule, were ineffective to stop the clan manipulations of power-hungry warlords who exploited clan affiliations and friction.[75]

With the collapse of Barre's government, Somalia "detached itself into a Fourth World Order by virtue of complete political and social collapse."[76] The disintegration of Somalia created horrifying human loss, desolation of infrastructure, the collapse of the health and educational structures and the death and displacement of millions of Somalis. Like other conflicts, there is no denying that the most vulnerable – minority groups, women, the elderly and children – were the most severely affected. When television broadcasted images of starving children struggling to suck a drop of milk from a mother's shriveled breast, Somali men were also on TV looking healthy, wearing sunglasses, toting weapons and chewing Qat.[77] Although, some women did participate in the fighting or incited their men to fight in the bloodbath that followed, this was a rare occurrence.

Violence and warfare establish, reinforce and exacerbate divisions within communities.[78] Once such divisions are created, they cannot be easily undone without the active participation of women. Since women are born into one clan and often marry in to another, they are in an ideal position to bridge the gaps that exist between these two clans.[79] Most "women are aware of the importance of the multiplicity of connections the warring communities have, seeing themselves now as mothers to children of one family, now as daughters of another, and on remarriage, as mothers to offspring from yet another lineage. [While] the men remain true to their father's ancestral identity, the women do not."[80] Thus, women should be an essential part of any lasting conflict resolution.[81]

Contrary to Somali traditions and signaling the breakdown of Somali Xeer and culture, women were targeted, raped, tortured and killed, not for themselves as women, but as a means to humiliate their male relatives. Hundreds of thousands of Somalis became refugees fleeing to neighboring countries in search of peace and safety. Many women braved the chaos and the killings, staying in Somalia and feeding those who were dying of hunger, looking after children, the sick and the elderly, and burying the dead. As conflict progresses, divisions develop between men and women: men become pre-occupied with military or strategic issues while women are often left to deal with the issues of subsistence and daily survival. While the men were vying for power and defending the honor and the name of their clan, Somali women effectively became the heads of households.

Transforming Patriarchy

A United States Institute of Peace report conducted in 1998 found that women had established committees and NGOs in Mogadishu and elsewhere. These women were playing a vital role in peacemaking where women were collaborating across clan lines and supporting health, nutritional and educational services. Since women were not expected to represent the clan who treated them as outsiders in public and political decision-making events, women played a neutral role, transcending the more destructive elements of Somali clannism. Since the civil war destroyed earlier livelihoods and the men were called for militia duty, the women assumed new commercial roles to support their children and relatives. The report finds that the special adaptability and resilience of women and women's groups have suggested a vital and generally overlooked role for women in bringing women about reconciliation. The report recommends that women's groups should be given support so that they can assume prominent roles and continue their constructive influence in rebuilding civil society.[82]

To increase women's earning potential, women's NGOs have also been vital in conducting training by providing micro-credit assisting women in starting small businesses. The breakdown of social norms allowed women to engage in activities that were considered male domains although women are still prevented from participating in the more lucrative markets such as livestock and frankincense trade. Other women have met their financial responsibilities by joining shalongo or hagbad, in which a group of Somali women pool specific amounts of money to be collected by each member in turn. Women then use this money to start up a business or invest in jewelry to guard against future hardship.

Before the civil war if a family did not have a son, the mother was told that she was *gablan*, implying that to have no son was a tragedy. Since the civil war, *gablan* has been used to mean a family without a daughter.[83] This clearly demonstrates women's central role in the survival of the family and that they have taken over responsibilities associated with men. When families are immigrating abroad, boys are often left behind because it is believed that women are much more likely to send money home and to take care of the family. Women in the Diaspora also benefit more from educational opportunities and job training, and they are more successful at locating and maintaining a job.[84] As such, women in the Diaspora bear a tremendous burden in supporting relatives in Somalia who send money every month to meet the needs of those who are unable to work in a devastated country. Indicating women's changed position, often the money is sent to female relatives because of the fear that men will squander the money on their needs rather than that of the family.

A major source of conflict in Somalia and the Diaspora, both within the family and in the community, is the habitual chewing of a stimulant called Qat (Cathis Edulis). Its impact on the Somali community has been devastating. Due to widespread addiction, it has resulted in the diversion of income and the loss of productivity and in many places has contributed to the prolonging of the conflict. While their wives, mothers, daughters and sisters work, men prefer to sit around drinking tea and gossiping for hours and sometimes for days on end. Despite this reality, Somali men perceive their role within the household as that of the primary income earner. This common misperception exists even though male unemployment is high and women's productive work actually provides the primary income.

Women have shown themselves to being a strong force in Somalia, but there is unanimity in all circles in Somalia, regardless of other disagreements men might have, to prevent women from encroaching on what is perceived as men's domain. If the clan is not effective in depriving women of their rights, then religion is used, although Islam has no laws against women participating in the political sphere. Yet men continue to use religious authority as an excuse to deny women's rights, despite the fact that Somali men have for the most part dismally failed to meet their God-given responsibilities as providers.

Somali women have been excluded or marginalized in the dozens of reconciliation conferences held in the past ten years. Even in the last conference held in Arta, Djibouti ending in the formation of a transitional government where women were touted as equal participants, only 25 out of 245 parliamentary seats were allocated to women and so far only one woman has been named as minister without portfolio while 3 others have been named as vice-ministers. While in Somaliland, women ran for the last two presidential elections as independents. It was only recently that Somaliland included a woman in its cabinet as Foreign Minister but as of yet, there are no women representatives in the parliament. In Puntland, although there a few women in the parliament, real power remains concentrated in the hands of men.

Sandra Harding criticizes the notion of "adding women and gender" to existing social and political structures without questioning their hierarchical and politically regressive agendas.[85] Other feminist scholars like Rhoda Howard also deplore the view that appointing special members of parliament, to represent women as "a means of incorporating potential political protests into a manageable forum."[86] In addition to Harding and Howard, Segers also

> cautions feminists not to view affirmative action as a panacea to the problem of discrimination and oppression reminding women that affirmative action is a single policy… a lonely policy, a voice in the wilderness that can achieve little without support of other policies directed at reducing disparities in wealth, status and power[87]

Although, affirmative actions may have limited impact, the alternative may be not to have women involved at all.

At the beginning of the formation of the transitional government both the prime minister and president made numerous public statements that women would be visible in their government. When questioned about the dismal lack of women representatives, they both resorted to the age-old excuse – no clan would agree to women representing them. Recently, the transitional government ratified the African Unity Treaty with the exception of two articles, one of which dealt with gender equality. In the latest ongoing reconciliation conference in Mbagathi, Kenya Somali women have refused to be marginalized and have actively attempted to participate in all aspects of the conference. However, they continue to face an uphill battle.

The international community has spent billions on Somalia and has very little to show for it today. There are thousands of studies documenting the roles, contributions, needs, aspirations, perceptions and perspectives of women in the world. The crucial question then becomes, what has been learned from all this activity as Somalia attempts to reconstruct itself?

In order to strengthen the position of women in Somali society effectively, each economic, political and social barrier they face must be overcome. It is no longer enough to assume that men's needs are identical or relevant to those of Somali women. By working with Somali women to identify and implement policies that promote gender equity, there is no doubt Somali society as a whole benefits.

For their greater contribution to the maintenance of households, Somali women should be given credit – literally. Access to substantial loans would allow Somali women a chance to compete in the more lucrative import/export business. Established women's NGOs should be promoted and encouraged by providing funding and training to meet women's specific needs such as education and health. "One of the most common problems in shaping development policies that affect women is the assumption that such policies are gender-neutral whereas in reality they greatly favor men at women's expense."[88] Donor countries should make women's active involvement in projects a condition for giving aid.

Women in Somalia, like women across Africa, have sought autonomy not only to demand policy changes but more importantly, to fight for greater equality. Women are at the forefront of struggles against patronage politics and corruption.[89] Nuruddin Farah writes that "to be a Somali and a woman fighting for equality and social justice in these times requires an even greater deal of courage than in times of peace. And yet it is more necessary than ever".[90]

There are however some positive signs that indicate that women's sacrifices and contributions are being slowly acknowledged. There are more people who are now saying that we should give women a chance to see if they can bring peace to Somalia, since men have only brought about destruction and misery.[91] Male poets have also paid tribute to women including one of the most renowned Somali poets Mohamed Ibrahim Warsame "Hadrawi", who in his poem *Daba Huwan* clearly recognizes the life saving role of women and prays to God to give them the leadership, subordinating men to them:

> And women are a bulwark
> Half of your gift they are
> What makes life possible
> Is their tolerance
>
> There is an obvious evil
> They were born in the hidden
> They dilute the sins of the man
> Oh Lord, accept my prayers for them
> Give the good (leadership) for us to women
> And put men under their wings
> What they destroyed, Oh Lord
> If they don't abstain from the wickedness
> Oh Lord, the impending travails
> A yet-to-be-seen accident
> Oh Lord prevent us from it.[92]

Jama Kediye, also a well-known poet, composed *Siyaasad* in which he also acknowledges that most women have met their responsibilities and asks God to reward them:

> And women are royalty
> Their reputation is greatest
> They carry the children

They raise the infants
They take care of the old
Allah made it easy for them (to do their job)
Ever hundred of them
There is a ninety
That perform their job dutifully
Oh Allah, the saatir
Give them their reward

Conclusion

This paper has attempted to lay out how women challenge, often successfully, patriarchal narratives. The gradual acknowledgement given to women's positive contribution to the society at large may be a product of this. Women create socially durable groups as a way to create counter-realities and identities and in the process defy patriarchy.

Unlike male poetry, a familiar theme within women's poetry is their constant concern for all Somalis and for Somalia. Their desire to see Somalia become successful in the world is also obvious. Somali women's poetry clearly demonstrates that they do not conform to the portrayal of the master narrative as inferior, incapable and unaware. Their poems reveal that Somali women have always played a positive and active role in the affairs of their communities and that of their nation. In fact, they have frequently challenged the men to confront tyrannical authorities whether external or internal. Due to their ability to bridge divisions within the society because of their weak links to the patriarchal clan system, their focus on meeting the needs of their families and creating an environment of peace and stability, women can be the solution to Somalia's problems. All that is needed is for them to be asked them for their advice and as Hadrawi recommends to entrust the leadership with them.

Notes

1. Adan, 115
2. All proverbs will be italicized
3. Haji Dualah, 14
4. One proverb states that "reason and a chest that has produced milk do not go together" See Kapteijns 1999, 45–46.
5. Ibid, 9
6. Ibid, 14
7. Choi-Ahmed, 158
8. Ibid, 159
9. In contrast, Somali men are described as "noble," Ibid, 161
10. Ibid, 162
11. In fact, Choi-Ahmed's article "Finely Etched Chattel The Invention of a Somali

woman" is littered with examples of these contradictions between master narratives and the reality of women; for example, see p.161; p.162–3; p.166 etc.

12. Berger and Luckmann, 163–180
13. For example, the story of Huryo Ugaas clearly demonstrates this counter-narrative. When Huryo agrees to elope with Hersi, he brings along his cousin Kabacalaf to come along. On the journey, Huryo decides to test Hersi's intelligence. She finds him wanting and instead chooses to marry Kabacalaf who was able to answer all her questions. See Haji-Dualah, 15.
14. In fact Berger and Luckmann note that children are socialized by the adults from their gender and that male and female children "will *know* the version appertaining to the other sex, to the extent that it has been mediated" to him/her by someone from the opposite gender, "but he will not *identify* with this version" 168
15. Hassan, 167
16. Ibid 167
17. Haji-Dualah, 19. That women valued these solidarity networks is also demonstrated in this song, in which women call on each other to help those among them who are less fortunate. Women why don't you; Give the fatty tails of sheep; To the poor among us? Ibid, 24.
18. Adan, 117 For the full lullaby see Kapteijns 1999; 58
19. Ibid 117
20. Adan, 6
21. Ibid, 59
22. Adan, 6
23. Haji Dualah, 17
24. Adan, 15
25. When he is his twenties, whenever he gets angry, just show him your thighs and he will forget. When he is in his thirties, don't ask him to divorce you, for he is already ready to marry another wife. When he is in his forties, he is in his prime; avoid being hit by him when he is angry… When he is in his eighties, do whatever you want. See Kapteijns 1999, 45
26. Bryden, 2
27. Smock 1997 as quoted in Tamale, 9
28. Kapteijns 1993, 11
29. In one case were H. Rayne was the colonial officer in charge of the court, he asks his interpreter to shut a Somali woman up, the interpreter responds "you cannot shut a Somali woman up. Beat her, yes. Kill her, yes. But as long as she has an ounce of breath left in her, she will talk"
30. Ibid, 13
31. Gordon, 64. For example, the British introduced a law called Nushuus laws, as part of Islamic law in which disobedient wives were confined to remain in the marital home, neither married nor divorced. Contrary to this, the Qur'an clearly states that men and women are to live with each other in peace or leave one another in peace.
32. Steiner, 194
33. Tamale, 9
34. Haji-Dualah, 30
35. Ibid, 30

36. Ibid, 30
37. Ibid, 30
38. Ibid, 34
39. Jama, 7
40. Dualah, 31
41. Haji-Dualah, 31
42. In 1951, a women's section was set up within the SYL and in 1959 in response to the impending coming independence women organized themselves in to the Somali Women's Association in order to create a platform with which to present their demands. Ibid, 36
43. Jama, 5
44. Ibid, 7
45. Tamale, 14
46. Haji Dualah, 38
47. Gordon, 63
48. Mubarak, 13
49. Jama, 189
50. Laitin and Samatar, 83
51. Somalia: Country Gender Profile, 3
52. Ibid, 3
53. See Lewis, 164. According to Islamic law, when inheriting from parents, women receive half of what their brothers receive, because the brothers are responsible for the welfare of their sisters from the portion that they receive (see Qur'an 4:7 & 4:11).
54. Ibid, 164
55. ILO, 75
56. Ibid
57. Translation by Zainab M. Jama and it is taken from a forthcoming doctoral thesis on the poetry of Somali women
58. Jama, 190
59. ILO, 82
60. Mubarak, 14
61. Elmi, personal communication
62. Gordon, 63
63. Gordon 63; Elmi, personal communication
64. ILO, 79
65. Ibid, 80
66. Haji-Dualah, 59
67. Jama, 190
68. Ibid, 192
69. Jama, 190
70. Ibrahim and Adan as quoted in Jama, 190
71. Farah, 1996
72. Marchal, 11
73. Lyons and Samatar, 28
74. Ibid, 21
75. Mubarak, 17

76. Horsman and Marshall, 144
77. Osman, 1993
78. Ramsey Marshall, 27
79. Kapteijns, 1999 59
80. Farah, 2
81. In fact, in order to cement truce agreements reached after fighting, clans would often exchange women for marriage.
82. Adam and Ford, 21–22
83. Even though, women in the pastoral tradition tended to value daughter over sons believing that girls were more likely to take care of them in their old age. Women would often pray "God save us from being a family without a girl" See Kapteijns 1999, 58
84. Adam and Ford, 22
85. Tamale, 23
86. Ibid, 23
87. Ibid, 25
88. Gordon, 138
89. Tripp, 2000
90. Farah, 1996
91. A novel titled "Has Anyone Asked Women for Advice" is part of this trend. This book is a loosely fictionalized account of what happened in Somalia. In the beginning of the story, a young boy is perched high on a tree, where the elders are meeting to discuss how to bring about peace and stability between the Soofmaal. The elders are unable to come up with a solution on how to recreate the peace that existed among the Soofmaal, when the young boy's question of "has anyone asked the women for advice" is met with shocked silence. See Ali, Abdibasihr
92. I thank Said M. Shire for providing me with a copy of the poem and Mohamud H. Khalif for the translation.

References

Adam, Amina (1989) "Women and words" Ufuhamu Vol. 10 (3): 115–142 Available at: http://web.archive.org/web/19991010230319/srv01.anaserve.com/~mbali/ Retrieved: January 10, 2001 Adam, Hussein, Richard Ford et al. (1998) *Removing Barricades in Somalia: Options for Peace and Rehabilitation.* Washington, DC: United States Institute of Peace.

Ali, Abdibashi (2003) Dumar Talo Ma Laga Deyey – Women: The Solution to the Somalia Crisis. Stockholm: Scansom Publishers 2nd Edition

Berger, Peter L. and Thomas Luckmann (1966) The Social Construction of Reality: A Treatise in the Sociology of Knowledge. New York: Anchor Books.

Bryden, Matt. (1998) Somalia between Peace and War: Somali Women on the Eve of the 21st Century. Nairobi, Kenya: UNIFEM

Choi-Ahmed, Christine (1995) "Finely Etched Chattel: The Invention of a Somali Woman" *The Invention of Somalia.* Ed. Ali Jimale Ahmed. Lawrenceville: The Red Sea Press, Inc.

Elmi, Zahra. (2001/02/14) Personal interview.

Farah Nuruddin. (November 15, 1996) "The women of Kismayo" *The Times Literary Supplement* (London), pp. Available: http://www.anaserve.com/~mbali/siteindex Retrieved January 10, 2001

Gordon, April A. (1996) Transforming Capitalism and Patriarchy: Gender and Development in Africa. Boulder, Co: Lynne Reinner Publishers, Inc.

Haji Dualah, Raqiya et al (n.d) *Women's Movements and Organizations in an Historical Perspective*. Research Project 1983–1985: Women and Development. The Hague, the Netherlands: Institute of Social Studies.

Hassan, Dahabo Farah, Amina H. Adan and Amina Mohamoud Warsame (1995) "Somalia: Poetry as Resistance against Colonialism and Patriarchy" *Subversive Women: Historical Experiences of Gender and Resistance* Ed. Saskia Wierenga. Atlantic Highlands, NJ, USA: Zed Books.

Horsman, Mathew and Andrew Marshall. (1994) *After the Nation-State: Citizen and Tribalism and the New World Disorder*. London: Harper Collins Publishers.

ILO International Labour Organization. (1989) *Generating employment and income in Somalia: Jobs and skills programme for Africa*. Geneva: International Labour Organizations. United Nations.

Jama, Zainab Mohamed. "Fighting to be heard: Somali women's poetry" African Literature and Cultures. London: School of Oriental and African Studies. Vol. 4 (1): 43–53. Available at: http://www.anaserve.com/~mbali/siteindex.htm Retrieved: January 10, 2001

Jama, Zainab Mohamed. *Muted by culture: the poetic voices of contemporary Somali women* From the 1970s to the 1990s. University of London: Ph.D. Dissertation

Kapteijns, Lidwien. (1993). Women and the Crisis of Communal Identity: The Cultural Construction of Gender in Somali History. Boston, MA: African Studies Center, Boston University.

Kapteijns, Lidwien with Maryan Omar Ali (1999) Women's Voices in a Man's World: Women and the Pastoral Tradition in Northern Somali Orature, c. 1899–1980 Portsmouth, NH: Heinemann.

Lewis, I.M. (1993) Understanding Somalia: Guide to Culture, History and Social Institutions. London: HAAN Associates 1993:

Lyons, Terrance and Ahmed I. Samatar. (1995) Somalia: State Collapse, Multilateral Intervention, and Strategies for Political Reconstruction. Washington, DC: Brookings Institution.

Marchal, Roland. (July 1998). "Let's Talk About Governance in Somalia" Written for *UNDOS*. Available: http://www.anaserve.com/~mbali/siteindex.htm Retrieved: November 11, 2001.

Mubarak, Jamil Abdalla. (1996) *From Bad Policy to Chaos in Somalia: How an Economy Fell Apart*. Westport, Connecticut & London: Praeger.

Osman, Hibaaq I. (March/April, 1993) "Somalia: Will Reconstruction Threaten Women's Progress?" *Ms. Magazine* Available at: http://www.anaserve.com/~mbali/siteindex.htm Retrieved: January 10, 2001. *The Holy Qur-an* with English translation of the meaning and commentary. Revised and Edited By: The Presidency of Islamic Researches. Kingdom of Saudi Arabia: King Fahd Holy Qur-an Printing Complex.

Ramsey Marshall, Donna. (2000) *Women in war and peace: Grassroots Peacebuilding*. Washington, DC: United States Institute of Peace. "Somalia: Country Gender Profile" (No date) Washington DC World Bank. Available at: http://www.anaserve.com/~mbali/siteindex.htm Retrieved: January 10, 2001.

Steiner, Martina (1997) "An Anthropological Outline of Gender relations and Politics in Somalia" *Pour une Culture de la Paix en Somalie* Eds. Mohamed Mohamed-Abdi and Patrice Bernard. Paris: European Association of Somali Studies.

Tamale, Sylvia. (1999) *When hens begin to crow: Gender and parliamentary politics in Uganda.* Kampala, Uganda: Fountain Publishers.

Tripp, Aili Mari. (2000) *Women and politics in Uganda.* Madison: University of Wisconsin Press.

Chapter Seven

Transformative Islam & Shifting Gender Roles in The Somali Diaspora

Rima Berns McGown, Ph.D.

W OMEN HAVE BEEN INSTRUMENTAL in keeping shattered Somali families and communities together, both in the Diaspora and in the homeland. They have been at the forefront of the redefinition of Somalis' practice of Islam as it has occurred in the Diaspora in the years since mass migration, and in the transference of ideas back into the homeland. As such, they have played, and continue to play, an enormously influential role in the developing Somali sense of self and identity.

Catapulted into the Diaspora in the late 1980s with the breakdown of civic society, Somalis in exile have tended to become significantly more religious than they had been in their homeland.[1] Their practice of Islam has changed, however, and been redefined in the process. And one of its most significant implications is that gender roles have shifted: women increasingly hold more power within households and within their communities as a result of their assumption of religious leadership within the household.

More – and Differently – Religious

Almost all Somalis in Somalia are Muslims. Prior to mass emigration, Somalis were depicted by I.M. Lewis and others as strong practitioners of Sufism.[2] However, over the course of the 1970s, Islamist movements grew up in the urban centers of Somalia – largely in response to the perceived ideological instability of the dictator

Siad Barre (1969–1991). These movements have proven to be influential both within Somalia in the aftermath of civil war and in the Diaspora, which has drawn the majority of its exiles from urban centers.

The author's research concluded that Somalis were forced to re-examine their identity as Muslims upon migrating to the West in the 1980s and 1990s. This re-examination occurred because they could not longer take their Muslim identities for granted, and because they and their children were faced, for the first time, with an apparently bewildering array of competing faiths and practices, dominant among them the West's particular brand of Judeo-Christian-based secularism. These challenges forced immigrant Somalis to wrestle with their identities and to answer questions for themselves about who they were and why. They did not have the luxury of time at their disposal. Even as parents hastened to secure housing, jobs, English training, and sources of *halal* meat for their families, their children were integrating – almost instantly – into schools and the world of their peers. Parents' greatest fear in the Diaspora was of "losing" their children to an alien culture, one that did not include Islam.

It was the immediacy of this fear, more than any other, that forced Somali parents to re-examine their Islam and to begin to understand it in a new way. If they were going to transmit it to their children, they could no longer rely on the wider society to do it for them or to reinforce their values; they had to do it themselves. Therefore they had to grasp, in a more explicit way, what it was that they wanted to transmit.

Exiled Somalis began to engage with the texts of Islam: to study the Qur'an and the *hadiths*, and to form study groups to discuss their relevance to their lives in the West. Women began to wear the *hijab* in a way that they had not traditionally done in Somalia.

Because of the pressures of refugee life, and the fact that many families became separated during the course of the war or escape from it, single women often found themselves at the head of families in exile. Sometimes their husbands were dead, sometimes they were still in Somalia or in refugee camps in Kenya, hoping to rejoin the family, and sometimes the couple had separated in the Diaspora, their relationship unable to withstand the hardships of refugee life. But even in the cases of intact families, the woman – taking traditional responsibility for the children while her husband sought employment, would still be the one to cope with the perceived 'loss' of culture among the children, and would therefore find herself becoming more – and differently – religious.

Women in Somalia have not traditionally been segregated or kept in purdah. Their work in the traditional pastoral society required that they be mobile. It was they who cared for the family's sheep, goats, and cattle, while the men took responsibility for the camels – considered the heart of a family's wealth. In addition, it was the women who struck and remade the family's portable housing every time a move was necessary. Somali head-coverings, such the gauzy *melchabad*, tended to be worn to beautify the wearer rather than hide her features, and often displayed her hair, neck, and breastbones.

A closer reading of the Qur'an on emigrating Westward, however, as well as a perceived need to emphasize their adherence to 'their' religion, culture, and values, has prompted many Somali women in the Diaspora to wear the *hijab*. This may take the form of the traditional opaque *garbasaar* or other thick cloth, folded in a triangle so as not to expose hair or neck. Or it may even be the *jilbab* (pl. *jelaabib*), the garb favored by the Islamist movements. The *jilbab* is a two-piece garment: a long, ankle-length gown, buttoned up the front, topped by *al-qimar*, the head-scarf, which is sometimes long and sweeping itself, as far as mid-calf or merely over the shoulders. It was designed to give women maximum flexibility and movement while covered from head to toe, and, like other Somali dress, *jelaabib* are found in strong, glorious colors in addition to shades of black and brown.

Many Somali women in the Diaspora participate actively in Qur'an classes and study circles. They pray five times daily. Moreover, they actively attend prayers at their local mosques, especially the Friday noon prayer, something that they were not wont to do – and that mosques were not built to accommodate – in their homeland.

Changing Attitudes to Sexuality

The combination of a redefined practice of Islam and the accommodation to living in the West has resulted in a re-evaluation of attitudes towards sexuality in several significant regards.

BIRTH-CONTROL

Almost all teenaged girls and women interviewed on the subject of birth control indicated that in the West it is both acceptable and unavoidable. Men tended to maintain that the number of children born to a couple was Allah's wish, and that the couple should not interfere, except to breast-feed babies for two years in the hope that this would prevent conception.[3]

Birth control, or family planning, is not viewed uniformly by Muslim jurists. Although large families have traditionally been encouraged in order to ensure a strong Muslim community, economic and development issues have prompted legal positions that allowed for family planning in many Muslim countries. The only birth control mentioned in the *hadiths* is *'azl* (*coitus interruptus*), which was frequently frowned upon in *fiqh* (jurisprudence) literature because it was seen to be detrimental to the woman.[4] On the other hand, Basim Musallam maintains that there is significant juridical support for birth control, based on hadiths which indicate the Prophet's tolerance of the practice, and on the writings of such respected jurists as al-Ghazali.[5] Many contemporary *'ulama* rule that the use of contraceptives is permissible as long as both husband and wife agree to it, and national family planning programs have been implemented in a number of Muslim countries. Many Islamists, on the other hand, discourage the use of birth control on the grounds that it contributes to immoral behavior such as pre- and extra-marital sexual activity.[6]

Pre-marital Sex

For most Somalis, this issue strikes at the heart of their fears for their daughters. Pre-marital sex for girls is a taboo in traditional Somali society. Somali parents frequently voiced fears that their daughters, in imbibing the 'freedom' of the West, would forego their Muslim and Somali values in favor of Western ones, and engage in pre-marital sex. (They did not voice similar concerns about their sons.)

Not surprisingly, attitudes towards pre-marital sex were varied across generational lines. Parents, and other people over thirty, by and large, were horrified of the possibility that they might not be able to keep their daughters' virginity intact until their marriages. Teenagers, too, were unanimous in their stated aversion to pre-marital sex. Women and men in their twenties, however, were not so sweeping in their pronouncements. While there were unmarried women and men who maintained that pre-marital sex was not acceptable to them as Muslims, others were not so unequivocal. Some women, as well as men, said that their views had shifted on this issue in the years since they had arrived in the West. These people said that they no longer believed it was wrong, as Muslims, to engage in pre-marital sex, although they acknowledged that it would pain their parents grievously to know of their views. The interesting point is that every person who held this view considered herself or himself to be a practising Muslim, and each of them maintained that they had grown more religious on moving to the West, rather than less so.

Extra-marital Sex

Similarly, many people – including adults who rejected the notion of their children engaging in pre-marital sex – were less condemnatory on the subject of extra-marital sex, particularly in circumstances where one partner in a marriage was dead or had been separated from the family for a lengthy period. Although considered not ideal, even objectionable, people accepted that it was unavoidable, particularly in times of societal upheaval such as the community in exile was experiencing. Again, it is interesting that the people holding these views considered themselves to be religious Muslims – more religious than they had been in their homeland.

Female Circumcision or Female Genital Mutilation

Both the terms 'female circumcision' and 'female genital mutilation' are problematic. The former implies a procedure that is as uncomplicated and without repercussions as its male counterpart, which it is not, while the second implies an intention to harm the victim, which is unfair and inaccurate.

Female circumcision has been expressly outlawed in Britain since 1985, and this step was taken in Canada in 1995. In 1994, for the first time, a Somali woman was granted refugee status in Canada due to the fear that her daughter would be infibulated were she to return to her homeland.[7] For Somalis, the particular issue is that in their oral Muslim society, infibulation was historically understood to be a requirement of being a good Muslim woman.

In her book *Infibulation*, Esther Hicks maintains that the practice, which pre-dated Islam, served as a mechanism to ensure virginity among unmarried girls in pastoral societies. These societies developed a physical chastity belt which was meant to perform the same function as seclusion because they were unable to separate the girls physically from possible violation. The importance of virginity and chastity outside marriage, the maintenance of family honor, and the perpetuation of patri-lineal lineage were all values which found a solid echo in Islam when the religion was adopted. As a result, the practice was maintained and reinforced,[8] even once the societies evolved into agricultural or otherwise settled communities. In closed pastoral-originated societies, she argues, there has been little reason for change.

The essential point about female circumcision is that, as Somali women in the Diaspora leave their 'closed' society, educate themselves about the texts of Islam, and become more religious, they find that female circumcision is not the Muslim requirement their oral society had taught them to believe it was, and they have begun to speak against it, and to end the practice. They have separated the religious from the cultural, and decided in favor of the religious. The Islamist groups reject the practice, and this is one area in which they have shown their influence.

There does exist a degree of backlash against the revulsion of the West to the practice, a backlash against the barrage of health clinics and television shows depicting the 'barbarism' of the practice and its practitioners. It is a backlash that is articulated by people – both men and women – who declare with pride that female circumcision is a Somali practice, and Westerners, who are guilty of their own 'barbaric' assaults on women (in the form of inflicting the ideal of impossible thin-ness on adolescents and subjecting them to a lifetime of dieting and such life-threatening conditions as anorexia and bulimia) have no right to preach to Somalis, and that Somalis alone will decide how and when to end the practice. This backlash is more pronounced in London than in Toronto, for reasons that will become apparent below. Nonetheless, it is but a minor phenomenon; by and large women are retreating from the practice.

More Power to Women

The power and status of women within the Somali Diaspora communities has increased since exile. The Somali novelist Nurrudin Farrah remarked on the strength of Somali women in a Toronto appearance in 1998[9], both in having helped their families through the war and its aftermath in Somalia, and in building the Diaspora communities. His remarks are born out by my observations.

Often it is the women who have found work, even in two-parent families, and support the families. They have done so in single-parent families as well. They have kept families intact spiritually, frequently by leading the re-imagination of Islam within the family. It is the women who have donned the *hijab* or even the *jilbab*, enrolled their children in Qur'an schools, instituted hours of prayer and study at home. They have set the examples in the home of what they want their children to be, and the children – although the mothers frequently decry them as lost – are keen not to disappoint their mothers, and follow their examples in re-imagining, even if that re-imagining happens in a way that distresses the mothers because it is such a different re-imagining – their relationship with their faiths. The children follow the letter if not the spirit of the mothers' example, and endow their mothers with greater household and community status as they do so.

This is particularly true given that the community has needed to adopt new patterns of parenting since moving to the West. Within Somalia, authority was traditionally assumed to flow from male to female and from elder to youth. Respect was expected to stream in the other direction. Authority was expected to be reinforced by corporal punishment where necessary. Somalis, however, found themselves in exile in societies which have witnessed their own debates over child-raising over the past half-century, and corporal punishment is out of favor in Britain and Canada. Parents are expected to respect their children as much as children respect them, and to spank them rarely, if at all. For Somali parents to be questioned, as many have been, on grounds of child-abuse, after enduring unendurable horror and hardship in their homeland and in the leaving of it, has seemed to many the ultimate insult. As one parent put it:

> This society has seen a breakdown in the family system. We don't have the tradition of a Children's Aid Society. This is an alien system. In Somalia if you abuse your kids, society will alienate you. This is a terrible sanction so the system corrects for people who would hurt their kids. Some kids use this system [in Canada] to gain additional freedom. The major thing is if the institution is there for the kids' welfare, and the parents are there for the kids' welfare, there is one objective, so the major thing is to mediate misunderstandings between parents and institutions.
>
> The thing is, parents who have taken their kids 20,000 miles from a war-torn country will never hurt their kids. Parents who have had to face dan-

ger – hunger, lions, fear, uncertainty, murder, the trauma of leaving everything behind and braving immigration to a new country – these people have faced things that social workers in Canada will never begin to understand – all to keep their children safe. Why would they then hurt their children? Of course they would not.[10]

Nevertheless, parents have had to learn to accommodate themselves to new fashions in child-rearing. Many parents mentioned a fear that one call from a recalcitrant child to Toronto's or London's emergency services ('911' in Toronto or '999' in London) would see the children removed from the home into the care of (non-Muslim) child welfare agencies. The fear of the loss of their authority has made it all the more important for mothers to set a good example for their children, and has them all the more frightened when their children do not appear to follow precisely in their footsteps.

Teenagers

Teenagers are a fascinating group, because they are so vulnerable and yet so bold. As proud of their identities and their heritage as their parents, they must yet infiltrate and live in the world of the school and their peers. It is not apparent to them – as it is to many of their parents – that these factors are irreconcilable. The teens see no reason why they cannot be Canadian or English, Somali, and Muslim, all at the same time, although they have found this to be an easier balancing act in Toronto than in London.

Parents cry that they have 'lost' their children. Their dress, their talk, their attitudes seem alien and unfamiliar, even unIslamic. However, the children themselves are fiercely proud of their Islam. There were many Muslim children in Toronto schools before the Somali exiles moved there, but it was Somali teenagers who asked for a prayer room and prayed in the halls until they were given one. Every teenager I interviewed had developed his or her own chart through the stormy seas of adolescence, using Islam as a compass. To be sure, there were differences in how they interpreted its signs, but in all cases they acted out of a belief that they were being true to what they considered to be essential to their faith. In one teen's case, this might mean no parties and no movies; in another's, this might mean parties but no dancing, or dancing but no alcohol (in fact, not a single teenager thought that drinking alcohol was acceptable). Some thought that no relations were possible with the opposite sex until marriage. Others thought that relations were possible as long as no touching was involved; for some touching was alright, so long as this did not include sex. Almost no-one in this age group sanctioned pre-marital sex. Similarly, although most teenagers said that their friends were mostly Somali, they also said that they believed it was possible and acceptable to have friends who were non-Somali, and non-Muslim. Almost all of them said that it would be important to them to marry Muslims (not necessarily Somalis) and to bring their children up to be Muslim. They identified their community – as did their elders – as the community of Muslims, and not just other Somalis.

Teenaged girls varied widely in their views on the importance of covering their hair. Some felt that it was extremely important, for the same reasons their mothers did. Others felt that it was not. It was what was in their hearts, not on their heads, that defined them as Muslims, they reasoned. And they were acutely aware that in Somalia that would not have been asked to wear the *hijab* at this point in their lives, and probably would not have covered their hair in any way until they married.

The question of praying was equally complicated for them. Many teenagers did pray five times daily, and declared proudly that they did so wherever they happened to be when it was time to pray (including subway stops). Others said that they found the five times daily requirement to be particularly onerous, and said that therefore they prayed intermittently. Others did not pray at all, but said that they thought about it frequently, and regretted that they did not, intending to begin when they were older.

The point again, as elsewhere, is that – however they practice – these teenagers consider themselves to be 'good' Muslims, even if they envision themselves practicing differently as they age.

London versus Toronto

Notwithstanding the facts that the Somali immigrant communities arrived in Toronto and London at roughly the same time,[11] and that London and Toronto are both large, multicultural cities, there are significant differences in how Somalis have been integrating into the wider societies around them. Somalis in London spoke continually of being isolated, distanced, and ghettoized by British society. Somalis in Toronto – while noting that Canada is not as racism-free as its residents might like to think – generally spoke of feeling Canadian, comfortable, 'a part of' their adopted society. In both cities Somalis tended to become more religious in exile: in London that change sometimes happened with a defiant and bitter twist; in Toronto that defiant edge was lacking. In London Somalis frequently said that no matter how long they resided in Britain, they could not see themselves ever feeling British. They envied relatives in Canada who spoke of Canadian politics as 'their' politics. They said that if there was an advantage to British prejudice it was that it helped them keep their culture and religion. In Toronto they spoke of a surprise at the ease with which their culture and religion was accepted by the wider society. One woman – in Toronto for seven years – declared her intention to learn French (she had barely mastered English) because, as a Canadian, she felt it her duty to be proficient in both official languages. Toronto Somalis showed a stunningly greater attachment to their adopted society than did London Somalis. Islamism in London has an unmistakably defiant edge; in Toronto, Islamism is interpreted as a legitimate expression of culture and identity.

These differences are important for two reasons. First, they are an indication that, just as Islam is not a monolith, neither is the West. There are as many examples of 'Westness' as there are political cultures in them. Political culture is a key determinant of how an immigrant-receiving society helps to integrate newcomers. Integration, in the sense in which I use it, denotes an accommodation on both the part of the newcomer and, significantly, of the wider society. I hold the view that immigrant-receiving societies are as changed over time by the inclusion of the immigrants who are enfolded into their midst, as are the immigrant communities.

A society's political culture describes how its political institutions are used in its own context. In other words, both Britain and Canada are both constitutional democracies, yet for any number of reasons their laws and institutions are used very differently to enfold, welcome, accommodate, and integrate immigrants and minorities into their midst. Britain has not been as successful as Canada in granting immigrants legitimacy to participate in the wider society, to feel that they are a legitimate and welcomed part of it, and therefore, in turn, to accept their contribution to the self-understanding of the "imagined community"[12] that is a nation.

This creates implications for the commitment to the life of the community and the adopted society experienced and felt by the immigrant community. Harmonious integration is bound to create more committed citizens, such as the Toronto Somali woman determined to learn French, than is a distancing, ostracizing environment.

IJTIHAD

Two concepts are important for understanding the religious shifts that are occurring within the Somali Diaspora community. The first of these is *ijtihad*. *Ijtihad* means independent reasoning, and it refers to the ability of individual Muslims to interpret the Qur'an and *hadiths* for themselves, without requiring the intervention of the *'ulama* in these interpretations. Or, even if the *'ulama* are taken into account, an ongoing diffusion of religious legitimacy within the Muslim world[13] means that different *'ulama* might be heeded than prior to emigration. In other words, as the Muslim Diaspora grows, and significant communities of Muslims grow up in cities throughout the Western world, those cities become legitimate and thriving Muslim centers. This is true of London and Birmingham, Toronto and Markham. Mosques, imams, Friday *qutba* prayers, competing traditions from different Muslim immigrant communities: all these factors combine to give the impetus to individuals to read the texts and decide for themselves how to interpret them. Somalis interviewed in London and Toronto took their religious cues from

Somali and non-Somali imams in their midst, and not from the Middle Eastern heart of the Muslim world or even from their Muslim-majority homeland. Toronto and London have become centers of Islam in their own rights.[14] Moreover, the interviews were full of the views of women who asserted their rights as religious Muslims to decide, sometimes with the help of imams as guides, how best to adapt Islam to their needs in the West. A pertinent example of this is a quote from Deeqa, a student in her twenties in Toronto:

> For us when culture and religion coincide, that's good, but when culture contradicts religion, that's difficult, because Somali culture has become so Arabized. It's difficult to distinguish one from another.
>
> I hope being here makes this process easier. As a woman if you argue through Islam it's more liberating than taking a Western stand. Men can't argue with the religion. And the religion says women, as much as men, must be educated. So long as your position is in the Qur'an, there is no obstacle. I hope other Muslim women read and learn to think this way.[15]

Hijra

The second term of importance is *hijra*. *The Hijra* refers to the movement of Muhammad and his followers from Mecca to Medina in 622 CE, and, following this, *hijra* refers to migration from a territory hostile to the practice of Islam to one that is accepting of it. Doctrinally, Muslims are not meant to remain in non-Muslim majority lands, as these are taken to be the lands of unbelief and therefore hostile to Islam (*dar al-kufr*). Good Muslims are meant, therefore, to move as soon as possible to Muslim-majority lands: *dar al-Islam*. However, this doctrine is increasingly being turned on its head as religious Muslims declare that they are, in fact, able to practice Islam as they see fit in the West and that sometimes they are better able to practice it in the West than in homelands that allow only for narrow interpretations of the practice of the faith. For many Muslims, the West has become *dar al-da'wa*, the land of preaching, as described by Shaykh Faisal Malawi.[16]

This is a huge and critical shift, and has allowed for the rapid transformation in the legitimacy of how Islam is imagined, and by whom.

Formal versus Informal Power Shifts

It is perhaps important to emphasize that the increase in status and power to which I refer is an informal, as opposed to a formal, one. One will not – at least in the short term – find women imams, or find women leading the work of the Islamists, or even working among them. The shifts to which I have referred are significantly more subtle. They have to do with the role women are seen to play within the family, the household, the community. In socioeconomic terms (as providers) and in religious terms (as leaders of the re-definition/re-imagination of Islam within the family) women are gaining esteem.

Somali women are playing – and are seen to be playing – significantly more important roles than was their wont in their homeland. This is true in spite of the fact that the religious orthodoxy itself assigns women a minor public role.

What is happening – beneath the formal surface of Diaspora Islam – is a wider example of Deeqa's creed. Muslim women are gaining strength, power, and status through their use, and not rejection, of Islam.

This has huge long-term implications for the Diaspora communities and for the development of what I have called 'transformative' – re-imagined Islam.

Two cautionary remarks are in order. The first is that this article has focused on women, but it does not mean to imply that it is Somali women, and not men, who have transformed their interpretation of Islam. Somali men have of course been involved in the same process. It is they who have been at the forefront of the Islamist movements, which have gained prestige in the Diaspora in large part because it is in the Diaspora that the movements' religious – as opposed to political – dynamic gains in importance.

Secondly, the inference of this analysis is not that Canada's is an ideal society from an immigrant/minority perspective. Far from it. As writers such as M. Nourbese Phillips and Dionne Brand express with eloquence, Canada has trouble admitting the extent to which racism – including systemic racism – exists within its borders.[17] Nor is it intended to cast an unreasonably rosy glow on the diasporic condition. Times of resettlement are times of immense personal and community stress. Moreover, in both Canada and Britain Muslims face significant anti-Muslim prejudice. Cultural or religious racism is frequently not recognized for what it is.[18] Interviews indicated that color was more of a barrier to integration for Somalis in London than in Toronto, but religion was an issue in both cities.

In fact, the very source of strength for Somali women within their communities – the *hijab* that endows them with Muslim legitimacy and therefore greater status – often stigmatizes them within the larger community. Many women reported that they have been refused employment because of their headscarves. One London respondent said that she has taken to removing her *hijab* before job interviews, and replacing it only three or four weeks after she has secured the position. By that point, she reasons, her employers will see her as a competent employee, and the *hijab* is more likely to be viewed as an irrelevant and legitimate personal choice. At the job interview, however, it can be seen as anything from a political statement to a sign of a woman's submission to her male relatives.

Deeqa, for instance, argued with her religious future husband to ensure that he saw her right to complete her education and work outside the home as Islamically correct and compatible. With the co-operation of an *imam*, she found it a much easier argument to win than the one that she continues to have with feminists at her university and her workplace, who insist on viewing her as an anti-feminist because of her decision to wear the *hijab*.

The tools of women's strength within the Somali Diaspora communities, therefore, appear to undermine it in the larger society. Not until the larger society understands that religious or cultural racism is as damaging to its victims as color racism, and not until it is more widely understood – and accepted – that integration is a process of change that involves immigrants and adoptive society both, is that likely to change. Nevertheless, it is important to keep sight of the possibilities for transformation and change that exist within the fluidity of life in the Diaspora.

Conclusion

Gender and power relationships have shifted within the Diaspora Somali communities, largely because women have been instrumental in leading the re-imagination of their practice of Islam. The communities have become more religious in the West, not less so, and they have become differently religious. Somalis have become Western, but not Westernized, Muslims, re-defining their definition of a 'good Muslim' and their practice of Islam in the process. Because women – in their quest to keep the children grounded in their religion, culture, and values, and out of a need to understand their own identities faced with the challenges of an alien culture – have been key to this religious re-definition, their power and status within the community has been, and will continue to be, enhanced. However stressful resettlement may be, it offers immense opportunities for the re-imagination and re-definition of both Islam, and the relationship between Muslims in the West and the wider society around them. It also offers unprecedented opportunities for a rebalancing of gender relationships in the homeland, as porous borders and the transnational flow of ideas mean that phenomenon developed in the Diaspora take root at home as well.

Notes

1. Interviews for this article were drawn from a larger study by the author. *Muslims in the Diaspora: The Somali Communities of London and Toronto* (Toronto: University of Toronto Press, forthcoming, 1999).
2. I.M. Lewis, "Sufism in Somaliland: A Study in Tribal Islam", in Akhbar S. Ahmed and David M. Hart, eds. *Islam in Tribal Societies* (London and Boston: Routledge and Kegan Paul, 1984), p. 159.
3. Breast-feeding has been shown to be an unreliable method of birth-control.
4. Donna Lee Bowen, "Family Planning", in Esposito, ed., *The Oxford Encyclopedia of the Modern Islamic World*, Vol. 1, pp. 464–465.

5.   Musallam, *Sex and Society in Islam* (Cambridge: Cambridge University Press, 1983), notably Chapter One, "Why Islam Permitted Contraception", pp. 10–38.

6.   Bowen, The Oxford Encyclopedia of the Modern Islamic World, Vol. 1, pp. 464–465.

7.   A similar decision was taken for the first time in the United States in June, 1996. *New York Times*, June 14, 1996, p. 1.

8.   Esther Hicks, *Infibulation: Female Mutilation in Islamic Northeastern Africa* (London, UK and New Brunswick, USA: Transaction Publishers, 1993).

9.   Harbourfront Reading Series, October 25, 1998.

10.   Interview with Rashid, an outreach worker who solves intercultural disputes between Somali parents and Toronto schools, Toronto, April 26, 1995.

11.   Somalis were employed by the British merchant navy to work in the engine rooms of steamships. While the ships were docked in London, the seamen stayed in lodgings in the East End, where a small transient community gradually built up. Similar communities grew in Cardiff, Liverpool, and South Shields. Shamis Hussein, "Somalis in London", Nick Merriman, ed., *The Peopling of London: Fifteen Thousand Years of Settlement from Overseas* (London: Museum of London, 1993), p. 163

12.   in Benedict Anderson's famous phrase, from Imagined Communities: Reflections on the Origin and Spread of Nationalism (London: Verso, 1983).

13.   Dale Eickelman and James Piscatori, *Muslim Politics* (Princeton: Princeton University Press, 1996), pp. 68–79 and 131–135.

14.   Barbara Daly Metcalf, ed., *Making Muslim Space in North America and Europe* (Berkeley: University of California Press, 1996).

15.   Interview, Deeqa, Toronto, March 24, 1995.

16.   W.A. Shadid & P.S. Van Koningsveld, *The Integration of Islam and Hinduism in Western Europe* (Kampen: Kok Pharos, 1991), p. 229.

17.   See, for instance, M. Nourbese Philip, *Frontiers: Essays and Writings on Racism and Culture* (Toronto: The Mercury Press, 1992) or Dionne Brand, *Bread out of Stone,* (Toronto : Coach House Press, 1994).

18.   See *Islamophobia: A Challenge For Us All* (London: 1997, Runnymede Trust).

References

Abdalla, Raqiya Haji Dualeh. Sisters in Affliction: Circumcision and Infibulation of Women in Africa. London: Zed Books, 1982.

Abdullahi, Abdurahman. *Tribalism, Nationalism and Islam: The Crisis of Political Loyalty in Somalia*. Unpublished M.A. Thesis. Montreal: McGill University, 1992.

Abu-Sahlieh, Sami A. Aldeeb. "The Islamic Conception of Migration". *International Migration Review*, Vol. 30, No. 1, Spring, 1996, pp. 37–57.

Adam, Hussein M. "Islam and Politics in Somalia". *Journal of Islamic Studies*, Vol. 6, No. 2, July 1995, pp. 189–221.

Ahmed, Akbar S. and Hart, David M. *Islam in Tribal Societies: From the Atlas to the Indies*. London and Boston: Routledge & Kegan Paul, 1984.

Ahmed, Ali Jimale. Daybreak is Near: Literature, Clans and the Nation-State in Somalia. Lawrenceville, NJ: Red Sea Press, 1996.

Ahmed, Ali Jimale. *The Invention of Somalia*. Lawrenceville, NJ: Red Sea Press, 1995.

Ahmed, Leila. *Women and Gender in Islam*. New Haven & London: Yale University Press, 1992.

Anderson, Benedict. *Imagined Communities*. London: Verso, 1983.

Anwar, Muhammad. *Young Muslims in a Multi-Cultural Society*. London: The Islamic Foundation, 1982.

Aqli, Abdirisaq. "Historical Development of Islamic Movements in the Horn of Africa". Paper presented to the First Conference of the European Association of Somali Studies. London: 1993.

Berns McGown, Rima. *Muslims in the Diaspora: The Somali Communities of London and Toronto*. Toronto: University of Toronto Press, 1999, forthcoming.

Bolaria, B. Singh and Li, Peter S. *Racial Oppression in Canada*. Toronto: Garamond Press, 1988.

Brand, Dionne. *Bread out of Stone*. Toronto: Coach House Press, 1994.

Breton, R., Isajiw, W., Kalbach, W., and Reitz, J. *Ethnic Identity and Equality: Varieties of Experience in a Canadian City*. Toronto: University of Toronto Press, 1990.

Cohen, Philip, and Bains, Harwant. *Multi-Racist Britain*. London: MacMillan, 1988.

Commission for Racial Equality. Living in Terror: A Report on Racial Violence and Harrassment in Housing. London: CRE, 1987.

Commission on British Muslims and Islamophobia. *Islamophobia: Its Features and Dangers*. London: The Runnymede Trust, 1997.

Dench, Geoff. Fighting with Numbers: Strategies of Somali Refugees in East London. London: Center for Community Studies, 1993.

Doi, 'Abdul Rahman I. *Woman in Shari'ah*. London: Ta-Ha Publishers, 1989.

Dorkenoo, Efua. Cutting the Rose. Female Genital Mutilation: The Practice and its Prevention. London: Minority Rights Publication, 1994.

Eickelman, Dale and Piscatori, James, eds. *Muslim Travellers: Pilgrimage, Migration, and the Religious Imagination*. London and New York: Routledge, 1990.

Eickelman, Dale and Piscatori, James. *Muslim Politics*. Princeton: Princeton University Press, 1996.

El Dareer, Asma. Woman, Why Do You Weep? Circumcision and its Consequences. London: Zed Books, 1982.

El-Solh, Camillia Fawzi and Mabro, Judy, eds. *Muslim Women's Choices: Religious Belief and Social Reality*. Oxford: Berg Publishers, 1994

El-Solh, Camillia Fawzi. "Somalis in London's East End: A Community Striving for Recognition". *New Community*. Vol. 17, No. 4, July 1991, pp. 539–552.

El-Solh, Camillia Fawzi. "'Be True to Your Culture': Gender Tensions Among Somali Muslims in Britain". *Immigrants and Minorities*, Vol. 12, No. 1, March 1993, pp. 21–46.

Esposito, John. *The Islamic Threat: Myth or Reality?*, revised edition. Oxford and New York: Oxford University Press, 1995.

Esposito, John, ed. *The Oxford Encylopedia of the Modern Islamic World*. Oxford and New York: Oxford University Press, 1995.

Gallo, Pia Grassivaro. *La Circoncisione Femminile in Somalia*. Milano: Franco Angeli, 1986.

Gilroy, Paul. *The Empire Strikes Back*. London: Hutchinson & Co., 1982.

Gilroy, Paul. *There Ain't no Black in the Union Jack*. London: Hutchinson & Co., 1987.

Glazer, Nathan, and Moynihan, Daniel Patrick. *Beyond the Melting Pot: The Negroes, Puerto Ricans, Jews, Italians, and Irish of New York*. Cambridge: MIT Press and Harvard University Press, 1963.

Glazer, Nathan and Moynihan, Daniel, eds. *Ethnicity: Theory and Experience*. Cambridge, Mass.: Harvard University Press, 1975.

Gordon, Paul. Citizenship for Some? Race and Government Policy 1979–1989. London: Runnymede Trust, 1989.

Haddad, Yvonne Hazbeck and Smith, Jane Idleman. *Muslim Communities in North America*. Albany: State University of New York, 1994.

Halliday, Fred. Arabs in Exile: Yemeni Migrants in Urban Britain. London: I.B. Tauris, 1992.

Halliday, Fred. *Islam and the Myth of Confrontation*. London: I.B. Tauris, 1995.

Hersi, Ali Abdirahman. The Arab Factor in Somali History: The Origins and the Development of Arab Enterprise and Cultural Influences in the Somali Peninsula. University of California, Los Angeles: Unpublished Ph.D. thesis, 1977.

Hicks, Esther, K. *Infibulation: Female Mutilation in Islamic Northeastern Africa*. New Brunswick, USA: Transaction Publishers, 1993.

Holmes, Colin. A Tolerant Country? Immigrants, Refugees and Minorities in Britain. London: Faber & Faber, 1991.

Hosken, Fran. *The Hosken Report: Genital and Sexual Mutilation of Females*. Lexington, Mass: Women's International Network News, 1979.

Husaini, Zohra. *Muslims in the Canadian Mosaic*. Edmonton: Muslim Research Foundation, 1990.

Joly, Daniele. Britannia's Crescent: Making a Place for Muslims in British Society. Aldershot: Avebury, 1995.

Kepel, Gilles. *A l'ouest d'Allah*. Paris: Éditions de Seuil, 1994.

Kymlicka, Will. *Multicultural Citizenship*. Oxford: Oxford University Press, 1995.

Lightfoot-Klein, Hanny. Prisoners of Ritual: An Odyssey into Female Genital Circumcision in Africa. New York: Harrington Park Press, 1989.

Lipset, S.M. Continental Divide: the Values and Institutions of the United States and Canada. Toronto and Washington: The Canadian-American Committee, 1989.

Mazrui, Ali. *Cultural Forces in World Politics*. London: James Currey, 1990.

Merriman, Nick, ed. The Peopling of London: Fifteen Thousand Years of Settlement From Overseas. London: Museum of London, 1993.

Metcalf, Barbara Daly. *Making Muslim Space in North America and Europe*. Berkeley: University of California Press, 1996.

Miles, Robert. *Racism after 'Race Relations'*. London: Routledge, 1993.

Modood, Tariq. *Muslims, Race and Equality in Britain: Some Post-Rushdie Affair Reflections*. Birmingham: Center for the Study of Islam and Christian-Muslim Relations, Selly Oak Colleges, 1990.

Modood, Tariq. *Not Easy Being British: Color, Culture and Citizenship*. London: Runnymede Trust and Trentham Books, 1992.

Modood, Tariq. *Racial Equality: Color, Culture and Justice*. London: Institute for Public Policy Research, 1994.

Modood, Tariq, Beishon, Sharon, and Virdee, Satnam. *Changing Ethnic Identities*. London: Policy Studies Institute, 1994.

Modood, Tariq and Werbner, Pnina. The Politics of Multiculturalism in the New Europe: Racism, Identity and Community. London: Zed Books, 1997.

Modood, Tariq. "Muslim Views on Religious Identity and Racial Equality". *New Community*, Vol. 19, No. 3., April 1993, pp. 513–519.

Musallam, Basim. *Sex and Society in Islam*. Cambridge: Cambridge University Press, 1983.

Muslim News. Monthly Newspaper. London: Multiple Volumes.

The Muslim Voice. Monthly Newspaper. London: Muslim Students Association, University of Toronto, Multiple Volumes.

Opoku-Dapaah, Edward. *Somali Refugees in Toronto: A Profile*. Toronto: York University Center for Refugee Studies, 1994.

Nielsen, Jorgen. Religion and Citizenship in Europe and the Arab World. London: Grey Seal, 1992.

Parekh, Bhikhu, ed. Color, Culture and Consciousness: Immigrant Intellectuals in Britain. London: George Allen & Unwin Ltd., 1974.

Parekh, Bhikhu. *Contemporary Political Thinkers*. Oxford: Martin Robertson, 1982.

Parekh, Bhikhu. *Britain: A Plural Society*. London: Commission for Racial Equality and the Runnymede Trust, 1989.

Parekh, Bhikhu. "The Concept of National Identity". *New Community*, Vol. 21, No. 2, April 1995, pp. 255–268.

Parekh, Bhikhu. "Minority Practices and Principles of Toleration". *International Migration Review*, Vol. 30, No. 1, 1996, pp. 251–284.

Peach, Ceri and Glebe, Gunther. "Muslim Minorities in Western Europe". *Ethnic and Racial Studies*, Vol. 18, No. 1, January 1995, pp. 26–45.

Philip, M. Nourbese. *Frontiers: Essays and Writings on Racism and Culture*. Toronto: The Mercury Press, 1992.

Pye, Lucian W., and Verba, Sidney. *Political Culture and Political Development*. Princeton: Princeton University Press, 1965.

Reitz, Jeffrey, and Breton, Raymond. The Illusion of Difference: Realities of Ethnicity in Canada and the United States. Ottawa: C.D. Howe Institute, 1994.

Rex, John. *Race and Ethnicity*. Buckingham: Open University Press, 1986.

Shadid, W.A.R. and Van Koningsveld, P.S., eds. *The Integration of Islam and Hinduism in Western Europe*. Kampen: The Netherlands: Kok Pharos Publishing, 1991.

Solomos, John. *Race and Racism in Britain*, 2nd. edition. London: Macmillan Press Ltd., 1993.

Soysal, Yasemin Nuhoglu. *Limits of Citizenship: Migrants and Postnational Membership in Europe*. Chicago and London: University of Chicago Press, 1994.

Spinner, Jeff. The Boundaries of Citizenship: Race, Ethnicity, and Nationality in the Liberal State. Baltimore and London: The Johns Hopkins University Press, 1994.

Toubia, Nahid. Female Genital Mutilation: A Call for Global Action. New York: Nahid Toubia, 1993.

Virdee, Satnam. *Racial Violence and Harassment*. London: Policy Studies Institute, 1995.

Werbner, Pnina and Modood, Tariq. Debating Cultural Hybridity: Multi-Cultural Identities and the Politics of Anti-Racism. London: Zed Books, 1997.

Werbner, Pnina. "Stamping the Earth with the Name of Allah: Zikr and the Sacralizing of Space Among British Muslims". *Cultural Anthropology*. Vol. 11, No. 3, August 1996, pp. 309–338.

Yamani, Mai. *Feminism and Islam: Legal and Literary Perspectives.* New York: New York University Press, 1996.

Young, Crawford, ed. *The Rising Tide of Cultural Pluralism: The Nation-State at Bay?* Wisconsin: The University of Wisconsin Press, 1993.

Yousif, Ahmad F. *Muslims in Canada: A Question of Identity.* Toronto and New York: Legas, 1993.

Chapter Eight

Landless Landlors, and Landed Tenants: Plantation Slavery in Southern Somalia (1840–1940)

"Murug Maahino ii Masiibo Aduunyo-Minaa Minin Keeyga Leegu Maamu-laaiyo." (Isn't it disheartening and reflective of the unfairness of this world that we are bossed around in our own abode). Mohamed Ali, a Jareer bard, 1988.[1]

Omar A. Eno
York University, History Department

Introduction

MOST STUDIES of East African slave plantations have concentrated on Zanzibar and Pemba, probably because they were the two most visible slave-holding centers in the region. Consequently, research on plantation slavery along the rest of the East African coast, in particular, the Benadir coast of Southern Somalia, has been less critically scrutinized. What is more problematic, though, is that most research projects carried out along the Benadir coast of Southern Somalia[2] operate from three epistemologically erroneous assumptions. The first suggests that the overwhelming majority of the Bantu/Jareer population of Southern Somalia were slaves imported from East Africa. This assumption has, in turn, created the belief, both among scholars and lay people, that these people are essentially either runaway or emancipated slaves, and therefore they have neither claim to full Somali citizenship nor any right to the farming land they occupy. On the contrary, however, oral traditions as well as available archival records indicate that the majority of the Bantu/Jareer people had occupied their present location as far back as the

10th century. This is not to suggest that some slaves were not imported from East Africa, but their numbers were very small in relation to the indigenous population. The second suggests that the Somali people did not partake in the enslavement of the Bantu/Jareer people, while the third assumption indicates that the reason the Italian colonial administration abolished slavery in Somalia was mainly for humanitarian reasons.

The purpose of this paper is to dispel these assumptions by (1) examining the origin and the historical background of the Bantu/Jareer people; (2) to examine the role of Somalis in the enslavement of the Jareer people; and (3) to examine the mutually reinforcing political and economic interests of both Somalis and the Italian colony in maintaining slave-like situations, so that they can retain the labor of the Jareer people.[3]

The first section of this paper examines the origins, historical background, and settlement patterns of the Bantu/Jareer people along both the Juba and the Shabelle Rivers and their historical and contemporary social and economic interactions with Somali nomads. The second section focuses on the process through which the Bantu/Jareer people on the one hand were enslaved by the Somalis and on the other later by the Italian colonies. The third and the final section deals with the political and economic conditions that hindered the implementation of the abolition of slavery as articulated through the Belgian abolition act.

The Origin of The Bantu/Jareer People

Written as well as oral traditions indicate that the Jareer people of Southern Somalia consist of three groups: (a) runaway slaves, (b) emancipated-slaves, and (c) indigenous population. The majority of available scholarship, however, has concentrated on the first two groups, possibly because of their lower social status among Somalis, or their alleged distinctive physical features, that is, the so-called "Negroid" look. The history and identity of the third group (indigenous) remains unaccounted for. This problem, according to available research, resulted from the difficulty of separating them from the Somali clan groups, with whom they were culturally assimilated.[4] This paper takes a different angle and divides the Bantu/Jareer people into two groups: (1) communities formed by runaway slaves, who were later emancipated groups, and (2) descendents of the Shungwaya kingdom, who today represent the Jareer indigenous population. The first group will be referred to as the Wazigwa,[5] (Gosha people of *Juba* River), while the second are Mjikenda.[6] The latter are believed to be the remnants of the Shungwaya Kingdom and residents along the *Shebelle* River. This distinction is necessitated by the fact that some scholars have often conflated them and broad-brushed them as one group of the same historical background, while in reality they are from two different historical settings and cultural backgrounds.

The Wazigwa Origins

The first group, the Wazigwa, consists of runaway and manumitted slaves. It seems that Arab slave merchants originally brought them from Tanganyika, Zanzibar, Pemba, and Mozambique into the coastal cities of Merca, Brava, Kisimayu, and Mogadishu early in the 19th century.[7] Some scholars suggest that they left Tanganyika, their country of origin (modern Tanzania), because of severe famines in the 19th century. Another possibility is that Arab traders may have duped them by promising to take them to work in a fertile land where famine and drought are never experienced.[8] Despite some of these suggestions, though, it is clear that these people were initially brought as slaves and sold to Somalia's coastal people, and later to the Hawiya Somalis in the interior of Southern Somalia.

After some time, many of the enslaved Bantu escaped from their Somali masters with the intention of returning to their homes (modern Tanzania).[9] They failed in this attempt and subsequently settled in the Gosha[10] 'Forest' region along the Juba River, where they established 'maroon' communities, erecting strong defenses against re-enslavement. It is also likely that, at the time of their escape, the Wazigwa found some indigenous Jareer population already dwelling in the vicinity of their newly-established resettlement (Gosha), which later developed as a state. The new state of Gosha became prosperous under the leadership of Majenderu, Wanakucha, Mkomo Maliku, Shungor Mafula, Nassib Bunde (a local hero who fought against the Somali slave-masters and the Italian colony), and Shaykh Murjan (a prominent religious leader) respectively.[11] According to R. Bricchetti, an Italian anti-slavery activist, the Wazigwa had sworn in the name of God and equality that they would fight to maintain their freedom to the last person and would never submit/surrender themselves to their ex-Somali slave masters. Their motto was "...*vivere liberi e liberi morire,*"[12] (we live free and die free). Another important run-away slave community was established in Avai near Barava. According to Barile, "...ex-Somali slave owners such as Tuuni, Beghed[i], Giddu, and Biyamaal tried several times to destroy [Avai], the new runaway slave settlement, but failed in their attempts."[13] As a result of their military might, the Italian colonial authority recognized Avai as an independent entity, and began to send fugitive slaves seeking protection under Italian authorities to this new haven.[14] It is also possible that Italy recognized Avai as an independent entity because of their rich agricultural estates, and Avai remained as 'free' Bantu communities until the imposition of Italian colonial authority.

The Mjikenda Origin

The second group of Bantu/Jareer people in Somalia are linked and believed to be the remnants of the Mjikenda people, who migrated to the Tana River in modern Kenya after being driven from Ethiopia by Oromo fighters in the 15th and 16th centuries. These Jareer people reside mainly along the banks of the Shabelle River in Southern Somalia. According to Cerulli, the Mjikendas could be the natives and descendants of the ancient and controversial Kingdom of Shungwaya, located in Buur Gaabo. Alice Werner and Cerulli suggest that Shungwaya is known to have been an ancient Kingdom and the headquarters of the then-King, Mze-Sagawambe Mkawma of the Bantu/Jareer people in Southern Somalia.[15] Despite the need for further research, it is safe to assume that Shungwaya was a well-established Kingdom with rules and traditions generally respected by all its residents, who at the time consisted of nine to twelve ethnic groups.[16]

Aside from those groups who migrated to the Tana River (in present Kenya), there were those who remained behind, and continue to live in their present locations in Southern Somalia. These are, according to oral tradition, the Pokomo, the Shidle, the Shabelle, the Eile, the Bajuni, and others. Most of these ethnic groups lived together,[17] alongside the victorious Oromo, who invaded their territory in the 15th and 16th centuries, and who were in turn invaded by the Somali-Hawiya. At any rate, the Mjikenda from the Shabelle River are believed to be the indigenous stock that has resided in their present area for several centuries.[18] A group of anthropologists have stated that "...we may reckon those [Bantu/Jareer] tribes in all probability represent remnants of a pre-Somali population going back to the first millennium of the Christian era."[19] Additionally, the Shungwaya Kingdom is also known to be a point of dispersal of the ethnic Somali Bantu in modern Kenya.[20] We must also add here, it is likely that this second group of Jareer, the Mjikenda, later absorbed some of the emancipated and runaway slaves (Wazigwa) from Somali slave-owners. This absorption could be seen as an indication of their long existence in the area. According to Luling: "Before the Somali [pastoralist] penetrated the area [in the south] in the 16th and 17th centuries, a population of Bantu-speaking cultivators inhabited the river lands."[21] They are described as being "[d]istinctly Negroid in physical type, whereas the [nomads] have the 'Hamitic' features typical of the Somali in general..."[22]

The Negroid features of the Bantu soon became a distinct identity where people with such features were classified as slaves and subjected to a variety of discriminatory practices[23] regardless of where they came from.[24] As a result, for the majority of slave owning groups, Negroid features became synonymous with inferior status, as Luling describes:

> "Traditional Somali society is famous for its egalitarian character, and yet it is known that some of its members were much less equal than the rest. [The] category of people whose status was traditionally inferior was the farming villagers of inter-riverine [Bantu] area."[25]

It appears that the notion of inequality between the nomadic and coastal peoples on the one hand and the Jareer on the other existed for centuries. These factors have further contributed to the creation of a strong and influential myth. A myth perpetuated by Somali officials and by some scholars suggested that the entire Jareer population in Somalia consists of a small number of imported slaves from East Africa, an argument not supported by any historical or anthropological evidence.[26]

More importantly, though, this myth has forced both scholars and lay people to put forward the claim that it is very difficult to separate the indigenous farmers from the other two groups (runaways and emancipated slaves). Historians believe that the difficulties in separating them are due to their physical resemblance, unrestricted intermarriage between the free and the emancipated, and their similar ways of life such as subsistence farming. Cassanelli, for example, elaborated on the difficulty of identifying and separating the indigenous Jareer people from the runaway and the emancipated slaves by saying that "…scholars found it so difficult to distinguish in this area between the remnants of prehistoric Negroid population [Mjikenda] and the descendants of 19th-century captives [Wazigwa]."[27]

The aforementioned difficulty in separating the ex-slaves from the indigenous has apparently worked in favor of the nomadic Somalis, who pretend that every Jareer Somali and their descendants are of slave origin. Although some scholars have indicated the existence of an ancient and pre-Hamitic group of Jareer existence along the Shabelle River, the dominant nomadic society seem to have downplayed this research. The nomads claim that these scholars have a cursory knowledge of the Jareer and their origins, and that further study was unnecessary.[28] Consequently, it has become commonplace among scholars and students of Bantu/Jareer history in Southern Somalia to conveniently label all Bantu/Jareer people as ex-slaves, overlooking their authentic status as indigenous people of the inter-riverine area in Southern Somalia. It is only recently that scholars such as Luling have claimed that this portrayal of Bantu history regarding their origin and social structures has no historical basis.[29]

Moreover, according to Cerulli, although some freed slaves might have later joined to dwell with the mentioned indigenous farmers does not mean they are all of slave descent. Cerulli argues that these Bantu/Jareer groups are not imported slaves but rather an ancient people. In one of his books, Cerulli suggests that at times the well-established Jareer villages used to absorb and assimilate other groups of non-Jareer origin.[30] It is therefore worth mentioning the relationship between these groups. There were rules and conditions of coexistence between these two groups (nomads and free Jareer). These rules included exchange of trading items, a tradition practiced until today in various locations in Southern regions. The nomads sold meat, milk, oil, and animal hides to the Jareer in exchange for maize, millet, and other subsistence products.[31]

One way to distinguish imported slaves from the indigenous population is to examine their cultural and social differences. For example, the first group, the Wazigwa, still maintain the languages and dialects of their country of origin (modern Tanzania) and their traditions and cultural dances, which are very similar to those in Tanzania.[32] Another important characteristic of the Wazigwa is that they were not absorbed by Somalia because they spoke and still speak a Tanzanian-related language and lived in isolation from other Somali nomads. Furthermore, they still maintain their cultural and genealogical links with the Tanzanian and Mozambique ethnic groups such as: the Yao, the Nyasa, the Mushunguli (or Zegwa), the Makua, and the Ngindu.[33] These are the Bantu/Jareer people that were brought into Somalia by the Arabs. One characteristic that both groups share, however, is that they are not fully accepted as first-class Somali citizens by the majority of Somali society despite the fact that the Mjikenda dwelling along the Shabelle River seem to have lost the authenticity of their culture, language, and most of their traditions because of their integration into other Somali ethnic groups.

Plantation Slavery in The Benadir Coast

In many African countries, plantation slaves were forcibly captured from different villages and locations regardless of ethnic affiliations. However, the situation in Southern Somalia is slightly different. Along the Shebelle River area, only the indigenous Bantu/Jareer communities were the targeted group for enslavement. As mentioned earlier, the slave owners were the nomads (Hawiya) who originally migrated from the Ethiopian highlands and the coastal people of Benadir from Arabia and Persia.[34] These slave owners (nomads and coastal people) had begun the use of indigenous slave labor in the Benadir plantations around the 19th century for economic gain.[35] Most of the Benadir plantations were privately owned by the Somali slave-owners with the average of 1–15 slaves per plantation. Some of the slave-owning groups most notorious for ill treatment of slaves are the Gaaljecel, the Wadan, the Biyamaal and the Mobilen, subgroups of the larger Hawiya group. According to Hess, citing materials from Italian colonial archives, "…slaves were harshly treated, often kept in manacles and fetters; overworked, and underfed."[36] Further, documents that are available in the Italian colonial archives suggest that:

> The prosperity of the war-like Biyamaal…who settled in the area between the Webi Shabelle and Indian Ocean and controlled the hinterland of Merca and Brava, was dependent on grain grown by Bantu slaves to trade for imported cloth and hardware in Merca. The Bimal, who possessed the nomadic Somali's traditional disdain for agriculture, would not have [subsisted] without Bantu slave labor.[37]

According to Lt. Christopher, a British naval officer who visited the Benadir in 1842: "Slaves and their wives, being laborers, were housed miserably in small, half-roofed huts, with their usual food [of] parched Indian corn and fish from the river."[38]

Apart from Somali nomads, there were other groups of slave owners in Somalia. These Somalia-Benadir were considered to be of Arab descent. These people, having interacted with Arabs of Yemen, Oman and those along the East African coast, spread Arab culture into Somalia.

By 1842, some Arabs along the Benadir coast were willing to put themselves under the Sultanate of Zanzibar to gain supremacy through the Sultan by imposing their authority upon factions operating along the Benadir coast of Mogadishu and its vicinity.[39] There were three factions that struggled for control of Mogadishu and control of the slave trade: the inhabitants of Shingaani area, the Hamarwein, and the Sultanate of Geledi from Afgoy.[40] Hence, the Hamarwein elders invited the Sultan of Zanzibar, Seyyid Said, to take control of the region and make the Benadir as part of his Sultanate. Mogadishu-Benadir later fell under the protectorate of the Sultan of Zanzibar.

While Arab influence was growing in Somalia, the Somali nomads from the interior already controlled the riverine areas in Bantu land and had established their supremacy.[41] Lewis expanded on this point by stressing the importance of the Somali alliance with the Arabs when he stated that: "The Somali [nomadic] ethnic groups have often become powerful through alliance with immigrant Arab 'Sheicks', of whom in retrospect [they] consider themselves the [irir] descendants."[42] In the first decades of the 19th century, the Somali clans that lived along the coastal cities of Benadir had increased their trade in ivory, cattle, hides, woven clothes, gum, and other goods. The main product in demand was grain; therefore the Somali coastal people, being the traders in the region, responded to this strong regional demand.[43] As a result, early in the 19th century, huge slave plantations were established along the Shebelle River to meet the increasing demand for grains, particularly sorghum, maize, and sesame seeds.[44] By the 1840s, European travelers were amazed by the large amount of grain produced along the Shebelle River for the Arabian and Zanzibar markets in the south. The average number of slaves per plantation in Somalia was very low. It was more or less equivalent to those small plantations in East Africa, particularly in Mombasa and Malindi.[45] However, the smaller number of slaves in the Somalian plantations should not detract from its identification as a *plantation*.

The transformation of the Shabelle valley economy was facilitated by the tapping of the large reservoir of non-free labor supplied by the resident Bantu population.[46] Part of the profits generated by the exploitation of these lands were used to purchase more slaves, who in turn led to a further expansion of cultivated lands.[47] Unlike in Mombasa, where production of grain in the plantations was limited because of scarcity of arable land,[48] in the Benadir, cultivable land was abundant. As a result, plantation workers were divided into two groups: cultivation and weaving were assigned to the men, and easier tasks of gathering the seeds and cleaning the husks to the women.[49] Beautiful female slaves were often used as household domestics and concubines.[50] It appears that during the Benadir slave trade women slaves were more valued than men because women were used for both domestic and plantation labor.[51] This corroborates with the domestic slavery in Africa, where female labor was extensively used in the farms and cottage industries. Lovejoy has also pointed to this phenomenon, in which women were categorized as major contributors in agricultural production in Africa.[52]

Slavery and the slave trade in Southern Somalia lasted until early in the 20th century, and subsequently were abolished by the Italian authority in accordance with Belgium protocol. However, the same Italian colonial authority that initially abolished slavery in Somalia, re-introduced coerced labor laws and the conscription of the manumitted slaves and the indigenous Bantu people for economic purposes in the Italian agricultural schemes.

The Abolition of Slavery in Southern Somalia

Around the 1890s, Antonio Cecchi, a popular Italian explorer and businessman, was probably the first to succeed in drawing Italian attention toward the Somali coast of Benadir. Based on his explorations in East Africa, he highlighted the importance of the river valley region as a place with promising agro-based economic potential for Italy. Based on this finding, late in the 19th century, the Italian government leased Somalia Benadir from the Sultan of Zanzibar for various reasons, which will be explained in the following section of the paper. The Italian colonial authority first occupied the arable land around Juba River and then in the Shabelle valley, where they soon appropriated the land for agricultural development.[53]

Therefore, the abolition of slavery in Southern Somalia by the Italian colonial government was not only based on humanitarian grounds but also on the Italian need for economic gains, and the search for legitimate commerce. As Robert Hess stated:

> Italian industry was insufficiently developed to absorb the vast number of unemployed workers. The country lacked the raw materials necessary for an industrial civilization, and there was little chance for improvement. [Thus necessitated] …finding overseas colonies in which to settle surplus population under the Italian flag. [That is why] in the second half of the 19th century more

than seventy Italian expeditions were sent to explore [economic opportunities in] Africa.[54]

As a result, Italy exploited Somalia and Ethiopia's fertile land and the labor force of the indigenous and manumitted people. This led to the establishment of immense Italian plantations, which were acquired by confiscating the indigenous arable land in between the two rivers, Juba and Shabelle.

As I said earlier, in 1892, the Italian colonial government leased Somalia Benadir from the Sultan of Zanzibar, Sayyid Said, and a few years later began the process of freeing the slaves who belonged to the Sultanate.[55] At the time, other European nations were also scrambling to colonize the African continent; Germany was among those who set their eyes on Somalia. However, the Sultan of Zanzibar did not want Germany to take over Somalia. According to an Italian official, the Sultan "hated and feared the Germans…not only would he be pleased if Italy took possession of the Somali region, but he would support it wholeheartedly."[56] As a result, Italy was able to acquire Somalia at a very low cost. The legal document for the transfer of Benadir was signed by Mr. Gerald Portal, a British diplomat who negotiated on behalf of the Sultan, and Mr. Cottoni on behalf of the Italian government.[57] On the strength of this agreement, the Sultan ceded all his sovereign rights in Benadir for a yearly payment of 160,000 rupees. He also received the sum of 40,000 rupees as a sign of good will for agreeing to sign the agreement.[58] Meanwhile, the slave trade between Zanzibar and Somalia continued intermittently, under the aegis of Somali nomads from the interior, the Somali coastal traders, and the Arab-slave importers. This trade was carried on through the Benadir coastal cities of Merca, Kisimayu, Brava, and Mogadishu.

Although it was part of the Italian colonial obligation in the Belgium treaty to abolish slave trade, Italy's initial concern was to promote efficient colonial administration in Somalia than to abolish slavery. As a result, some of the Italian officials turned a blind eye to the ongoing slave trade. Like other colonial regimes in Africa, the Italian administration acted with restraint on the abolition question. Initially, the Italian officials often returned fugitive slaves to their former masters, even though Italy claimed to be abolishing slavery. This appears to be a conflict of colonial policy,[59] and a breach of the Belgium abolition act to free the slaves. In this agreement, Italy was a member country among the signatories that agreed to abolish slavery in Africa. Over time the abolition question acquired external momentum because of the pressure from other European governments and the ongoing slavery debate in the Italian parliament.[60] This problem was highlighted by the revelation of Gustavo Chiesi and a lawyer Ernesto Travelli, who were sent to Somalia by the Italian government to investigate the operations of the chartered company, V. Filonardi, to abolish slavery. Chiesi and Travelli discovered anomalies in the way the chartered company was being administered.[61] Their investigation also uncovered the existence of an extensive slave trade in Southern Somalia.[62]

In 1894, there were over 2,000 domestic slaves in Mogadishu alone awaiting emancipation, without even taking into consideration those in other cities and plantations, where most of the slaves were kept. The first 45 slaves were freed by the Italian colonial authority under the administration of the chartered company, V. Filonardi, in 1895. Massive emancipation of slaves in Somalia only began after anti-slavery activist Robecchi Bricchetti informed the Italian public about the practice of slavery in Somalia. Bricchetti appealed to the Italian public through the media in Milan, and exposed the lackadaisical attitude of the Italian government toward emancipating the slaves and stopping the slave trade.[63] During Bricchetti's short stay in Benadir in 1903; he witnessed the emancipation of about 50 slaves in some coastal cities. Bricchetti himself also bought freedom for two slaves.

In 1896 a new company by the name of the Benadir Company, which replaced the V. Filonardi, administered Somalia until 1904.[64] When the new company (Benadir) began to experience financial difficulties because of insufficient funding from the Italian government, the colonial government decided to administer the colony (Somalia) directly.[65] Upon assuming this new responsibility in 1905, the Italian government acted vigorously to put an end to the slave traffic due to parliamentary coercion and incessant pressure from Italian anti-slavery organizations such as "Anti-schiavista."[66]

As Italy progressed with abolition of slavery in Somalia, local slave dealers in the Benadir coast embraced the Italian proposal with less resistance, but the Somali nomads (Hawiya) in the interior tried to resist the Italian policy intensively. Those who resisted the abolition included the Wadan, the Bimal, the Moblen, and the Gaaljaal, just to mention a few. These resisters described the Italian colonial government as infidels who were against the Islamic faith and who were trying to infiltrate into the Somali society to convert them from Islam into Christianity.[67] Unlike the nomads, the indigenous Jareer people and the emancipated slaves regarded the Somali nomad's resistance as propaganda and as a means of maintaining slavery and the status quo.[68] Resistance by the nomadic Somalis led to several confrontations between them and the Italian colonial government. To note a few of the significant combat locations between the Bimal and the Italian regiments in 1893, which was mainly composed of locally recruited soldiers, are Merca, Danane, Jilib, and Jesira. The Italian soldiers also encountered the Wadan combatants/warriors in 1897 at Afgoy, Mallable, Audegle, and Barire.[69] One of the well-remembered incidents, which occurred in 1896–1897 between the Wadan and the Italians, is known as 'The Lafoole Massacre,' locally referred to as *Axad Shekki* (the "Sunday year of Cecchi"). This incident took place on the road between Mogadishu and Afgoye, where Wadan warriors ambushed a convoy of Italian travelers, including a top official, Antonio Cecchi, who died in the ambush.[70] The Italians retaliated against the Somali nomads, deploying heavy arms to the scene (Lafoole), bombarded surrounding villages, and inflicted several casualties upon the local Wadan residents.[71] In order to overcome the nomadic resistance and slavery, the Italian government in 1906 issued an ultimatum ordering the Somali nomads of every region to surrender their weapons within a short period of time. One of those who ignored the order was Sheik Hagi Hassan, a religious leader of Gaaljeel nomadic clan, and a representative of the larger Hawiya groups who argued that we would:

> …not accept your [un-Islamic] order. We will not come to you at any cost because you have broken our pact. All our slaves escaped and went to you and you have set them free. We are not happy with the [abolitionist] order. We abandoned our law, for according to our law, we can put slaves in prison and force them to work. The [Italian] government has its law and we have ours. We accept no law other than our own. Our law is that of God and the Prophet.[72]

Surprisingly, the Islamic law that Sheick Hassan referred to did not allow or accept any kind of violation of another Muslim's basic civil rights. Therefore, it seems that the violation of the Jareer's rights by the nomads was itself anti-Islamic.

Refusal to accept the ultimatum led to wars and hostilities between the Italian government and Sheik Hassan and his followers. In the ensuing battle, the Sheik was captured and disarmed while the total emancipation of slaves was decreed. Most of the ex-slaves went to join with other Bantu/Jareer communities who were already settled, while others moved away from the nomads to one of the safe havens (Gosha or Avai) to establish a new life.

Around 1907, a new concern emerged among the indigenous groups after they noticed a strong and willful effort from the Italian colony to exploit the agricultural potential of the inter-riverine area.[73] Subsequently, the indigenous people's fears became a reality. When the Italian foreign minister Pasquale Mancini was asked by the parliament about the delay of the agricultural progress in Somalia, he told the Italian parliament that the popular explorer's, [Antonio "…Cecchi's] mission and that of others would surely discover vast fertile areas awaiting peaceful cultivation and commercial penetration [soon]."[74]

Post-Abolition: The Italian Colony's Land Confiscation

During the first quarter of the 20th century, the Italian government decided to hire a young economist and agronomist by the name of Romolo Onor. He was sent to the Juba and Shabelle region of Somalia to conduct feasibility studies regarding the possible exploitation of the area's agricultural potential.[75] He concluded his report by recommending large-scale agricultural development in the area. However, Italian officials had informed Onor that the local indigenous Bantu people preferred to work on their own farms rather than work on the Italian plantations.[76] The Italians considered importing workers from India, Arabia, China, and even Ethiopia, but all these alternatives were subsequently rejected.[77] Onor advised that unless the Italian government was prepared to confiscate all Bantu farmlands and use forced labor, it would not succeed in implementing their agricultural scheme. Another option for Italy was to provide huge wage subsidies to attract farm workers or wean away the Bantu from their own land; otherwise, the agricultural exploitation of the Benadir plantations would be difficult. The Italian government rejected Onor's suggestions and opted instead for a settler-based plantation system.[78]

Another Italian official, Carletti, suggested that villages be organized for emancipated slaves, who would be classifiedinto labor brigades to work in the Italian plantations.[79] In 1906, these villages were established with the help of a few clan leaders (former slave owners) near the farm areas occupied by Italians.[80] In view of the use of the forced labor of the former slaves by the Italian government, in collaboration with ex-slave owners, the sincerity of the Italian government's abolition measures is questionable, Therefore, one can conclude that Italy leased Somalia Benadir from the Sultan of Zanzibar in order to exploit the indigenous arable land and their labor force. In accordance with the Italian coerced labor and exploitation, when the Italian government was pressured by the opposition party for failing to show a tangible benefit from Somalia-Benadir, "...the [Italian] Foreign Affairs Minister announced to the Chamber of Deputies, on February 13, 1908, that exploitation of [the] alleged immense resources [in Somalia] could forthwith begin."[81] In view of the Italian ill-intent in confiscating the native land in the inter-riverine area, Pankhurst described the Italian agricultural scheme as an initiative "...to deprive the natives of ownership of the land and to compel them to work for the Italian concession holders who were to replace them."[82] However, I must also mention that there is a scholarly disagreement with Pankhurst's views towards the Italian land confiscation in Somalia. Cassanelli says, there is a possibility that Pankhurst might be biased against Italy, since she is British, and the British too had their interest and involvement in Somalia's affair. However, Barile's statement seems to support Pankhurst's view; he says, after confiscating the farmlands from its native owners, Italy did not waste much time in establishing about 107 small and large plantations.[83]

In 1911, De Martino, the new Italian governor in Somalia, decreed that all uncultivated lands within the vicinity of Italian government plantations would be at the disposal of the government.[84] Before De Martino arrived in Benadir, the first agricultural concession was 5,000 hectares along the Juba River. This had been granted and leased to an Italian businessman by the name of Gustavo Carpanetti in 1907. He had arrived in Somalia a year earlier and had conducted some experiments on how to cultivate cotton in the vicinity of Brava City.[85] Over the following years, many more concessions were approved and released to other Italians.[86] These Italian concessions founded by Governor De Martino in 1912 included the sugar plantation (SAIS) in *Jowhar*;[87] another one was AAGG, which was the core of a number of plantations that grew various products. One of the main products grown in this plantation was bananas, for export, which was directed by Romolo Onor until the year 1918. This plantation (AAGG) was located within a reasonable distance to the south of Mogadishu.[88] Another important and well-known plantation in Southern Somalia is called Avai, locally known as *Asaili* (Sorrow); where many Bantu laborers were drowned in the irrigation canals.[89] Avai is not very far from the other plantation at *Genale* (AAGG).

All the above noted plantations were worked exclusively by emancipated slaves and conscripted Bantu natives who were virtually expected to supply their labor to the Italian colonial government. The Italian agricultural schemes would not have succeeded without the collaboration of non-Bantu ethnic groups (the ex-slave owners). The Bantu were forced to abandon their own farms in order to dwell in the established villages around the Italian plantations.[90]

It is also worth noting that before the Italians began the conscription of the emancipated slaves, many of them had been assimilated by the local Bantu population.[91] Therefore, they (the emancipated) too became landowners and had access to the land that belonged to their respective and affiliated clan areas. Besides, most of the emancipated slaves had already returned willingly to farm in their areas.

Those who re-enforced the Italian forced labor against the Bantu/Jareer people were the Somali nomads and the coastal people, who created slave institutions prior to the colonial period and later, collaborated with the Italian authority to conscript the very emancipated Jareer people for Italian plantations. The Somali nomads (the ex-slave owners) still wanted to maintain a continuity of slavery after its abolition by the Italians.[92] The argument here is that the abolition of slavery in Somalia was a mere exchange of masters only. After the abolition, slave-mastership was transferred from the Somali nomads and the coastal people to Italian plantation owners. As a British official in East Africa, Rennel, stated:

The conception of these agricultural enterprises as exploitation concessions engendered under the [Italian] fascist regime a labor policy of considerable severity in theory and actual brutality in practice. It was in fact indistinguishable from slavery.[93]

The non-Bantu Somalis did not have the expertise for farming, and in fact they held agriculture in contempt, so they were not conscripted. That is probably why the Italian authority saw the Somali nomads as the major factor limiting colonial agricultural development.[94] As a result, the colonial authorities concluded that an end to slavery would liberate a population that could help Italy build a new agricultural economic empire.[95] Therefore, the colonial administration in Somalia was an imperial power that came claiming to be abolitionist, when in reality it sought to impose its authority and exploitation upon the indigenous (Bantu/Jareer) people.

Conclusion

I have attempted to highlight the societal differences between the two Bantu/Jareer groups in southern Somalia, namely, the Wazigwa or imported slaves from Tanzania and the Mjikenda or the indigenous farmers in Southern Somalia. These groups have always been referred to by historians as one group of the same origin; on the contrary, they are very different. I have also tried to indicate the uniqueness of the type of slavery that took place in Somalia, which was unilaterally directed against the Bantu/Jareer people only. Additionally, I have examined plantation slavery in Benadir, its protagonists and the causes that created the need for plantation slavery, as well as the emancipation of slaves in Somalia by the Italian colonies. I have also shown the resistance the Italians encountered from the interior (Hawiya) nomadic clans while implementing the abolition acts against slavery.

In this paper, I have also tried to elucidate the social difference between the Wazigwa, runaway slaves who established their own independent entity within Somalia, and the indigenous Mjikenda farmers who became culturally incorporated within the milieu of the Somali nomads, which continue to discriminate against indigenous farmers. Finally, I have underlined the implicit and explicit Italian colonial objectives to confiscate and exploit the land and the labor force of the indigenous and the emancipated slaves.

Notes

1. Although Mohamed Ali's (1988) poem is an innuendo directed against the 'land reform policy' of the late Siyad Barre's military regime, it is also relevant in retrospect to colonial land confiscation policies (see Ahmed Qasim, Land Rush in Somalia, in this volume). As this Jareer poet's complaint indicates, and as we shall see in the paper, land appropriation has always been an unabated apprehension among the native Jareer population. Because, the livelihood of the river valley people heavily depended on land cultivation.

2. Enrico Cerulli. *Somalia: Scritti Vari Editi Ed Inediti* 3 Vols. Roma, 1957; Cassanelli, Lee. *The Shaping of Somali Society. Reconstructing the history of a pastoral people, 1600–1900.* Philadelphia; University of Pennsylvania Press, 1982; Cassanelli, Lee. "The Ending of slavery in Italian Somalia," in Miers, Suzanne and Richard Roberts, eds. *The End of Slavery in Africa.* Madison: University of Wisconsin Press, 1988: 308–331; Cassanelli. "The distant frontier as refuge," in Kopytoff, Igor, ed. *The African Frontier.* Bloomington: University of Indiana Press, Indiana, 1987: 216–238; Besteman, Catherine. "The Invention of Gosha: Slavery, Colonialism, and Stigma in Somali History," in Ahmed,

Ali Jimale, ed., *The Invention of Somalia*. Lawrenceville NJ: Red Sea Press, 1995: 88–99; Besteman, Catherine. "Land Tenure, Social Power, and Legacy of Slavery in Southern Somalia." Ph.D. Thesis, University of Arizona, 1991; Luling, Virginia. "The Social Structure of Southern Somali Tribes." Ph.D. thesis, University of London, 1971; Grotanelli, Vinigi. "I Bantu Deli Giuba Nelle Tradizioni Dei Wazigwa," *Geographica Helvetica*, 8, 1953: 249–60.

3. Besteman, Catherine L. *Unraveling Somalia: Race, Violence, and the Legacy of Slavery*. Philadelphia: University of Pennsylvania Press, 1999: 120–21.

4. Grotanelli, Vinigi. "I Bantu del Giuba nelle tradizioni dei Wazigwa," *Geographica Helvetica* 8. 1953: 249–60; Cassanelli, Lee. *The Shaping of Somali Society. Reconstructing the history of a pastoral people, 1600–1900*. Philadelphia: University of Pennsylvania Press, 1982; Cassanelli, Lee V. "The Ending of slavery in Italian Somalia," in Miers, Suzanne and Richard Roberts, eds., *The End of Slavery in Africa*. Madison: 308–331; Cassanelli, Lee V. "The distant frontier as refuge," in Kopytoff, Igor, ed., *The African Frontier*, Indiana. 216–238; Luling, Virginia, 1971. "The Social Structure of Southern Somali Tribes," Ph.D. thesis, University of London.

5. Most scholars believe that the Wazigwa are the founders of Goshaland along the Juba River-a safe haven for runaway slaves. Late in the 19th century, Egypt, Zanzibar, Italy, and Britain recognized this haven as an independent entity. Although other communities like the *gamas* later resided in Goshaland and constituted the largest part of their confederacy, the Wazigwas remained as an autonomous society with a distinct political structure. That is probably why the Goshaland people are generally known by the name of their founders, the Wazigwa. Until the 1920s, the Bantu people of Goshaland were divided into nine *gamas* groups, which constituted the core of their confederation. They are Makua, Nyassa, Yao, Mushongoli, Makale, Ngindo, Nyika, Nyamwezi, and Molema. Later, a small number of this group has been assimilated to the indigenous Bantu/Jareer of the Shabelle River.

6. According to Cerulli, the Mjikendas consist of approximately twelve tribes while Thomas Spear and others assert only nine tribes. These groups presently reside along the Tana River in Kenya-while their remnants are scattered around the interior of southern Somalia-the inter-riverine areas. These remnants are believed to be the Jareer groups that originally resided in Shungwaya in southern Somalia. According to Spear, their location in Shungwaya is believed to have been near the contemporary location of Buur Gaabo-southwest of Buur Hakabo. Also, other scholars have suggested that Shungwaya was the center where Bantu people autonomously exercised their Kingdom up until the sixteenth century. Later that century the Jareer, who were not experienced in warfare, were pushed by the warlike nomad "Galla" (Oromo) and Hawiya tribes from the interior from northern regions, and lost control of the grazing land between the rivers Juba and Shabelle. In the same century, the warlike Hawiya Somalis attacked both the Gallas and the Jareer. However, the "Gallas" stayed behind while most of the Jareer people decided to move away from the Somalis and ended up in Tana River in modern Kenya. The Jareer who presently reside along the Shabelle River in southern Somalia are therefore the remnants of those who left Somalia. For more information about the Mjikenda, see for example: Spear, Thomas T., 1981. *Kenya's Past: an introduction to historical method in Africa*. Longman, London and New York.

7. Guilain p.537 cited in Virginia, Luling. 1971. "The Social Structure of Southern Somali Tribes…" 116.

8. Grotanelli, Vinigi L., 1953. "I Bantu del Giuba nelle tradizioni dei Wazigwa," *Geographica Helvetica*. Vol. 8: 249–60. Also, see Cassanelli, Lee V., 1987. "The distant frontier as refuge," in Kopytoff, Igor, ed., *The African Frontier.* Indiana: 216–238.

9. Grotanelli, Vinigi. *Geografica Helvetica*. Vol. 8 (1953): 254.

10. The word Gosha in Somali language means forest. This word insinuates that the inhabitants of Gosha-land are the runaway slaves who hid in the forest. The terms Wazigwa and Gosha are interchangeably used, since they refer to the same group of people. For more information about the Gosha people also-see Cassanelli, Lee V. "The Distant Frontier as Refuge," 214, in *The African Frontier.* Igor Kopytoff., ed. Indiana University Press, 1977; Besteman, Catherine. *Unraveling Somalia: Race, Violence, and the Legacy of Slavery.* 1999.

11. Menkhaus, Kenneth J., 1989. "Rural Transformation and the Roots of Underdevelopment in Somalia's Lower Jubba Valley." Ph.D. thesis, University of South Carolina. p. 128.

12. Bricchetti, Robecchi L. *Dal Benadir. Lettere illustrate all societa' antischiavista d'Italia,* La tipografia societa' editrice. Milano, 1904: 146.

13. Ibid. p. 125.

14. Bricchetti, Robecchi L. *dal Benadir: lettere illustrate alla societa' antischiavista d'Italia.* Milano: societa' editrice, La Tipografia, 1904: 142–45.

15. Cerulli, Enrico, 1957. *Somalia: scritti vari editi ed inediti.* Roma. Vol. I: 254 & 255; Warner, Alice. 1912–1913. "Some notes on the Wapokomo of the Tana Valley," *Journal of African Society.* 12: 359–384.

16. Warner, Alice 1912–1913. "Some notes on the Wapokomo of the Tana Valley". *J. Afr. Soc.*, 12: 359–384. Also see: Prins, A.H.J., 1952. *The Coastal Tribes of North-Eastern Bantu.*, London. Also, Introduction of Enrico Cerulli, 1957. "Il libro dei Zenji" in Somalia Vol. I: 54 & 259. Also, Prins, A.H. 1972., "The Shungwaya Problem: Traditional history and cultural likeness in Bantu northeast Africa," *Anthropos*, 67:1/2–6. Luigi V. Grotanelli, 1976. "Una Metropoli perduta dell'Africa," in *Gerarchie etniche e conflitto culturale; saggi di etnologia nordest Africana.* Milan: Franco Angeli, Editore: 285–301; I.M. Lewis, 1988. *Modern History of Somalia.* Boulder: Westview Press: 28; Steiner, Martina I., 1994. *La Grande Faida: I processi di etnicizzazione e di segmentazione in Somalia.* Roma: Centro Analisi Sociale: 68.

17. Ibid. 264.

18. Bulletin of the International Committee of Urgent Anthropological and Ethnical Research: 28–29. N3, 1960, with the help of UNESCO.

19. Ibid.

20. Turton said, the Somali nomads from around the coastal city of Merca expanded and occupied both the west and the south in order to gain total control over much of the riverine area between the Juba and Tana rivers long before the Gallas (Oromo) from Ethiopia came to the coast. In the process both the Somalis and the Gallas found Bantu-speaking communities to be their main rivals for control over the grazing areas. This is why it has been suggested that a constant Somali and Oromo pressure initially caused the Bantu-speaking groups to retreat to the Tana river, towards the modern Kenya, in the 16th century. Also see: E.R. Turton, 1975. "Bantu, Galla and Somali migrations in the Horn of Africa: A Reassessment of the Juba /Tana area." *Journal of African History*, Vol. 16: 519. Also, Robert L. Hess made a similar argument, see 1966, *Italian Colonialism in Somalia.* Chicago: Chicago University Press.

21. Luling, Virginia., 1976. "Colonial and Post colonial Influences on a South Somali Community," *Journal of African Studies*, 3, 1: 491–511.

22. Ibid.

23. This information was obtained through personal communication with Mohamed Ali Adan, a former student of Aligarn Muslim University, Bombay-India. 1988. Faculty of Social Science.

24. Martina, Steiner. 1994. La Grande Faida, Centro Analisi Sociale: 79–81.

25. Luling, Virginia., 1983. "Studies in humanities and natural sciences," in Thomas Labahn, ed. *Proceedings of the Second International Congress of Somali Studies*. Germany: University of Hamburg: 39.

26. For more information, see, for example: Luling, Virginia. 1983. "Studies in Humanities and Science". Vol. IV, Paper presented in *The proceedings of the Second International Congress of Somali Studies*. Thomas Labahn. (ed) University of Hamburg- Germany.

27. Cassanelli, Lee. 1987. "Social Construction on the Somali Frontier: Bantu Former Slave Communities in the Nineteenth Century.," in *The African Frontier*. Igor Kopytoff., ed. 233.

28. Eno, Mohamed A. 1993. This information was extracted from a "fact-finding" report for the vulnerable groups in southern Somalia. The said study was sponsored by the international organization-ACORD.

29. For more information, see: Luling, Virginia. 1994. "The origins of the 'Jareer' people of the Shabelle: the implications of some rituals." (Unpublished) Paper presented at the Somali Inter-riverine Studies Conference, at Sidney Smith Hall. University of Toronto.

30. Cerulli, Enrico. *Somalia*. Vol. 3 (1964): 86–90.

31. Cassanelli, Lee V. and Catherine Lowe Besteman. *The Struggle for Land in Southern Somalia: The war behind the war*. Colorado, 1996: 124.

32. Declich, Francesca. "Identity, Dance and Islam among People with Bantu Origin, in Ahmed, Ali Jimale., ed. *The Invention of Somalia*. Lawrenceville, New Jersey: Red Sea Press, 1995: 191–222.

33. Besteman, Catherine L., 1991. "Land Tenure, Social Power, and Legacy of Slavery in Southern Somalia," Ph.D. Thesis, University of Arizona, 1991. 129.

34. This information was obtained from Hassan Gumbow, a native of Dhajalaq village along the Shabelle river. Gumbow is among the well respected village elders, and he is 85 years old who still goes to work in his farm every morning. 1988.

35. Cassanelli, Lee V. *The Shaping of Somali Society. Reconstructing the history of a pastoral people, 1600–1900*. Philadelphia, 1982: 147–150. For a similar argument of economic enslaving in West Africa, see for example: Klein, Martin. 1992. "The Impact of the Atlantic Slave Trade on the Societies of Western Sudan." in *The Atlantic Slave Trade: effects on economics, societies, and peoples in Africa, the Americas, and Europe:*. 25–41. Inikori, Joseph E. & Stanley L. Engerman., eds. Duke University press, Durham & London.

36. Hess, Robert. 1966: 87–99.
Some of those nomadic tribes from the interior who wrested control of the Bantu land and then enslaved them are from the Hawiya tribes, of which their sub-clans are: the Moblein, the Biamal, the Waadan, the Abgaal, the Gaaljeel, the Baadiadde, the Murusade, and some of the Digil & Mirifle. These are the tribes that classify themselves as "Bilis" (Nobles).

37. ASMAI (Archivio Storico del Ministero degli Affari Esteri, Rome, Italy) 1905. (position

75/6 f. 58.) – While the Biamal were busy making war against the neighboring tribes for territorial expansion, often imbued with the belief that they should control the whole South, Bantu slaves were used in the plantations to produce food for subsistence and commercial purposes. For a similar argument and for comparative purposes see for example: Cooper, Frederick. *Plantation Slavery on the East Coast of Africa*. Yale University Press, 1977. Also see: Lovejoy, Paul. 1979. "The Characteristics of Plantations...." *The American Historical Review*. Vol. 84. # 5. (1979): 1267–73.

38.   Christopher, Lt. "On the East Coast of Africa". *Journal of the Royal Geographical Society*. V.14. (1844): 80. For more comments of brutality against the Bantu slaves in southern Somalia, see for example: Robecchi, Bricchetti. 1904. *dal Benadir*: 30–31

39.   Alpers, Edward A. "Muqdisho in the nineteenth Century: a regional perspective." *Journal of African History*. 24: (1983): 441–459.

40.   Afgoy is a small city located about 30 km from the capital city of Somalia (Mogadishu). Afgoy was the head office of the Sultanate of Geledi (Geledi is the name of the tribe led by Sultan Yusuf). Yusuf was among the factions that were striving to gain control of Mogadishu to put it under his Sultanate. He faced resistance from the Hamarwein and Shingaani elders. The power struggle between these three groups resulted in the intervention of Zanzibar's Sultan, presumably to counterbalance the hostility of the stronger Sultan of Geledi.

41.   Robert, Hess. *Italian Colonialism in Somalia*. University of Chicago Press: Chicago, 1966: 1–12.

42.   Lewis. 14.

43.   Menkhaus, Kenneth. 1989. "Rural Transformation...": 103.

44.   Cassanelli, Lee V., 1982. *The Shaping of Somali Society*. 166. Also, see Menkhaus, Kenneth. 1989. "Rural Transformation..." 102–105.

45.   Cooper, Frederick. *Plantation Slavery on the East Coast of Africa*. Yale University Press, 1977.

46.   Kenneth, Menkhaus. 1989. "Rural Transformation....". 103–104.

47.   Robecchi, Bricchetti. 1904. *dal Benadir*. p. 63 & 107.

48.   Lovejoy, Paul E. Transformations in Slavery. A History of Slavery in Africa. Cambridge, 1983: 226.

49.   Faay Muudeey Shongow and Madina Muddey Dhurow. Interview. 1989. These two women are of Somali Bantu origin.

50.   Besteman, Catherine. "Land Tenure..." 1991: 69–78.

51.   Faay Muudey Shongow, 1988. This information was obtained by interviewing an old lady from Afgoy City in 1988. This lady is considered as one of the few living Jareer persons who mastered the local oral history in her area, around the Shabelle River.

52.   For a similar argument see: Lovejoy, Paul. 1983. *Transformations in slavery*: 12.

53.   Hess, Robert. 1966: 15.

54.   Hess, Robert. 1966. Italian Colonialism in Somalia. 2–3.

55.   Robecchi, Bricchetti. 1904. *dal Benadir*. 45–50.

56.   Filonardi report, Zanzibar, October 20, 1886, ASMAI, pos. 55/1, f. 4.

57.   Ibid.

58.   Robecchi, Bricchetti. 1904., *dal Benadir*. p. 48. For more information regarding the involvement of both Italy and Zanzibar as protectorates in the Benadir colony, see for example: Pankhurst, Sylvia E., 1951. *Ex-Italian Somaliland*. London.

59.   For more information on this issue see for example Lovejoy, who made a similar argu-

ment about the European colony's conflicting policies in Africa towards abolition, see Lovejoy Paul., *Transformations in Slavery*. pp. 246–268.

60. Pankhurst, Sylvia. 1951. *Ex-Italian Somaliland*. 46.
61. Ibid.
62. Robecchi, Bricchetti. 1904. *dal Benadir*. 266–67.
63. Ibid. 72.
64. Cassanelli Lee V. *The Shaping of Somali Society: Reconstructing the History of a pastoral people, 1600–1900*. Philadelphia: University of Pennsylvania Press, 1982. For more elaborated information regarding the Filonardi Company, see for example Hess, Robert. 1966. *Italian Colonialism in Somalia*. chap. 2.
65. Hess, Robert., 1966. *Italian Colonialism in Somalia*. Chap. 2. Also, see Cassanelli, Lee V., 1982. *The Shaping of Somali Society*.... 183–207.
66. Hess, Robert., 1966. *Italian Colonialism in Somalia*. Chap. 2.
67. Ibid.
68. Faay Muudey Shongow and Madina Muudey Dhurow. Interview. Afgoy. 1989.
69. Hess, Robert. 1966. Italian colonialism in Somalia. 87–91.
70. Cassanelli, Lee V. 1982. *The Shaping of Somali Society*. 204–208.
71. Ibid. p. 208.
72. De Vecchi, De Val Cismo, Cesare Maria. *Orizzonti d'Impero: Cinque anni in Somalia*. Milano, 1935: 25–27.
73. Onor, Romolo. La Somalia Italiana: l'esame critico dei problemi di economia rurale e di politica economica della Colonia. Roma, 1925.
74. Hess, Robert., 1966: 13.
75. Cassanelli, Lee V. in *The End of Slavery in Africa*. Miers, Suzanne and Richard Roberts, eds. University of Wisconsin Press, 1988: 308–331.
76. Guadagni, Marco. *Xeerka Beeraha/Diritto Fondiario*. Roma. 1981: 179.
77. Cassanelli. 1988., in *The End of Slavery in Africa*. Miers and Roberts, ed. 311.
78. Romolo, Onor. 1925. *La Somalia Italiana: esame critico dei problemi di economia rurale e di politica economica della colonia*. Turin: Fratelli Bocca. For more elaborate information see for example Cassanelli V. Lee. 1988. "The Ending of Slavery in Italian Somalia: Liberty and the Control of Labor 1890–1935." in *The End of Slavery in Africa*. Suzanne Miers and Richard Roberts. (Eds): 308–331. Also, see Hess, Robert., 1966.
79. This information is from a confidential letter written by Gustavo Carletti to Italy's foreign ministry while he was in Brava. It was later filed in the ASMAI account. July 19, 1907. ASMAI pos. 75/6, f. 64. NB: The word "Webi" is a Italianized Somali language which means river.
80. Ibid.
81. Pankhurst, Sylvia. 1951. *Ex-Italian Somaliland*. 90.
82. Ibid.
83. Barile, Pietro., 1935. *Colonizzazione Fascista*...166.
84. Royal decree No. 695. June 8, 1911. ASMAI, pos. 75/11,f.122. For more information on land tenure by Italian Colonial Authority in Somalia-Benadir see for example De Martino's report, "Report to H.E., the foreign minister: "The present and the future of the colony". Mogadishu. Oct. 10, 1910. ASMAI, pos. 75/12.
85. R.D. n. 334 del 19 Carpanetti, Luglio G. "il cotone nella valle del Juba." Agricultura coloniale, 1907. pp. 51–53. Also, see for example, Manassei, T. 1910. "\La ripartizione delle terre concesse in Somalia. Rivista Coloniale, 1907: 67–69.

86. Guadagni, Marco. 1981. Xeerka Beeraha/ Diritto Fondiario Somalo. 145.

87. SAIS (Societa' Agricola Italiana in Somalia). This is an exclusively sugar cane grower plantation which was totally owned by Italian government and Italian investors. It is located about 150 km north of Mogadishu, (the present capital city of Somalia). Jowhar is the largest city near SAIS Jowhar also has the biggest and only sugar factory in Somalia. The name Jowhar was given to that city after the independence of Somalia in 1960; its original colonial name was Duca degli Abruzzi-(The Duke of Abruzzis). Jowhar and its surroundings is known to be a Bantu area; along the Shabelle river. The Italian colony had established small villages for the conscripted, coerced, and freed Bantu slaves to work in this plantation. There were no workers from other non-Bantu tribes. Jowhar, in the Somali language, means a stupendous place where you can grow or find almost every product.

88. AAGG (Azienda Agraria Governativa Genale). The word "Genale" in Somali language means "Paradise"; this refers to the fertility of that land along the Shabelle river. As on any other Italian plantations, the workers are from Bantu people.

89. Awaile is a well-known plantation among Somalis, particularly in the Bantu community, because so many young men lost their lives at this plantation. Its famous local name is "Kili Asaile" (the canal of sorrow and death). This was one of the worst plantations in Somalia-Benadir: it was here where the Italian government gained a very bad reputation with regard to death, brutality, and re-enslavement of the freed Bantu slaves. The name Awaile (Asaile) still reverberates in the minds of many Bantu families in Somalia because it was at Awaile that many Bantu brothers died. Most of the death on this plantation occurred during the period when they were manually digging huge and gigantic canals for irrigation. These canals diverted water from the main river; most of the time the water was uncontrollable: workers were trapped in the depth of the canals and drowned. The name Awaile carries a strong negative connotation among the Bantu community in Somalia. The reason why the locals named this plantation as Asaile (sorrow), is because anyone who was conscripted for Asaile was considered dead by his family. Other brutalities include when Italian officials came to visit or to survey the progress of the plantations, in order not to dirty their shoes with the mud soil, they used to lay down the Bantu workers on their chest so that the Italian official could walk on them.

90. Cassanelli, Lee V., 1988, in *The End of Slavery in Africa*. Miers and Roberts eds. 308–331.

91. Enrico, Cerulli. *Somalia*. Vol. 3 (1964): 86–90.

92. Cassanelli, Lee V., 1982,1987, 1988; Bricchetti.1899 & 1904; Luling.1964; Menkhaus. 1989; Besteman. 1991; Cerulli. 1957; Lewis. 1994; and Hess. 1966.

93. Rodd, Rennell. "British military administration of occupied territories in Africa." Londra, 1948: 162.

94. Foligno, Fazi. To colonial Minister, August 18, 1915. ASMAI, pos. 171/4, f 97.

95. Cassanelli. 1988. In *The end of slavery in Africa*. Miers & Roberts. Eds. 310–11.

Chapter Nine
Land Rush in Somalia

Ahmed Q. Ali

THE LATE DICTATOR Mohamed Siad Barre, in his last address to the Somali people on January 26, 1991, called on the people to refrain from the insane idea of opposing the regime and to instead farm the land for the nation was blessed with unlimited amount of agricultural land and water resources. The above statement represents a long-standing master narrative that begun with the onset of the Italian Colonial Administration, and continued throughout the successive post-colonial Somali regimes and has its roots in a highly organized myth intended to dispose land from its rightful owners. The implicit motive behind the narrative, however, was to legitimize the expropriation of farm land form the less powerful and redistribute it to those clans that had political and economic connections with the slogan that land belonged to all Somalis and all citizens of the country had the right to acquire land wherever it was available. What the slogan, again, implicitly meant was that Somalis of certain clans with the support of the state could confiscate land without any due process.

The purpose of this chapter is to trace the historical and political misappropriation of land in the Riverine and Interriverine regions of southern Somalia. The chapter specifically examines how tenure policies enacted by both colonial and post-colonial regimes led to the total alienation of land from its original owners. The chapter further agues that the current social and political crisis in Somalia owes its source to the unjust land tenure processes that begun during the Italian Colonial Administration, and adopted and later intensified by the successive post-colonial Somali regimes and the activities of the masses to resist. I specifically argue that the collapse of the Somali social structure resulted from the contested ways in which the above mentioned narrative defined and delimited the social boundary of land ownership and the definition of land tenure.

Background

The total area of Somalia is 638,000 sq. km (246,000 sq. mi). Between 10 to 13 percent of the total land is classified as arable. A very small part of this area is irrigable. The area under cultivation is estimated around 700,000 hectors (1.73 million acres). About 80% of that is located in southern Somalia, mainly in the interriverine and riverine regions. The main sources of irrigation water are the Shabelle and Juba Rivers. The Shabelle is not a permanent river and normally dries up from January to March, while the Juba is a permanent river with soil limitations. With normal irrigation practice and cropping patterns, the Shabelle River can irrigate about 50,000 ha, while the Juba Valley can provide about 150,000 ha of irrigated land. This situation makes irrigable land very valuable in Somalia. Water availability, scarce precipitation, and soil quality are also limiting factors. Southern Somalia is a semi-arid region with average maximum temperatures ranging between 30° c to 40° c and minimum temperatures between 20° c to 30° c. Rainfall is far below evapotranspiration; thus few crops can grow without irrigation. Most of the region receives 500 mm of rain yearly; Jilib and Baidoa get 600 mm, while the western part of the region receives 300 mm. Rainfall occurs in two seasons and the river peaks are bimodal, approximately matching the rainy seasons. This situation allows two farming seasons – irrigation and rainfed. In the irrigated areas, the most common crops are maize (corn), sorghum, beans, sesame, cotton, rice, fruits and vegetables, while rainfed agriculture provides mainly sorghum and beans. In the middle Juba, farmers exploit the recession of river flooding from adjacent depressions called *Dhesheeg*. Most of the farmers are small holders, relegated to marginal lands, who employ mainly family workers and little hired labor. These farmers produce for subsistence with a small surplus to the market, but they provide most of the staple food in Somalia. The average size of a small farmer's property in the riverine regions ranges from 0.5 to 3.3 ha (1.23–8.15 acres), but more and more farmers are becoming landless as larger estates spread out rapidly. Large estates account for about 90 percent of irrigated land. These employ capital, hired labor and equipment, and produce cash crops for profit.

The Italian Colonial Administration

The present condition of agricultural land and, therefore, the condition of the small farmers in Southern Somalia, is the consequence of a long process of expropriation of farmlands and eviction of farmers. This process began with the Italian colonial administration and was aggravated by successive post-colonial Somali administrations. It had two peaks, characterized by coercion and violence. These peaks came about during the Italian fascist era and during the Military Regime (MR) in the 1980s, but every other administration did its share.

This study is confined to the problems of farmlands in the Shabelle and Juba Basins. The riverine region is linked to the larger region of the interriverine. In fact, the land issue is among the factors that have generated great resentment among the interriverine people and are at the root of today's regional aspiration for autonomy. The demand for a federal state in the 1950s had its roots in the agricultural land problem.[1] Besides the sources cited in the endnotes and a long list of others not reported because of space, the author, a native of the interriverine, has drawn on his own experience as a hydraulic/irrigation engineer for about 20 years in the region.

The Italian colonialists affected the life of the farmers in the lower Shabelle even before the conquest because they evoked fear of land expropriation among the riparian farmers. They expropriated and evicted farmers and pastoralists from their lands for establishing plantations for a handful of Italian settlers. The small farmers and the ex-slaves were the first to be used as forced labor on the plantations. Later on, during the fascist era, compulsory work was extended to other social strata and groups living in regions such as the interriverine.

Despite the atrocities perpetrated by the Italian colonialists who subjugated these people with superior firearms, confiscated their lands, and burned their villages, colonial historians have not done justice to the afflicted people. Writers of colonial history in southern Somalia instead minimized or totally concealed the confiscation of farmlands, the eviction of farmers and pastoralists from their lands, and all other related crimes. This issue is discussed in this chapter at some length because of its relevance to the land reform in Southern Somalia. The denial by the colonial historians of land confiscation, expropriation of farmlands and eviction of peasants by the Italian colonialists justifies only the failure of the successive Somali administrations to affect a land reform. These administrations denied the claims of the indigenous farmers and refused to reestablish justice through land reform, i.e., to re-distribute land confiscated before and after independence. These administrations, in essence, asserted that land in Somalia was abundant; therefore, there was no need for confiscation.

I.M. Lewis, for instance, based his account on Italian fascist sources, deliberately avoiding Somali sources and Italian sources, which were critical to the colonial expansion. Instead, he preferred the official reports of the very governors (Carletti, De Vecchi, G. Corni, and the like) who were responsible for such crimes. I.M. Lewis, referring to the first 10,000 ha of land seized by Governor Carletti in the Lower Juba stated, "This land had been formerly cultivated by the Tuni clan bondsmen and serfs." About forced labor, Lewis wrote, "…contrary to all expectations, [local labourers] proved far from being easy to attract". He continued, "This led …to force people – mainly former slaves and serfs – to work on plantations... Despite salaries which were not low, voluntary recruits were hard to come by, and those who were induced to work for the Italian farmers had to be supervised by guards otherwise they simply stopped work or fled."[2] First of all, the alienation of a land belonging to others is called confiscation, but I.M. Lewis stops short of accusing the Italians of this crime. Since Italians had no right to expropriate land, the act deserves condemnation not an excuse. Second, historic records show that the forced labor was not limited to ex-slaves and serfs; even if it were so, it would not lessen the crime of the Italian administration who was a signatory of the Brussels' Act and who claimed to "civilize" Somalia. Lewis admitted later on that forced labor was widespread and lasted for a long time, "This tradition of largely compulsory labour recruitment, mainly from the sedentary Bantu tribes of the riverine regions, continued throughout much of the Italian colonial period, although the conditions of service of plantation workers gradually improved, in theory at any rate, if not always in practice." It seems that Lewis can only sympathize with the "nomad pastoralists" and not with "sedentary Bantu". But forced labor was not restricted to "sedentary Bantu" alone. Compulsory labor also affected Bur Hakaba and Baidoa. Elders in Huddur, Bakool, have recounted that Italians ventured as far as Huddur where there is evidence of a massacre of people who resisted abduction for forced labor. Third, it is hard to believe that someone who practiced forced labor would offer high salaries or "gradually" improve working conditions.

Sylvia Pankhurst described the domination of lower Shabelle and the Benadir coast area as follows: "The tribes, who had been promised 'protection,' friendship and trade were taken unaware and by superior arms and were overcome district by district. Neither the Hague Rules, nor any other international convention designed to mitigate the barbarism of war was applied in their case. Defense of their homes and farms was punished as rebellion to a government in regard to whose advent they had not been consulted."[3] But Lewis left out this author because, as he stated, she is "anti-Italian" and "pro-Ethiopian". Lewis carefully avoided not only Somali sources, but also all Italian sources, which were not apologetic to the Italian conquest. He instead preferred to refer to British colonial sources.

Another defender of Italian colonialism is Robert. L. Hess who wrote a book totally based on colonialist and fascist sources. "Official" colonial documents alone cannot provide a clear picture of the colonial administration. The very existence of an opposition to colonial expansion at home is but one of the many unreported indications that the official documents did not tell the entire story. A historian worthy of the name should have known more than that. Hess wrote, "Perhaps because the Shabelle did not become Italy's Nile in Somalia, the Somali[s] were spared the hardship of being deprived of large areas of their land. Although the Filonardi ordinances set a precedent for state seizure of all unoccupied lands, there was no reason for the Italians to confiscate land." The reason for this is that, "Only one-tenth of the land area of Somalia was suitable for agriculture of any kind. A Somali had more to fear from other tribesmen who coveted his clan's grazing area and water holes than he did from the Italians."[4] This would suggest that the land is limited. In Somalia water is also limited and to irrigate the six million ha mentioned by Mr. Hess, Somalia would really need a river as great as the Nile. Additionally, it is very hard to explain how the Italians found all that unoccupied land near the villages and along the rivers. A glance at the shapes of the plantations, all of them precisely rectangular, does not suggest that the Italians avoided "cultivated farms." Leone Iraci, author of a critique of the book, commented on Hess' statements as follows: "It is absurd to hold that Somalis did not have to fear expropriation of land because the Italians did not have reason to confiscate them. The land was indeed confiscated, it certainly constituted a limited portion of the Somali territory, but indeed it was the major part of the arable land..." Iraci also added, "In the 1930s the fascist Italy used brutalities which were not common even in the Portuguese colonies, such as a merciless expropriation of the little irrigable lands."[5]

Catherine L. Besteman explained, that, "...the purpose of the colonial legislation was to eliminate tribal collective tenure and to set the conditions for individual ownership, particularly by foreigners."[6] The Italians achieved this process through what they called the *Native Tribunals* beginning in 1911. According to Hess, "The *Indigenato* [tribunals for natives] enforced its decisions through confiscation of goods or through collective punishment." He added almost admiringly, "Both methods were extremely effective because they were refinement of the Somali custom of tribal and clan responsibility for the behavior of the individual."[7] This shows that the Italians imposed private property to alienate the land and collective punishment to impose forced labor. A similar policy is reported in Eritrea by Haile M. Larembo who pointed out that, "Land was appropriated for colonization following the guidelines set by the Royal Commission which recommended that settlement be directed towards better State lands, demanding that land legislation should be enacted with the ultimate goal being 'to facilitate the colonization and the agricultural progress. In other words, to easy transfer of lands into the hands of the Italians, and among the Italians, of those who could best cultivate it." This policy aimed at a gradual erosion of the traditional land system to serve the settlers' interests. As a result, in order to 'remove a great obstacle to colonization', private property among indigenes was encouraged at the expense of prevailing communal or village ownership, as the latter hindered the sale of long-term concession because of the need to secure unanimous consensus of the community."[8]

In June of 1908, Governor Carletti ordered the occupation of the lower Shabelle (Afgoy-Malable), and by September the occupation was consolidated. The occupation was achieved with military force and continued until the entire middle and lower Shabelle were totally subdued to Italy by 1914.[9] Lee V. Cassanelli, in his book, described and mapped the extent of the cultivated area along Shabelle before and during the colonial occupation (1850–1911). According to this map, the whole Shabelle Valley was cultivated.[10] Most of that land was later on occupied by the Italian colonial administration. Many villages were burnt solely for reprisal. Immediately after that Italians began to clear the land to access roads using the defeated as laborers. On the Juba Basin alienation of land started even earlier. By 1909 almost 50,000 ha were in Italian hands along the Juba.

In a second campaign in 1912, all fertile land between Balad and Mahadday was occupied by 4,000 troops and "uncounted irregulars" (irregulars differed from the regulars only by the length of the contract, which in their case was three years). By 1914, the only portions of the interriverine not yet occupied by the Italians were Bakol and upper Shabelle. During World War I, Governor G. De Martino prepared a series of laws and decrees. Italy declared all land "Crown property" and even land owned privately could be confiscated if not "cultivated on a permanent basis." In other words, most of Somalia became the property of the state. Land was confiscated from any Somali farmland even those with standing crops. All the laws (Law of 1895, Law of 1911, Law of 1912, Law of 1929, Law of 1932) made during the Giolittian period and during the fascist era allowed the Italians to expropriate farmlands at their pleasure. Riparian farmers claim that Italians not only confiscated farmlands for concessions, for access and other roads, for military purposes, for canals, drains, dykes etc., but they also moved entire villages for security reasons. In the 1920s, the size of the Italian concessions on the Shebelle alone, as shown in the following table, was considerable.

Table 1: Italian Concessions along the Shabelle River in the 1920s

City	Number of Hectors	Number of Individual Holdings
Afgoy	2,000 ha	15 holdings
Genale	27,000 ha	136 holdings
Jowhar	25,000 ha (SAIS)	– – – – – – –
Haway	800 ha	– – – – – – –
Total	**54,000**	**151**

Thus, the impact of colonial domination in the riverine area is characterized by loss of land and forced labor in the very farmlands that were confiscated. But this is not a novelty in the African arena. Most of the colonized African countries have experienced a similar situation. A. Adu Boahen explained in his book, "All the colonial administrators also ensured that land was made available to Europeans, mainly through confiscation, expulsion and resettlement of the indigenous peoples. In all such areas, compulsory labor was practiced on a very large scale, especially during the early decades of the system, while migrant labor was provided and the pass system was introduced to ensure the availability of labor."[11] This is exactly what happened in Somalia. Italy was not the exception that I.M. Lewis, R.L. Hess, and Co. wanted to claim it was.

The Fascist Era

The advent of fascism in Italy rekindled the Italian dream of a "settlement colony." Cesare Maria De Vecchi, "a fascist head of the punitive squads who in the 1920s, soiled themselves in Italy with bloody deeds against communists, socialists, and other antifascist leaders"[12] was appointed Governor of *Somalia Italiana* by Mussolini, in 1923. De Vecchi, who proudly defined himself as "a fascist and nothing but a fascist and less than ever a liberal or democratic," was as the Somalis remembered him a ruthless fascist, a racist who permanently tied his name to the consolidation of the fertile Jannale irrigation district.[13]

The implementation of the first phase of the fascist plan was completed in 1926. It consisted of a barrage across the Shabelle at Genale (Jannale) and a complete irrigation system network for more than 20,000 ha. All the infrastructures were implemented with compulsory labor. The major canal was named after De Vecchi. Subsequently, a large canal for irrigation and flood relief was added on the right riverbank. This canal was named *Assayle* because of the large number of women who were widowed during its execution. The land was distributed to Italian settlers on the basis of political merits rather than entrepreneurial skill or capital investment. In this way, the administration founded an absurdly inefficient colonial agriculture. The government guaranteed availability of local forced labor and a protected market in Italy. The size of the "concessions" was large and each estate consisted of two parts: *azienda fiume* along the river and *azienda madre* along one of the canals. Normally, these parasitic settlers lived in sumptuous houses in the *azienda madre* and most of them developed exceptional skills in how to keep "bankrupt" records and a life of splendor. The colony had a rudimentary land registration system in which the settler was to undertake the surveying of his/her land to be plotted on the "cadastral map". This meant that the settler decided on the boundaries between his/her property and indigenous farmlands. The settlers were entitled to move farmlands and houses according to their needs. In the 1930s, further racist laws were introduced to psychologically strengthen the perpetration of forced labor. Law 2590 of 1937 forbade mixed marriages while allowing Italians to keep concubines, and Law 1009 of 1939 was introduced for "the defense and prestige of the race" granting the settlers more abusive power. There were also ordinances allowing all sorts of injustices including corporal punishment such as whipping natives. The local people remember settlers such as Bufow and Abayle (Bufalo and Availe) for their abuses.

As the acreages grew the provision of compulsory labor also increased and was extended to the interriverine region. In the Lower Juba area labor was imported from middle Juba and also from Bay upland. Besteman stated that, "Colonial land tenure laws did not affect land holdings in the middle Juba, as no European settlers expressed interest in establishing plantation so far upriver."[14] There may be some truth in this, but the author is demonstrating a colonial perspective on Somali history. In the first place, World War II unexpectedly interrupted the colonial domination of the country, i.e., before the implementation of Italy's plan that included the regulation of the Jubba (with a dam upstream at Bardhere) and the development of the Juba Valley. Secondly, indigenous land holdings may have not been affected, but the landowners were indeed affected since the compulsory labor affected the middle Juba. In addition, Dujuma-Bo'aale was a military zone for both colonial powers until the Jubaland was ceded to Italy in 1924, with negative consequences to the local population and the agriculture. Both powers have destroyed immense forestall wealth by clearing for military purpose one of the few tropical forests of Somalia. The rest was done by the Military regime during the resettlement in Dujuma in 1975.

The Duke of Abruzzi

Often pro-colonialist literature is consistent in exalting the Duke's business in the middle Shabelle. There, he founded an estate of 25,000 ha. Instead of seeking a concession from the administration like other Italian settlers, he directly negotiated with the local elders. Thanks to the subjugation of the indigenous people, he could count on their cooperation. In March 1912, Governor De Martino announced to the inhabitants of Mahadday that from that date the region was to be subjected to Italian authority. Colonial rule implies coercion, institution of a superior-inferior relationship, dismantling existing authority and leadership and its substitution with a docile, collaborative leadership, with whom "treaties" could be signed. It is not surprising that the elders agreed to let the Duke of Abruzzi, a prince of the Italian crown, seize 25,000 ha and establish a giant plantation.

Luigi di Savoia was nothing more than an ordinary capitalist whose methods differed somewhat from those of the parasitic pre-industrial type of colonialism carried out by Giolittians and Mussolinians. The Duke also reverted to compulsory labor in times of crisis. He used a system of tying the farmer to the land of the master with immoral criteria that were contrary to the ethics of a civilized society.

For example, those practicing polygamy and heads of families with many children were offered incentives or bonuses.

Colonial historians try to depict a totally different image of the Duke and his colonial enterprise. Lewis wrote, "Unlike earlier attempts at plantation farming in Somalia where settlers had obtained their land from the Administration of the colony, S.A.I.S. acquired both its land and much of its labor by direct contract with the local tribesmen (the Bantu Shidle)..." Lewis did not tell us explicitly why he praised the Duke of Abruzzi for acquiring the land directly or what was wrong with the administration's acquisition. The colonial Administration confiscated the land purely by force.

The Trusteeship Period (AFIS)

In 1949 at the UN, during discussions on the trusteeship of the former "Italian Somaliland," the US representative proposed the inclusion of a clause on "Land and National Resources" for the purpose of preventing Italy from continuing land confiscation in Southern Somalia. The proposal did not pass. S. Pankhurst described the proposal as "locking the stable after the horse is stolen" since all members of the Committee knew "that the native people had been evicted from the best of the land long before and that all natural resources believed to be capable of yielding a profit had passed into Italian hands." The Italian representatives Brusasca and Cerulli were however able to include in Article 15 the following provision, "The Administrating Authority shall not, without consent in each case of a majority of the members of Territorial Council, permit the acquisition by non-indigenous persons, or by companies or associations controlled by such persons, of any rights over land in the territory save on lease for a period to be determined by law."[15]

During the first five years of the Trusteeship, Italy administered Somalia through use of colonial systems and military occupation. When the Italian endeavor and repression could not curb the thrust of the independence movement after the mid-1950s, Italy moderated its policy. In the meantime, the banana monopoly was in place. Somali farmers and Italian consumers alike were penalized with this anachronistic institution. All the attention and input were going to the banana plantation, sacrificing the indigenous agriculture.

While the indigenous farmers who had lost their land were awaiting justice, the Italian administration (Amminstrazione Fiduciaria Italiana della Somalia-AFIS) drew up a new plan, which caused further harassment for farmers in the Shabelle area. The aim of the plan was to safeguard the Italian properties and divert the attention of the emerging Somali leadership to new opportunities. They were given irrigated farmlands along the river and provided with infrastructures such as roads; canals, drains and flood escape facilities. In essence, the Italian administrating authority lured the new Somali leadership at the expense of the local farmers by distributing plantations to them, a fact that would have dramatic consequences in the future agricultural development of the country.

Two barrages across the Shabelle River at Qoryoley and Falkero were built in 1958. Two main canals to irrigate "new lands" were diverted: Qoryoley canal (later called *Liibaan)* on the right bank and *Bulo Bokore* canal on the left bank. Upstream Jannale, beyond the Jannale barrage backwater, was provided with two smaller canals: *Jiddo,* to be used partly by the banana plantations, and *Malable* canal. *Fornari* canal (called by the locals Madulow) was opened on the right bank but exclusively for the existing banana plantations. All these works were realized in record time without proper surveying and up-to-date design. These works turned out to be a very inefficient hydraulic system. In addition, they were responsible for a series of adverse effects on the river, the consequences of which continues to be felt.

Liibaan canal has an average bed slope of zero and, therefore could hardly irrigate a small part of the claimed area. Falkero barrage paradoxically was located just six km downstream from Qoryoley barrage because of the lack of adequate topographic surveying. In addition, *Bulo Bokore* canal has an insufficient bed slope and is, thus, prone to excessive sedimentation. The designer also ignored the existence of a flood channel, *Far Fruqley,* which was offtaking just upstream of the new barrage and was able to divert about half of the river discharge into a swampy area.

All these works meant more expropriation of farmlands without compensation. After completion, the land was distributed to the emerging political class. The list of the new *aziendas* along B. *Bokore* canal resembled the roll-list of the Legislative Assembly. None of these new owners had been farmers before or could claim land in that area except for Hon. Ibrau Talassio. The poor peasants living in the villages of Abdi Ali, Bulo Bokore, Jerow, etc., who all were directly or indirectly victims of the previous Italian land seizure and compulsory labor, saw history repeating itself. Some of these farmers moved downstream just to be harassed by floods for another two decades until the expropriation for the resettlement of nomads stricken by famine in the mid-1970s caused them further disaster.

During the British military administration after World War II, many farmers became squatters in the Italian plantations and became successful farmers when they were allowed to farm the land. Others, joined by farmers from the Interriverine, who had also provided compulsory labor for the Italian plantations in the past, founded new villages further downstream on the river and collectively constructed small hand dug canals. Some of these small hydraulic works deserve admiration. On the middle Shabelle, small farmers moved upstream to found new farming villages. Also religious communities, *Jamea,* old and new ones, were established. Floods became a major enemy in all these areas, and until the mid-1970s, no administration provided them with flood protection schemes. But these farmers lived with the hope that better days of justice were on the horizon.[16]

The First Republic

The First Republic (FR) was responsible for the absence of land reform and for the deterioration of the conditions of riverine and interriverine farmers. But this will hardly surprise anyone familiar with the formation of the leadership of the FR. The fate of the FR was decided during the Trusteeship and its leadership was shaped by the AFIS. The change of attitude of the AFIS after the mid-1950s worked very well with the major independence movement, SYL, which became very cooperative with Italy. The new leadership of the SYL, led by the moderate Aden Abdulle Osman, surprised the country by cooperating with the Italians. The major opposition party to the SYL, the HDSM which was supposed to represent the interests of its constituency, the riverine and interriverine (*Digil and Mirifle*), disappointed everybody as well, and thus is equally responsible for the betrayal of the farmers of these regions.

As far as the land question is concerned, the possibility of revisiting the past land alienation effected by the Italians has become remote. The civilian regime, which inherited the monoculture of bananas from the past, exhibited great determination to continue export of bananas as a source of foreign currency. In its first Five Year Plan, bananas were at the top of the list in agriculture. Another intervention was the creation of ADC (Agricultural Development Corporation), which was supposed to alleviate the effects of cereal price fluctuations artificially created by merchants. The farmers most hit were those of Bur Hakaba and Baidoa.

The leadership of the FR, because dominated by *compradores* (a social class keen to speculative business with negligible interest in establishing the foundation for a national economy) did not show sensitivity to the problems of farmers. High officers, ministers and deputies themselves became plantation owners. Many Italians, in view of the future dismantling of the AMB (azienda monopolio banane) in Italy due to the conflict with the EEC (European Economic Community) policy, were ridding themselves of plantations by selling them or just appointing Somali representatives. The government took over the majority of the shares and participated in the sugar estate SAIS of Jowhar.

For many poor peasants in the riverine area, squatting on abandoned plantations was the only way to get access to irrigated land. Squatters often had to abandon plantations because of change of ownership or for other reasons, just to squat on another abandoned plantation. Some owners established agreements with the squatters to allow them to temporarily cultivate the land.

The FR was by no means the right government to solve the problems of agriculture in southern Somalia. It maintained the status quo and contributed to the decline of production and consequent deterioration of farmers' livelihood. It also postponed land reform indefinitely.

The Military Regime

The agricultural policy of the Military Regime (MR), if any existed, was undefined from the beginning. The MR attributed the failure of agriculture to the generic *mussuq-maasuq* (corruption) of the civilian regime and to middlemen and promised the elimination of the latter. On the other hand, the MR – contradicting scientific evidence that agricultural land is scarce in Somalia – asserted the thesis according to which Somalia is blessed with unlimited quantities of land and water resources, enough for those willing to tap them through hard work. The SRC (Supreme Revolutionary Council) admitted there were some land problems and established a "Justice Committee" to handle the matter. On the first anniversary of the coup, the SRC declared the adoption of Scientific Socialism as a panacea for all problems. Rhetoric about how to free the country of the evil of the exploiters (*dhiigmiirad*) and the middlemen was unleashed. The famous *Iskaa-wax-u-qabso* (self-help) schemes were launched. The riverine farmers were called to participate in a vast campaign to clear silt sedimentation from canals, construct new canals (without proper technical support), and fix mobile sand dunes, etc. Every type of soil was declared suitable for cropping. The MR, abusing the initial enthusiasm of the masses, dissipated farmers' energies in futile and gross schemes that became *hal bacaad lagu lisay* and which will be remembered for their lack of any scientific basis.[17]

The MR never admitted that banana plantations occupied the best soil of the valleys and that most of these plantations were uncultivated. Instead it vowed to boost the production of bananas. In fact, in 1970, a state banana board (*Ente Banana)* was established to be in charge of its export. In 1970, the production was 146,000 metric tons; in 1972 it rose to 186,000 tons; and by 1973, it was 156,000 tons. The contribution of banana to hard currency earning declined steadily from 1960 when it accounted for 75% of the total country's exports. Instead, livestock exports grew fast until, in 1979, they made up 75% of total exports. Livestock exports rose from 19 million So. Sh. in 1970, to 160 m So. Sh. in 1972, 10,589 m So. Sh. in 1978, while bananas were dropping to below 25% of the total export.

To improve crop production, the MR strengthened the ADC (Agricultural Development Corporation) by giving it the monopoly on cereal marketing. Farmers were ordered to sell all their harvest to the agency. The new price was fixed arbitrarily by the agency and soon became inadequate. Farmers were re-buying their products with tax added. This policy proved to be a real tragedy for food production because it forced many farmers – especially middle sized farmers who employed labor – to abandon farming.

With the adoption of "scientific socialism", the state was in control of all economic sectors. Agricultural Crash Programs were established on large areas of land to absorb unemployed youth from the urban areas. As the ultimate solution for agriculture the MR also identified the creation of large-scale state farms. State farms meant further expropriation of land, eviction of farmers, and drainage of resources. Besides these, state owned mega projects, several government agencies, and military and para-military corps seized land to "increase production of food." Land appropriation by these agencies was the cruelest acts of land expropriation since the colonial domination. Cooperatives Law No. 70 of 1973 was launched followed by Land Law No. 73 of 1975. The creation of state farms and the two laws definitely proved that the MR by no means was willing to undertake a land reform.

In 1973–74, the country experienced a severe drought. About 90,000 pastoralists were re-settled in the lower Shabelle and middle Juba, further expropriating small farmers. The three sites chosen were Kurtunwarey (downstream of Qoryoley), Sablale, (further downstream) and Dujuma in the middle Juba. At the first site, expropriation mainly affected small farmers in Madulow, Baarow, Kurtunwarey, and Iidow Guudow who lost their land. Baarow lost 300 ha. The land belonged to a community of mixed farming. Madulow farmers had lost their land at the end of the 1950s for *Fornari* canal, and now again they lost their land again. The majority of Kurtunwarey farmers lost their land. The resettlement in Kurtunwarey with "northern nomads" constituted a very cruel and shocking experience for the *Jiiddo* community. The loss of land and the disruption of livestock routes and ranges were combined with harassment by government officers and by newcomers who had no understanding of the plight of this community. Communication and conflict resolution were impossible because the *Jiiddu* people speak *Jiiddu* language and use *May* as a *lingua franca*. At the second site, Sablale, most of the land was not cultivated because of flooding, but persons living in and around Brava claimed the land, and no compensation was paid. Some farmers even had titles. In the 1950s and 1960s, Sablale was a swampy area. The biggest crime was committed against the environment at Dujuma. The area was covered by one of the rarest examples of tropical forest in Somalia with rare vegetation. In the 1920s, the British at Dujuma/Bo'aale had affected a similar land clearing for military purposes. The land was cleared without any plan or technical information and had to be abandoned. The only suitable land for cropping belonged to local farmers who were eventually evicted.

After the long drought the MR became addicted to food aid, which grew from only 5,000 tons in 1972 to 82,000 tons of cereal food in 1976. The figure grew to a record of 330,000 metric tons in 1980/81, 186,000 in 1981/82, 189,000 in 82/83, 177,000 in 83/84, 262,000 in 84/85, and 128,000 metric tons in 85/86. Somalia received as much aid as Ethiopia, a country with a population six to eight times larger. The failure of the state farms further encouraged the regime to rely on food aid, and this is believed to have had a negative effect on production because the food was flowing from refugee camps to the markets. From the 1970s, cereal production (sorghum and maize) increased, "but not fast enough to keep up with growth of urban population and demand."[18]

In the 1980s, pressure to move to privatization came from western countries, the International Monetary Fund (IMF), and the World Bank. Instead of distributing the land of the state farms to the original tillers, the MR prepared a program named *Ujahaynta Wax Soo Saarka* (orienting toward production). The land was distributed to government employees and other individuals. The program was preceded by the liberalization of cereal prices in 1984, which made food grain cropping attractive.

Land Law and Land Tenure

At the beginning, the regime allowed landless farmers to occupy abandoned or uncultivated plantations. (In the previous period, plantation owners or their representatives had prevented farmers from occupying these lands.) The cooperative law launched as the panacea for poor peasants did not help them, however. The *Ujeeddobadan* (service cooperative) required the peasants to own land. The *Tacabwadaag* (labor cooperative) in which the Ministry of Agriculture was supposed to provide land was not enforced. In some cases peasants were allowed to cultivate abandoned plantations, and, in other cases, unsuitable land difficult to irrigate was bush-cleared for cooperatives.

When the land Law No. 73 was introduced in 1975, it appeared to meet neither the needs of small farmers nor those of plantation owners. Small farmers were for no apparent reason required to own land and go through lengthy, expensive, and discouraging procedures just to have their land registered. Plantation owners with large areas often found that the law heavily trimmed their properties unless they associated with other individuals to establish a company for which they were not prepared. Thus, they found Law No. 73 an attempt to confiscate their land. Article 8 of the Law limited the size of the land that could be granted to individuals or families to 30 ha and to 100 ha for the banana plantations. However, these size limitations were not applied to state farms, cooperatives, or private companies.

Practice showed small farmers that possession of ownership title had little legal value and did not prevent expropriation by third parties or by the government. There was also a technical problem. The government failed to establish a cadastre system or an appropriate map to record and adequately plot farm boundaries of the land registered. In 1976, a topographic map of the country to the scale of 1:100,000 were prepared which was unsuitable for cadastre purpose because of the scale. This means that boundaries of registered farms were not plotted on the official map, thus leaving the properties exposed to claims from whomever.

In the mid-1980s, an unprecedented race for land took place both in rural and urban areas, especially in the capital. By the end of the 1980s, it is believed that there was not a single piece of land along the two rivers that remained unclaimed. Law No. 73, which could not be an instrument for land acquisition for small farmers, became a formidable means for upstarts and profiteers to become new owners of land. Even traditional access to water livestock (*hilo*), stock routes, and village lands were seized. Farmers who resisted and tried to protect their land were threatened or imprisoned and lost their land.

In her survey in a village of the middle Juba, Besteman gave shocking details. Only two out of 400 farmers were successful in achieving titles for their land. 217 farmers (60% of total) initiated the registration process without being able to complete it for lack of funds. She explained, "Titles in the district are being issued disproportionately to newcomers to the area and not to people who are permanently settled farmers."[19] The Department of Land Use and Irrigation in the Ministry of Agriculture was the most hostile office to the riverine farmers and after the mid-1980s was the main instrument for the expropriation of their land.

State Farms and Planatations

Excluding farms seized by Crash Programs, cooperatives, and autonomous agencies, the major irrigated state farms realized by the MR in the Juba Valley are:

Table 2: State-owned Plantation during the Military Regime

Project	Hectors
Juba Sugar Project (JSP)	10,000 ha
Mogambo (Phase I and II)	3,600 ha
Fanole	8,000 ha
Hoboy	5,000 ha (planning stage)
Total	

Due to the size of these projects, each one affected several villages. The late Ibrahim M. Abyan, in his study on the social impact of agricultural development in lower Juba, showed how minimal the benefits of these projects were, compared to the great harm they did. The Mogambo project affected villages such as Mogambo, Mana Moofe, Bulo Yaaq, Koban, Mashaqo, and some banana farms. Abyan reported that most of the village farmland was taken over by the first phase of the project without compensation, but only 40 farmers were offered land and only 20 persons were employed by the project. In 1979, the author, who was part of the Mogambo irrigation design team, surveyed and plotted on the map the farmland of these villages that fell inside the project boundary, which were more than 400 ha. Abyan reported that Juba Sugar Project (JSP) and Fanole affected about 56 villages in which "most of the peasants were expropriated of their land; others had their sources of water diverted or blocked, or their fields deliberately flooded to drain off the project farms." At Fanole some of the farmers were offered land in very poor soil, the "marine plain soil," which is a saline, compacted soil with poor drainability and therefore not suitable for farming. On Marerey, Abyan reported, "The villagers are traditional peasants. They used to farm 4,200 ha of land; all of it was taken over by the Project."[20]

Table 3: Shabelle Valley State Farms and Plantations

Location	Hectors
Afgoy-Mordile	1,500 ha
Barirre (Gizoma)	12,000 ha
Jannle-B.Marerta	2,500 ha
Balad Irrigation	5,000 ha
Jowhar Sugar Estate (SNAI)	10,000 ha
Baarrow	1,000 ha.
Shalambood	5,000 ha
Farxaane	5, 000 ha (planning stage)
Total	

In the Shabelle flood plain, all state projects had expropriated farmlands and evicted farmers without compensation. The Jannale Bulo Marerta project was developed not as a state farm, but when the land was distributed, many farmers did not get land. Farmers with political connections had the lion's share. Others benefited without even being inside the project area. To the poor peasants who were occupying abandoned plantations, an insufficient piece of land was given to be cropped as cooperative.

Not only did farmers lose land to these state farms, but also they were not even employed by them. The appointed managers and the officers were always strangers to the area, unable and unwilling to communicate with indigenous people who either spoke *May* or used *May* as *lingua franca*. Mogambo project headquarters was located at Mogambo village where people spoke *Chiziguli* and used *May* to communicate with outsiders, and the project officers spoke standard *Maxaatiri* Somali. Communication often required a chain of interpreters. Often villagers were expelled from government offices because they were not able to speak "Somali", as was the case in the interriverine regions where people speak *May*. This shows how the cultural values of specific clans are imposed as the "real" values of the nation. Abdi M. Kusow explains in detail in chapter one of this book how language and literature are used to remove segments of the society from the social boundaries of *Somaliness*.

In 1987, the *Ujahaynta* program was launched and state project lands were distributed to "private farmers" and the villagers witnessed their land being given away to "outsiders" who had never lived in the region. The effect was devastating. The families became dismembered because the youth abandoned the villages. In the late 1980s many young *Chiziguli speaking* were doing the most regarding jobs in the capital. Similar fates befell other villagers who lost their land to state farms. In the "locally financed projects" (Crash Program and farms of government agencies), the situation was similar. Afgoy suffered most from these projects because of its closeness to the capital. Farmers who used to have farms near the river were pushed to areas previously reserved for dry land farming.

Land Rush

Despite the fact that 10 to 13 percent of the total land is arable in Somalia, only a small portion of this land is irrigable. However, the MR and, before it, the civilian regime, insisted that there was an abundance of land and water resources in Somalia. In fact, hydrological studies carried out in the 1960s, 1970s, and 1980s showed that only 40 to 50,000 ha were irrigable by the Shabelle in *Gu season*, though a larger area can be irrigated during *Deyr* season. Juba Valley suffers from limited soil availability rather than limited water.

The civilian regime was preparing a land law before it was ousted by the coup. The law drafted in 1968 by the Ministry of Agriculture assisted by FAO was similar to Law No. 73. Somali entrepreneurs were limited in number in the 1960s, yet land acquisition took place during that period; land transactions however, were limited. In the 1970s, the MR discouraged and interrupted land alienation. Clause (e) of Art. 15, which authorized the government to confiscate any land which remained uncultivated for two years – which was applied in several cases-constituted a real threat to land owners in general. The provisions restricted land transactions. Art. 12, paragraph 1 and Art 14 paragraph 1, sub (c) forbade the transfer, the selling or the leasing of agricultural land.

The political and economical situation of the country changed dramatically in the 1980s. These changes greatly affected the land tenure in southern Somalia. It is hard to identify the factors that most contributed to the race for land after the mid-1980s. The following paragraphs contain a review of some changes, which may have paved the road to the land rush.

In 1983, Saudi Arabia stopped the import of live animals from Somalia for health reasons. The decision dramatically affected the country and the trade balance. Livestock exports had constituted 75% of the total export. The deficit of the trade balance became huge and inflation climbed. In 1984, the foreign debt increased by 143% and inflation rose by 92%, while agriculture sector growth was 10.6%. The pressure from the IMF and World Bank forced the MR to accept conditions that according to IMF were supposed to lead to a free market economy. The monopoly on agricultural product marketing by ADC was broken in 1984.

Despite the prevailing misery of the country, the MR allowed some social groups to accumulate a great deal of wealth. A new class emerged from the bureaucratic clique who became rich by accumulating a fortune from the empire they managed. Government contracts and supplies to the army, and easy bank loans without guarantees became heaven for privileged businessmen and profiteers of all kinds, especially if they had clan affiliations with the presidency. Before, the "pie" was limited to the clan affiliation of the strong persons of the regime led by Siad Barre, the sharing was somehow a cross-clan affair. After Siad Barre's car accident in 1986, the circle was restricted. However, for those in Barre's family, getting rich was made even easier as no rules or laws were observed in their case.

After the liberalization of crop prices in 1984, farming became profitable. The internal fruit market also expanded due to changes in the transportation sector and the diet of the town population. Transportation was partially left by the MR to the private sector. In the 1980s this sector grew fast, alimented by the "import" of vehicles and trucks from the gulf market. This had a great impact on the rural areas. Light trucks and busses, *sitey, xaajiya, caasi* pushed by the competition, adventured more and more onto rural roads, making possible the flow of commodities and persons to markets. Crops and other commodities could be rushed to standard and improvised markets.

Remittance from some 150,000 workers in the Gulf, combined with favorable exchange rates in the black market, contributed to the accumulation of capital. Many emigrants rebuilt their family homes and started small businesses. Privates also established a number of successful factories producing construction materials or other goods without assistance from the government. The state factories, undersold to persons with connections to the "ruling family" during *Ujahaynta*, did not show any signs of life. Equipment and machines were idle until they were looted during the civil war and sold abroad.

Cultivation of fruit trees expanded dramatically and was aided by the facilities offered by the Grapefruit Project, as well as a sometimes-forced campaign, which was launched by the Ministry of Agriculture to encourage planting of fruit trees. The response of small farmers to the campaign was excellent because they hoped to protect their farms in this way. New fruits and vegetables, such as avocado, cantaloupes, etc. were introduced and appeared on the market. Despite the disaster experienced in state farms, farming bananas and other fruits was profitable for private entrepreneurs. In the 1980s, Italy invested in the banana sector. Somalfruit, an Italian-Somali joint venture established for the export of fruits, swallowed most of the Italian investment in the sector.

In the 1970s and in early 1980s, land transactions were limited. They never stopped totally since transactions in which land values were declared zero and the selling of farm facilities such as housing, infrastructures, fruit trees, etc. were legal. After 1984 there was a drastic change in land transactions, land transfers and registrations. A race for land started which reached its peak after the mid-1980s. A similar "land rush" occurred in urban land in major towns and was massive in the capital and major towns. During this period the city of Mogadishu expanded enormously. In the late 1970s, the capital had 600,000 inhabitants, and in the census of 1986, the population was 1,200,000 inhabitants. "Land hunters" swallowed the small farms, *goof*, for the production of fodder for livestock, located near the capital, and their owners were forced to undersell and move to the interior. With the expansion of the city, services also expanded greatly. What triggered the "land rush" has not been fully understood and this subject deserves more attention by researchers. Besteman reported that perhaps considering the high rate of inflation; land offered certain security in maintaining the value. The task force "Land Tenure Rearrangement" of the Somali National University in Italy asserted that cornering land had a speculative aim since lack of irrigation water makes land limited. The report also stated that by 1988, 65% of the irrigable land in Somalia was registered as concessions.[21] The figure is in agreement with those given by Besteman.

The data gathered by Besteman for the middle Juba show clearly that land registration rose drastically in 1984.

Whatever the real cause behind the race to agricultural land, its violence and speed were unprecedented. Those who were not willing to sell their land were coerced. Small farmers who could not afford to buy pumps in areas where gravity irrigation was not possible were stripped of their land and pushed further into the bush. Farmers with farms close to the river and main roads were targeted. Fallow and grazing lands were declared uncultivated. Luuq farmers lost their land (400 ha) in Halbo for a refugee settlement in 1978. Since that time, they have lost even more land because the land race did not spare that region. The land race on Juba reached the proposed Baardhere reservoir site. In the Upper Juba, the indigenous people no longer have farms on the right bank. In the Upper Juba region (luuq and Bardera) things were exasperated by the announcement of the Bardera dam project. This unleashed a rush by the president's clan to forcefully grab land and disposes farmers in the region.

Land Registration from 1980 to 1987 (# of Farms Registered)

Year	1980	'81	'82	'83	'84	'85	'86	'87
Middle Jubba	23	43	(17)	31	81	247	157	127
Jilib	7	8	(1)	12	17	40	58	44

* Total registered farms nationwide: 13,561 – 256,000 ha – of which 75% irrigable.
** Adopted from C. Besteman.
*** 1881–82 was a flood year in Middle Juba.

Government agency lands and states farms were not spared either. For instance, the Foreign Minister seized land belonging to the Agricultural Secondary School that was adjacent to the main bridge of Afgoy. The *Generalissimo's* son seized farmlands at Barirre to make a large and fortified estate. He also obstructed a traditional livestock right of way to the river. The access road and the farm were implemented with government equipment. To meet the needs of the new land holders, the MR implemented four bridges on the Shabelle which were financed by the EEC in 1989.

The Fall of the Military Regime

Except for the Bakol region, the people in the riverine and interriverine did not engage in armed struggle although they opposed the military regime. After the seizure of the capital they welcomed USC (United Somali Congress) in the hope of defending their homes and farmlands. When the army of M. Siad Barre fled the capital to seek refuge in the south, it looted crops and animals and killed hundreds of interriverine inhabitants. Bay region, following the example of Bakol, organized it and established the SDM (Somali Democratic Movement) knowing that the events of January were only the prelude to a series of battles and a full-blown war.

A self-styled SDM leadership made headquarters in Mogadishu far from the interriverine and detached itself from the riverine populations. Delegations from the agricultural riverine and the coastal areas such as Jannale, Qoryooley and Brava requested that local SDM leadership to be organized and trained so they could defend themselves and their farms. But they went back disappointed. Later on, the SDM leadership split into two factions. The faction allied to USC-Aydeed was assisted and the interriverine region was liberated from the remnants of Mohamed Siad Barre in May of 1992. However, the USC militia occupied the interriverine and committed crimes against the masses.

During the civil war, not only were the riverine people killed and looted but also the whole area was subjected to a total clean up. USC militia, followed by SNF (remnants of the regime) militia, took anything worth taking and the region was left bereft of all goods. Generators, agricultural and construction equipment, machines, etc., were taken away by a well-organized "looting incorporations." The riverine people saw their land again occupied by all types of factions, especially SNF and USC. When the USC elements were asked the reason for the occupation of farmlands, their answer was that the farmlands they occupied belonged to the *faqash* (remnants of the MR). The factions, in their reconciliation conferences, have included the land issue and looted properties in their agenda of discussions. However, they are not questioning the legality of the MR on the land issue at all.[22]

Conclusion

The riverine and the interriverine people have lost their land and suffered from the land rush. While they were being stripped of their land, they have been emarginated, oppressed and humiliated. Appointees of the MR-individuals from far regions and strangers to there culture and customs-administered their regions. These were "strangers" with whom they were not even able to communicate due to the language barrier.

It is a common belief among riverine and interriverine people that a great deal of the civil war was nothing but a continuation of the land rush at its highest stage, i.e., one faction eliminating another in order to take possession of the fertile farmlands. All transactions, land transfers, concession grants, and all registrations, which occurred under Law No. 73, must be reversed and declared illegal and invalid.[23]

Notes

1.   For more information about this issue, see Mukhtar, M.H. "The Emergence and the Role of Political Parties in the Inter-riverine Regions From 1074 to 1060." *Ufahamu*, 18, no. 2 & 3, UCLA Press, Los Angeles 1989.

2.   Lewis, I.M. *A Modern History of Somalia*, (*Boulder*, Westview Press, 1992) 92–94.

3.   Pankhurst, S.E., *Ex-Italian Somaliland*, (New York, Philosophical Library, 1951) 88.

4.   Hess, Robert. L., *Italian Colonialism in Somalia*, (Chicago: University of Chicago Press, 1966) 186.

5.   Iraci, Leone, "Per una demistificazione del colonialismo italiano: il caso della Somalia", *Terzo Mondo* Gen-Mar. (1969): 66.

6. Besteman, Catherine L., "Land Tenure, Social Power, and Legacy of Slavery in Southern Somalia, (Ph.D. diss., University of Arizona, 1991), 389.

7. Hess, Robert L., Italian Colonialism in Somali, 110.

8. Laredo, Haile M., the Building of an Empire, Italian Land Policy and Practice in Ethiopia 1935–1941(Oxford: Clarendon Press, 1994) 16.

9. Hess, R.L., Italian Colonialism in Somalia, 91.

10. Cassanelli, L.V., *The Shaping of Somali Society* (Philadelphia: University of Philadelphia Press, 1982)

11. Bohen, Adu A. *African Perspective on Colonialism*, (Baltimore: John Hopkins University Press, 1992) 60.

12. Cremascoli, Bruno. *Il Paese di Punt*, (Milano: Edizioni Unicopli, 1987) 214.

13. De Vecchi, C.M., *Orizzonti d'Impero*, 323.

14. Besteman, C.L., "Land Tenure, ..." 391.

15. Pankhurst, S.E., *Ex-Italian Somaliland*, 379.

16. The author in 1974–76 designed and supervised the execution of the first flood bund in the Qoryoley area and a river cut-off project for the purpose of reclaiming the swamps of Afgoy Yarey. None of the 5000 ha reclaimed land went to the local farmers. Ironically, the land race combined with inefficient use of irrigation water has greatly reduced floods in the lower Shabelle basin.

17. Literally: "A she-camel milked in the sand."

18. Raikes, Philip, *Modernizing Hunger*, (Portsmouth, NJ: Heinemann, 1988) 191–192.

19. Besteman, C.L., "Land Tenure, ..." 404.

20. Abyan, I.M. , Development and Its Social Impact on the Local Community in the Juba Valley, *Proceedings of the third Congress of Somali Studies*, Rome, 1986, 404–409.

21. Mohamed, Khalif S., "Riassetto Fondiario, in Programma per docenti dell'Universita' Nazionale Somala, Sottogruppo: "Somalia-Emergenza in Campo Agro-zootecnico", Firenze, 1993.

22. For more on this subject see African Rights publication: Land Tenure and the Creation of Famine, and the Prospects for Peace in Somlia, Discussion Paper no. 1, 1993.

23. An earlier version of this study was presented at the 37th Annual Meeting of the African Studies Association (ASA). In Toronto, Ont. Canada in November 5, 1994.

Chapter Ten
The Collapse of the Somali Banking System

Abdulqadir Arif Qassim

THIS ESSAY WILL EXPLORE the reasons behind the collapse of the Somali Banking system. The paper will establish that the legacy those colonial rulers bequeathed the country contributed to its failure. It will explore how the monetary policies and banking system pursued by the parliamentary regime continued that legacy. Finally, it will analyze how the military regime's shifting policies and nomadic management affected the Somali banking system.

Pre-Colonial Somali Currency

In ancient times, Somalia was well connected by sea routes with the eastern coast of Africa, the Middle East, southern Asia and China. Sea travel was facilitated by its geographic location and by the regular monsoon winds. Many studies confirm that the coastal cities of Somalia had trade relations with the Ancient World, especially with Egyptians, Arabs and Persians. A Greek guide for mariners of the Red Sea and Indian Ocean, written about 150 AD, tells about regular trade between Red Sea ports and East Africa (Somalia, Kenya and Tanzania).[1] Ibn Battuta, a Moroccan traveler, visited Zeila, Mogadishu and other ports in 1331. He described Mogadishu as a flourishing trade center with a large textile industry.

In the nineteenth century the Somali coastal centers not only exported commodities but also acted as an intermediary between the overseas traders and overland African traders. Long distance caravan trade flourished throughout regions of Somalia and attracted Western and Arab merchants to its network system.[2] It is not known when the bartering system ceased to exist in the coastal cities, but coins were used in the Benadir as far back as 1200 AD. There is a record of more than seven thousand coins minted in Mogadishu. The mint operated between the 13th and 16th century under 23 different rulers of Mogadishu. Also, Chinese coins dating from 960 to 1279 have been found in the southern coast, while Egyptian coins of the 1300s have been found in the Adal towns of the northern regions.[3] The Maria Theresa Thaler coins, issued in Austria after 1780, were used widely in Somalia. The rural and pastoral community of the horn of Africa esteemed the Maria Theresa not only for its intrinsic silver value, but also for its easily recognizable design. Also, Mombassa and Zanzibar "besas" were used in Benadir as fractions of the Thaler. The Indian rupee was also used in Somalia.[4] In the pastoral communities, particularly in northern Somalia, the traditional system of barter exchange remained until the colonial occupation.[5]

The Colonial Economy

The opening of the Suez Canal in 1869 granted the Horn of Africa a new economic opportunity. It created competition between European colonial powers desiring raw material to feed their industries and markets for selling manufactured goods. In Somalia, British middlemen took an interest in the northern regions, using them as supply centers for fresh meat for their garrison in Aden. Meanwhile, Italians took an interest in the southern regions, establishing huge plantations for export crops. Both colonial administrations imposed taxes not only to increase their revenues but also to drive Somalis from rural and pastoral activities. Somalis received very few social services in return for their money. In fact, the first veterinary service in the northern regions did not appear until 1924, after the United States of America threatened to embargo skin imports from Aden and neighboring countries unless provided with veterinary health certificates.[6] In addition, neither colonial administration invested much capital for development. From 1901 to 1920, Britain devoted its resources, grants and revenues, to military expenditures. Italians allocated 55% of their budget to military expenditure between 1931 and 1940.

The Italian administration was determined to promote foreign settlers' interests at the expense of the native Somalis. The colonial policy focused on production of cash crops. The consequence of that policy was confiscation of farmlands and compulsory labor recruitment, which adversely affected the native economy.[7] The production of subsistence crops, which had been developed long before colonial occupation in Somalia, received only negligible attention. Therefore, food for local consumption had to be imported. The colonial currencies caused a flood of imported goods into Somalia, which jeopardized local output. These colonial currencies facilitated tax collection and development of colonial banks, but the lending policy of these banks excluded Somali traders and entrepreneurs. Somalis were also denied job opportunities in the colonial banks. As A. Adu Boahen observed:

"[Finally] the monetary policies pursued by all the colonial powers must be held partly responsible for the present underdeveloped state of the continent. Under these policies, all the colonial currencies were tied to those of the metropolitan countries, and all their foreign exchange earnings were kept in metropolitan countries and not used for internal development."[8]

The Colonial Impact

Until 1920, the Italian colonial effort was spent on the domination of Benadir and the inter-riverine regions. The conquest of Benadir and the inter-riverine area coincided with the time when in Italy the Fascist wind was blowing. The colonial army completed its occupation of the northeastern portion of southern Somalia in 1927, when it consolidated its power in Benadir and the inter-riverine regions. The Fascist regime's goal in the southern regions of Somalia was mainly to settle a sizeable number of Italian farmers in the Shebelle and Jubba fertile lands. Before December 8, 1910, the Indian rupee and Maria Theresa coins were used for trade in Somalia and the coastal cities of Aden, Mombassa and Zanzibar. On June 26, 1911, the Italian Colony administration issued the Italian rupee in silver coins based on a fixed nominal value of 1.68 lira.[9] The new rupee replaced both foreign currencies in circulation as well as the Italian "besa." The Italian "besa," issued in 1905 and made of nickel and bronze, was used as a cent but failed to circulate after local traders rejected it.

As World War 1 affected the Italian economy, the depreciation of the lira posed difficulty for the colonial monetary system in Somalia. Besides, the high cost of silver caused the rupee's intrinsic value to exceed its nominal value. In September 1919, the Italian rupee was re-valuated. In 1920, Banca d'Italia established a branch in Mogadishu functioning as a colonial central bank designed to promote its interest in Somalia. The branch became the first foreign bank in Somalia, and immediately issued the first bank notes of the Italian rupee.[10] In June 18, 1925, the Italian lira was put into circulation; meanwhile, the rupee, which had lost ground in East African markets, continued as legal tender until July 1, 1926. The introduction of the lira in southern Somalia served as a connection between local consumption and Italian markets. When Italy gained Juba land from the British administration in 1925, Banca d'Italia opened a second branch in Kismayo.

The fascist policy in Somalia, the availability of fertile land for agriculture, and the introduction of metropolitan money instruments attracted many Italians to settle in Somalia. In 1932, the Cassa di Risparmio di Torino established in Mogadishu the first commercial bank in Somalia. In 1938 Cassa di Risparmio di Torino transferred its activities in Somalia to another Italian bank, the Banco di Napoli. Before 1940, Italian bank lending to Italian firms amounted to 1,014,139,910 liras of which 22% was for agriculture. Although direct grants by the Italian government to Italian firms are not known, two Italian companies enjoyed loans of about 131,000,000 liras.[11] Private banks denied loans to Somali traders because the lending operations were under the control of the colonial administration. The Fascist administration was devoted to promoting the foreign settlers' interests at the expense of the native population. Moreover, they introduced a law that excluded Somalis from competition with Italians. Para-state monopolies were created to pass every profitable activity into Italian hands.

The British Currency and Banking

After the defeat of Italy in World War II, the British gained control over all Somali territories except the French protectorate. At that time (1941), the Italian lira was the only money in circulation, and it continued to be used as a credit instrument together with the East African Shilling. In 1943, Barclays Bank (D.C. & O.) started to operate in Mogadishu, replacing the Italian banks. The Mogadishu branch of Barclays Bank became the first British bank operating in Somalia. The Italian banks were forced to close their Somali activities after the defeat. In the early stages of British occupation in Somalia, the lira was exchanged with the East African shilling at the rate of 3.50 lira for 1 EA shilling. But the lira was losing ground day by day until it lost market value and was no longer accepted as a means of payment. As the Italian lira failed to circulate, the East African shilling became the sole currency circulating in Somalia. The EA shilling had been issued after 1920, when one currency board was established for the British East African colonies.[12] It had been introduced into British Somaliland during the early 1940s. The East African shilling was linked with the value of sterling in London and after the Italian defeat; its circulation was expanded in Somalia, Eritrea and Ethiopia. The circulation of the British colonial currency facilitated the penetration of British banking institutions in Somalia. Before the 1950s, banking business in British Somaliland was conducted through an Aden branch of Messrs. Cowasjee Dinshaw Bros.[13] In 1952; the National Bank of India established a branch in Hargeysa and in 1954 in Berbera. In 1959, the National Bank of India transferred its activities in British Somaliland to National Grindlays Bank. Despite the fact that Britain dominated northern Somalia for about a century, the colonial power and its banking institutions gave negligible attention to the development of the infrastructure of the local market. The British colonial administration lending policy was not much different than the Italian colonial one.

Trusteeship – The Limited Program of AFIS

In the 1950s the former Italian Somaliland became a United Nations Trusteeship territory. The obligation of the Italian Trusteeship was to administer the territory for a transitional period of 10 years leading to independence. During that transitional period, the Italian administration (Amministrazione Fiduciaria Italiana della Somalia) was requested to foster the development of free political institutions and promote the economic advancement and self-sufficiency of the inhabitants.[14] In the early years of the trusteeship, the administration's effort was primarily directed toward suppressing the nationalist opposition. The AFIS invested much capital in maintaining law and order. The limited programs of AFIS, incompetence, corruption and colonialist sentiments hindered the development of the economy.[15] The AFIS supported Italian plantation owners in regaining the land they had abandoned during the British military occupation. The plantation owners emerged with a speculative aim, leading to a banana monoculture in the best-irrigated land at the expense of diversified agricultural production.

It was in 1954 that a Somali credit institution, "Credito Somalo" was founded in Mogadishu. The new bank, Credito Somalo, was designed to provide short-term loans to the private sector. In that year a seven-year development plan was instituted for the first time in Somalia. The plan advanced by the United Nations and USICA (United States International Cooperation Administration, later US-AID), was mainly concerned with the livestock and agricultural sectors.[16] In the 1954–55 budget, a plan was proposed to establish a credit institution for medium and long-term loans, but it was rejected. Somali currency was issued as legal tender under the ordinance No. 14 of May 15, 1950. The new currency "Somalo" (commonly called the Somali Shilling) was covered with fine gold of 0.124414 gr. and was convertible to Italian lira. One Somalo was equivalent to 87.50 liras.[17] The Somalo became the single monetary unit of the country and replaced the East African Shilling circulating in Southern Somalia. As the British, after the arrival of AFIS, withdrew their involvement in Somalia, Barclays Bank closed its Mogadishu business. In the meantime, Banca d'Italia and the Italian private banks (Banca di Roma and Banco di Napoli), which had ceased their activities during the British occupation in Somalia, restarted their business during AFIS. Later in 1957–58, 60% of the Somali currency was covered with convertible currencies (Pound sterling and US dollars).

During the AFIS administration, the Credito Somalo opened branches in Kismayo, Merka and Baidoa. Although banking institutions had been operating in Somalia for about half a century, it was Credito Somalo which first recruited native employees. Previously, colonial banks had denied job opportunities to Somalis, preventing them from acquiring training and experience in the banking field. The Credito Somalo's management was in Italian hands before independence. The low level of staff training and lack of managerial knowledge and experience contributed to the failure of the bank after independence. A Somali fund "Cassa per la Circolazione Monetaria della Somalia-Somalcassa" was created in Rome. Its first task was to control Somali currency in circulation and to lend short-term credit to the trusteeship administration. The Somalcassa was represented in southern Somalia by the Banca d'Italia branch in Mogadishu. In 1959, the function of Somalcassa was further extended to issuing of banknotes and foreign currency exchange. The rate of exchange between the Somalo and the Italian lira became subject to market.

Post-Colonial Era – The Beginning of The Crisis

The Somali National Bank was created on June 30, 1960, under the decree No. 3/1678.[18] The bank was designed to be an independent central bank and replaced both the Somalcassa and the Banca d'Italia branch in Mogadishu. On July 1, 1960, the northern and the southern regions (British and Italian Somaliland) merged as one independent and sovereign state. Neither of the colonial administrations had prepared skillful cadres to lead the banks after independence.[19] As a result, the bank's executive management was in the hands of expatriates, even though the president (who later became governor) was Somali. Until independence, each region has had its own currency, trade, payment, and fiscal systems.[20] These were substantially different. The First Republic's monetary policy focused primarily on the unification of those systems left behind by colonial administrations. To achieve that objective, the Somalo was introduced in the northern region, although the East African shilling continued to circulate under an agreement with the British. Subsequently a unified national customs tariff was established.

In August 1961, the Somali National Bank opened a branch in Hargeysa. The head office of the bank as well as all its branches carried out both central and commercial banking operations. A special law authorized the Somali National Bank to perform commercial bank business in order to compete with foreign banks operating in Somalia. In the same year, the Somalo was substituted for the East African shilling, and from that time on, the whole country had only one currency. An Egyptian bank established a branch in Mogadishu in that year. The Bank de Port Said became the first Arab commercial bank to operate in Somalia. After 1960, the management of the Credito Somalo was taken over by Somalis and a branch was opened in Berbera. The Somalo was substituted, after a few years of independence, with a new currency named "Somali shilling." The new currency had the same denomination of banknotes and coins as the Somalo, but the designs were completely different.

In 1963, a credit section for medium and long-term loans was established within Credito Somalo. The section, which later became the Somali Development Bank, was designed to promote new economic activities. Collaterals as well as personal guarantees secured these local and foreign commercial bank loans. Subsistence producers, farmers and pastoralists, however, did not possess the necessary requirements (improved farm land or improved urban real estate) to qualify for bank grants. This lack of investment capital hindered the small local producers' attempts to increase their production. In 1964, the government introduced an integrated system of trade and payment. Yet the monetary policy did not attempt to liberalize the lending system restrictions. Moreover, the standardization of a national custom tariff and the equalization of government salaries had an adverse effect on the standard of living of the employees in the northern region.[21] Neither of the development plans launched by the civil regime granted appreciable attention to the production sector. The leadership of the First Republic focused on export, which was the main foreign resource of the country. The livestock industry was entirely in the hands of private Somali producers and dealers, while Italian settlers owned the banana plantations. After 1960, privileged bureaucrats and traders purchased some of the plantations. Although the ownership changed hands somewhat, the banana crops raised for export remained in the hands of the Italian monopoly.

In 1967, the Middle East War adversely affected Somali exports and the Somali National Bank's reserves. The closure of the Suez Canal doubled the length of the sea route to Italy. As a result, Somali bananas faced more intense competition in the sole importer market. The devaluation of the British pound sterling caused another loss to the bank's reserves.[22] Despite the decline of foreign exchange earnings and bank reserves, the trend of import-dependence increased. Intermediaries connected to the parliamentary arena dominated the importation business. The State petit bourgeois was the major holder of private assets. Many politicians and bureaucratic officers were directly or indirectly controllers of business activities. The post-independence state inherited a chronic budget situation, which led it to remain dependent on debits (internal and external) and foreign aid, not only for development projects but also for budgetary support. The Somali National Bank had standby arrangements with the International Monetary Fund in order to meet the deficit in the balance of payments.

In 1968, the Somali National Bank absorbed the Credito Somalo, which was on the verge of bankruptcy. The absorption of the bank was not caused solely by debtors' insolvency, marginal profit and competition. Lack of savings collection, lack of awareness of market dynamics, and the colonial legacy (see page 8) also contributed to its failure. In the same year, the National Grindlyas Bank opened a branch in Mogadishu. In the post-colonial government, the expatriate commercial banks concentrated their business in the main urban centers. They engaged in granting medium and short-term credit to the elite farmers and traders. These banks avoided appointing Somalis to decision-making positions. The Somali National Bank, however, carried out intensive training programs (internal and external), which contributed to the formation of the bank's professional cadres. The bank attempted to extend its activities through the regional capitals, but poor communication appears to have deterred banking development in the remote districts. During the colonial administrations, bank savings from small traders, urban working classes, city dwellers, and rural and pastoral producers were almost nonexistent. In the First

Republic bank, domestic savings strategies for attracting new domestic investors were inefficient; also traditional financial practices and illiteracy may have prevented some native customers from investing.[23] The Somali banking institutions underestimated or were incapable of soliciting grass-roots participation in the economy. The vision of monetary policy of the country was based on nomadic thoughts and practices, since pastoral folks dominated the policy-making positions. Their tradition has limited saving tendency comparing with other local customs – city dwellers and agricultural culture.

In March 1969, the constitution of the Somali National Bank was amended and its functions, commercial and central, were separated. The bank's lending policy was also revised. The Somali National Bank and the Somali Development Bank were allowed to extend medium and long-term credit, while the commercial banks were limited to granting only short-term credit to the private sector, particularly outside of the main urban areas. Before the civil government could implement this reform, a military coup d'etat seized the country.

The Socialist Banking System

The monetary policy of the military regime primarily focused on the rehabilitation of the banking system. The former government had suffered from economic instability, which partly explained the military coup d'etat. The new regime introduced an austerity program to reduce budget deficits. The budget cut off affected mainly the salaries and allowances of civil servants. That policy was largely aimed at settling the external and the internal debts of the country, as Somalia had inherited a chronic budget deficit situation from the colonial administrations. The regime introduced *Xisaabi xil ma leh*[24] policy aimed to crackdown national resource looters of civilian administration. This policy created perplexities among the business elite connected with the former administration. The result was a banking panic, which led to a shortage of the Somali shilling in circulation at the end of 1969.[25] On May 7, 1970; the Government nationalized foreign banks, petroleum companies, the Mogadishu Power Station and the Jowhar Sugar Factory. These firms had been criticized for exporting high profits out of the country instead of reinvesting them in the further development of the country. The nationalized banks included the Banca di Roma, Banco di Napoli, the National Grindlays Bank, and the Bank de Port Said. The regime defined their act as being in the national interest. The military junta believed that the seized assets could best be operated by the state-owned enterprises for the benefit of the country. In fact, nationalization facilitated efficient exchange control measures, which considerably increased the reserves of the Somali National Bank in 1970 and 1971.[26]

The military government attempted to reduce unemployment through the introduction of crash programs and self-help schemes. The implementation of these projects resulted in a considerable increase in domestic production. Nevertheless, the regime continued its national public plan and took over the food importation business and the banana export industry. On October 21, 1970, the first anniversary of the coup d'etat, the military regime declared that the country would follow the path of "scientific socialism." The regime's aspiration was to make the country self-sufficient through centralized planned economy. Under this system, a number of programs were launched which brought the country's economy under the control of state-run monopolies and cooperatives. In January 1, 1971, the banking system was again restructured and two commercial banks were established – the Somali Commercial Bank and the Somali Savings and Credit Bank. The new banks, as public owned institutions, were designed to promote the socialist economy. Nevertheless, the monetary policy of the regime also considered the need for a mixed economy.[27] the commercial banks attempted to extend credit facilities to the private sector, particularly to the light industries, but the Somali Development Bank lending policy continued to promote mainly state-owned industries and socialist cooperatives.

In 1975, the banking system was further reorganized. The Somali National Bank became the Somali Central Bank. The Somali Commercial Bank and the Somali Savings and Credit Bank merged as one commercial bank, the Somali Commercial and Savings Bank. The main objective of the unification was to rationalize the activities of the two state-owned commercial banks operating in a small market in the same line of business. In the same year, Somalia and Libya agreed to establish a joint bank for international trade development, which would be based in Mogadishu.[28] However, the project was aborted before it was implemented. After the failure of the trade development bank project, the Somali Commercial and Savings Bank became the sole commercial bank of the country. Although management was unified, the Somali Commercial and Savings Bank failed to eliminate the superfluous staff inherited from the former banks. Moreover, the banking institutions, as public-owned institutions, were required to annually recruit a certain number of high school graduates without considering their staffing needs. The regime adopted policy to maximize employment while ignoring cost reduction strategies for state-owned enterprises. Besides, the Somali Commercial and Savings Bank was required to further extend its domestic branches throughout the country. The establishment of new branches was partly based on political reasons rather than business opportunities. The Siyad Barre policy was devoted to promoting certain clan's interests at the expense of the remaining population.

In the mid 1970s, the Somali Commercial and Savings Bank credit instruments were expanding, in spite of the growing trade imbalance in some public enterprises. The bank institutions attempted to resist requests for loans from state-owned enterprises', but the government pressured it to cover their financial needs.[29]

The commercial bank's credit system was periodically subject to the auditing control of the central bank. The Central Bank of Somalia had power to regulate national banking institutions and their credit system. But day to day operations in the banking institutions were conducted using obsolete methods which could not keep pace with the rapid expansion of financial markets. The state owned enterprises were inefficient and wasteful, placing a significant drain on the resources of commercial banks. Military officers held the top management positions of publicly owned enterprises. President Siyad Barre used to appoint his opponents to the executive positions of the state monopolies to eliminate them from military headquarters.

The banking system of the socialist regime continued to grant funds to public owned enterprises and tolerated their financial malpractice. The Somali Central Bank issued new banknotes to replace those inherited from the post-colonial government, while encouraging the socialist projects. The design of the banknotes incorporated pictures of local agricultural and industrial production and Somali script. This was aimed at encouraging the self-sufficiency production program. The agricultural programs' expenses were elevated from 10 percent to 29.1 percent of the budget within a couple of years. Despite the regime's attempts to increase the self-sufficiency of the country, the introduction of state price controls (retail trade and farm production) and periodic droughts created a severe food shortage. A black market continued to develop at the expense of the grass-roots population, particularly civil service workers with fixed salaries.

Although the regime was the largest employer in the country, the government failed to readjust employees' salaries.[30] Consequently, the high remuneration of the oil boom Arab countries attracted Somali workers (qualified, skilled and unskilled labor). As Somali workers in Arabia began to remit funds to Somalia, private hard currency collectors started to operate in Saudi Arabian markets and later in the Gulf countries. The Somali Commercial and Savings Bank, as a public monopoly, failed to improve its networks sufficiently to compete with the private collectors. Moreover, inefficient exchange control measures, lack of property rights and the fixed exchange rate prevented workers' hard currency earnings from channeling into the banking system. This gave a comparative advantage to remittance collectors who used to transfer money at some favorable rates. The workers earned enough money to support their families and relatives in Somalia and their remittances, "Hawaalad", constituted the largest source of foreign exchange in the country.[31]

In 1976, the regime introduced the Franco Valuta system, despite the considerable foreign exchange reserves of the Somali Central Bank.[32] The purpose behind that policy was to stop underground trading activities and to cover the importation of certain local needs with the remittances. This system allowed Somali importers who had available foreign currency outside the country to import certain commodities under special license. The goods imported through the Franco Valuta system were mostly luxuries and did not reduce the need for capital equipment for development. While the workers' remittances in foreign currency remained for the most part outside the banking system, domestic savings increased as families and relatives of migrant workers received Hawaalad in local currency.

In 1977, the regime mobilized the country's resources for the Ethiopian conflict. The war situation and clientelist politics of the regime (using public enterprises' resources for recruiting and maintaining support) gave advantage to some loyal speculators who easily enriched themselves. Ali K. Galaydh rightly observed:

> "The special circumstances of the war gave Siyad Barre almost a free hand. At the time very few suspected that he was diverting the funds for his personal use. But Abdi Hoosh, among others, who had direct access to the president, became wealthy members of the "merchants of the war." The patronage horse was very much out of the barn, and this obviously had an impact on the functioning of the state institutions and the perceptions of the public."[33] XIII, New Jersey 1990, p. 18.

In 1978, the demand for foreign currency increased and terms of payment for workers' remittances changed. The workers' remittances were to be paid (in local currency) to their families in advance or at least upon receipt of hard currency. The new terms were not convenient for most businessmen's local accounts (liquidity position). The merchants and traders used to collect workers' earnings on a promissory system based on trust, which allowed them a large volume of business activity. Escalating inflation, however, influenced the market terms, and the high demand of war speculators and public-owned enterprises that had a favorable financial position compared to that of most merchants. Some businessmen took advantage of the circumstances and avoided the bureaucracy of the banking lending system by arranging for illegal private transactions with some opportunistic bank branch managers.[34] It was then that certain branches of the Somali Commercial and Savings Bank began to lend merchants underground credits through "Ok funds."* Despite the political orientations and the introduction of the death penalty, corruption, looting, and nepotism within the apparatus of the government continued.[35]

Uncoordinated Lending System – What Went Wrong?

The regime was reluctant to abandon its business culture, which had become a heavy burden on the banking system, despite the economic and social consequences of the Ethiopian war of 1977–78. Government finance was dominated by endless security problems, which increased the dependence of the state upon the Central Bank.[36] Moreover, the increase in world oil prices adversely affected the weakening resources of the country and fueled inflation. The economic instability and the impracticality of public-owned enterprises, among others, forced Siyad Barre regime to consider the need for a market-oriented economy. In 1980, the regime, acting according to its hidden agenda, undertook a stabilization program backed by the International Monetary Fund (IMF) in the form of stand-by credit. The conditions of the IMF included devaluation of the Somali shilling and restriction of domestic credit.

In 1981, the Somali Commercial and Savings Bank prohibited the use of the "Ok funds" as a credit instrument and enforced the use of draft check (money order). In 1982, the regime prohibited the Franco Valuta System entirely in the hope that the foreign earnings from workers and exporters would be channeled through the national banking institutions. But the Somali Commercial and Savings Bank business was deteriorating because of its policy based on clan affiliation and loyalty to the regime rather than customer relations and credit evaluation. The implementation of a market-oriented economy increased the regime's interference and the politicalization of the banking business. The regime exhibited a growing tendency to engage in policies, which aimed at using clan loyalty to manipulate individuals and groups. As H. Adam has noted:

> "Siyaad Barre was not interested in building a "state class" as some radical analysts have argued; he [Siyad Barre] used every means necessary [banking facilities and public enterprise's resources] to establish a "state clan," obviously a contradiction in terms."[37]

This policy gave the decision-makers of the Somali Commercial and Savings Bank a free hand to discriminate against its customers on the basis of clan affiliation. While the decision-makers of the bank were granting loans on the basis of favoritism, the local and international auditors were obstructed in their efforts to examine the bank's records. This gradually jeopardized the Somali Central Bank's power to regulate the banking system and the IMF's intention to stabilize the economy.[38] The openly clan-based politics of the top management of the commercial bank lowered the morale and job performance of the staff and increased discontent among customers. Some senior officers of the banking institutions opted to retire, and others were forced into retirement, due to their clan origins or their opposition to clan business policies in the bank. In addition, inflation adversely affected the most vulnerable part of society.[39] Absenteeism hit its highest level. Underground credit revived and gained ground to develop. The financial institutions remained stuck between the centralized economy and free market, because the government was unwilling to dissolve some money-losing programs. In 1986, the Central Bank of Somalia agreed with the IMF to introduce an exchange rate system based on auctions of available foreign currencies. The IMF program increased the greed of the privileged elite. Many of the state politicians and bureaucratic officers were at the same time major borrowers of the banks (commercial and development). They were directly or indirectly controllers of the lucrative import-export business and other economic activities. The state-owned commercial bank was pressured into granting loans on the basis of political favoritism, despite the IMF domestic credit restrictions. The top management of the commercial bank abused the grant of uncollectible loans, and instead of tackling the problem of corruption advanced a clan recruiting policy. The increasing nepotism contributed widely to the inefficiency of the bank. The regime appointed loyal executives who had no knowledge or experience in the banking business to the top management of the financial institutions.

When the foreign exchange auction was abandoned in 1987, uncertainty grew among businessmen. Shrewd depositors, annoyed by the regime's policy toward the opposition and the bad business practices of the Somali Commercial and Savings Bank, began to withdraw their money. The clan business and high interest rate prevented real producers and the small business communities from accessing loans. The central bank attempted to cover the incompetency of the Somali Commercial and Savings Bank before its insolvency became public knowledge. However, the Minister of Finance opposed the plan and insisted on continued financial support for the bank. The eruption of the civil war in May 1988, in the Northern regions, seriously affected the banking system. In addition to the looting of the Hargeysa and Burao branches, military expenditures increased the budget deficit. The central bank was compelled to cover the deficit of the regime. The continual borrowing of the government not only fueled inflation but also increased the central bank's banknote printing cost.

No members of the top executive management of the Somali Commercial and Savings Bank showed a willingness to heal the disease, which was threatening the bank's reputation. They continued to grant unconditional loans, without paying attention to the financial position of the bank, to individuals and companies without commercial bases or established credit records. The regime's clan-based politics openly endorsed the creation, the implementation and the development of irregular lending systems. As a result, branch managers fraudulently granted huge amounts of credit to non-customers of the bank without any collateral. The branch managers perpetrated the illegal lending of *Xisaab caseen* (overdraft) and issue of *"jeeg-wareegga"* circular checks (demand drafts) without corresponding funds. None of the banking auditing systems and the regime's anti-corruption organs had a mandate to investigate the mismanagement, despite public knowledge of the scandalous affair. Abdalla O. Mansur has pointed out:

> "[Also] nomadic segments of the population, moving into the cities and constituting the new ruling class, kept the worst aspects of there nomadic mentality,

which became, in my opinion, the major obstacle to the growth and development of modern state. They are not easily satisfied and their desire is to get rich in the shortest time possible, even if this means by illegal methods."[40]

The uncontrolled domestic credit of the Somali Commercial and Savings Bank contributed to its bankruptcy. A banking panic created queues in front of the bank's branches as well as its main office. Consequently the Somali Commercial and Savings Bank lost ground as local traders and merchants refused to accept their credit instruments. The bank became unable to pay its depositors' checks. In May 1990, the Somali Elders stated in their document the "Manifesto 1" that:

"The Somali Commercial and Savings Bank has practically closed its doors to all customers for the past eight weeks as of March 15, 1990. It is now widely believed that the bank is totally bankrupt and in fact is thirty billion shillings in the red. This has resulted from political, tribal interference and unbearable pressures on the management of the bank from the highest circles of the government who facilitated easy credit to the tune of hundreds of millions of shillings to the wives, sons, daughters, brothers and other relatives, as well as tribesmen and other political favorites of the governing echelon. Most of these loans are irrecoverable, since they were not guaranteed by any assets or equities."[41]

The government hesitated to close the Somali Commercial and Savings Bank officially, even though news of the bankruptcy was widespread. This undermined the people's confidence in the state-owned banking system. Uncertainty among the people increased, and led to a shortage of the Somali shilling in circulation, despite the continual money supply of the Somali Central Bank.[42] Siyad Barre regime used the state-owned banks' loans and foreign currencies as "clientelist politics" to maintain support, oppress the opposition and destabilize clans. The Somali Commercial and Savings Bank of Djibouti was a typical example of the politicization process of the regime. This branch served as a clientelist politics-funding source for some individuals and interest groups who cooperated with the regime in different ways. The Somali Development Bank was not immune to mismanagement either. Most of the bank's investments did not go to development. A former Director General of the bank, Mr. Osman Yusuf "Dhabarey," voluntarily returned almost all the properties he derived from bribery as religious repentance; this act, however, was uncommon in the high circles of power. Despite the numerous scandals of the state owned banks, Siyad Barre's own family took control over the financial institutions (the Somali Central Bank and the Ministry of Finance) of the country. Fanon writes:

"We no longer see the rise of a bourgeois dictatorship, but a tribal clan] dictatorship. The ministers, the members of the cabinet, the ambassadors [the bank decision-makers] and local commissioners are chosen from the same group as the leader, sometimes directly from his own family. Such regimes of the family sort seem to go back to the old laws of inbreeding, and not anger but shame is felt when we are faced with such stupidity, such an imposture, and such intellectual and spiritual poverty. These heads of the government are the true traitors in Africa, for they sell their country to the most terrifying of all its enemies: stupidity. This tribalizing of the central authority, it is certain, encourages regionalist ideas and separatism."[43]

The failure of the Somali Commercial and Savings Bank necessitated the establishment of a new bank. On July 1, 1990, a new commercial bank was established, the Somali Commercial Bank. Although the bank was totally invested by the government, it was designed to sell 50% of its shares to the private sector immediately, while the remaining shares were designed to be transferred to private hands after one year of activity. Siyad Barre and his entourage, however, remained disinclined to liberalize the banking sector. There was little evidence that the regime would properly implement the privatization of the adjustment program. In fact, the regime offered as a candidate for a local privately owned bank a cooperative bank owned by the Somali Cooperative Movement.[44] The Somali Cooperative Movement was a branch of the Government Party SRSP, which was controlled by Siyad Barre. In addition, there is doubt that domestic investors were willing to risk taking over the inefficient public-owned banks without prior assurance of private property rights and macroeconomic stability. The dictatorial regime's refusal to undertake any reform effort and the economic-political instability of the country contributed to the collapse of the Somali state.

Conclusion
The collapse of the Somali banking system was caused by several factors. The colonial legacy, mismanagement and clan manipulation lies at the heart of the collapse. First, colonial rulers imposed their banking systems without considering the country's financial tradition and Islamic heritage. Second, the colonial rulers, who dominated the country for about half a century, neglected to prepare native banking professionals. The lack of managerial knowledge and experience contributed partly to the failure of the banking system.

Third, post-colonial monetary policy continued along the path laid down by the colonial administrations. This policy did not identify and direct long-term accumulation and underestimated the importance of the financial tradition of the country as well as grass roots participation in the economy. The post-colonial regimes' policy making vision were based on nomadic attitude and practice, which has limited saving tendency comparing with the rest of the Somali society customs – city dwellers and agricultural.

Fourth, Somalia inherited a chronic budget deficit situation from the colonial rulers. This made the post-colonial civil regime a state without the capacity to carry out the basic functions of statehood that leaned heavily on debts, internal and external. The economic instability of the civil regime partly caused the military coup d'etat. The monetary policies pursued by the military regime (Nationalization and Franco Valuta System) were not sufficient to channel domestic savings and workers' foreign currency earnings into the public-owned banks and domestic productivity investments. The clientelist politics of the regime indirectly allowed the use of the state office for private gain. Consequently, mismanagement, corruption and nepotism spread in all sectors. This created imbalance in public owned enterprises, which became a heavy burden on the banking system.

Finally, the politicization of the banking business endorsed an openly uncontrolled lending system based on clan hegemony and political favoritism and denied credit access for real producers and the small business communities. The bank decision-makers' wrongdoing endorsed the creation and the development of an irregular lending chain, which contributed to the failure. Moreover, the government abuse of the debit limits of the central bank and lack of a genuine macroeconomic stability policy finalized the collapse of the banking system and the state.

Future Prospect

The dilemma of the State-owned bank in the past decade suggests the need to rethink the shape of the banking system in the future. What is the prospect of a successful banking model in the future? It is conceivable that a competitive private bank will provide the confidence needed. But can some private banks guarantee an economic growth that will promote sustained development in Somalia? The solution to the banking system in Somalia will depend upon the future reshaping of the country and the role of the state. Future reforms, which guarantee a private property rights and accountability, stabilized macro-economy and an independent central bank institution are indispensable.

Notes

1. Davidson, Basil *Africa in Historical Perspective,* Africa South Sahara 1990, edition No. 19, page 6.
2. Casanelli, Lee V. The *Shaping of Somali Society,* Philadelphia 1982, University of Pennsylvania Press, page 150.
3. Cremascoli, Bruno 11 *Paese di Punt,* Milano 1987, Edizioni Unicopli, page 150.
4. Hess, Robert 1. Italian Colonialism in Somalia, Chicago 1966, The University of Chicago Press, pp. 36–120.
5. Samatar, Abdi I. *The State and Rural Transformation in Northern Somalia 1884–1986,* Wisconsin 1989, University of Wisconsin Press, page 27.
6. Ibid. page 51.

7. Ali, Ahmed Q. Land *Rush in Southern Somalia,* Paper presented 37th Annual Meeting of African Studies, Toronto 1994, page 2.

8. Boahen, A. Adu *African Perspectives on Colonialism,* Baltimore 1987, The Johns Hopkins University Press, page 103.

9. De Vecchi, Cesare Maria *Orizzonti d'Empero,* Milano 1935, Mondadori, pp. 295–6.

10. Somalia Africa Orientale Italiana, Immagini di Storia, Campobasso 1993, Italia Editrice, page 22.

11. Pankhurst, Sylvia page 199.

12. Boahen, A. Adu General *History of Africa,* Berkeley 1985, Heineaman Educational Books Ltd. Volume IIV, page 404.

13. Britannica *Book of the Year,* British East Africa, London 1938, Encyclopedia Britannica Inc., page 611.

14. United Nations, Draft Trusteeship Agreement for the Territory of Somaliland Under Italian Administration, Supplement no. 10 All294 19150, page 5.

15. Del Boca, Angelo-Gli Italiani in Africa Orienrale, Mondadori 1984, pp. 220–235.

16. Somalia a Country *Study,* US Government Printing Office, Washington, DC 1980, p. 136.

17. Angelo Del Boca, page 225.

18. The decree was converted to law by the law no. 2 of January 13, 1961.

19. In 1959, for the first time, the AFIS administration sent 10 young staff to Italy for clerical training for about 9 months.

20. Lewis, I.M. A Modern History of Somalia: Nation and State in Horn of Africa, Boulder, Westview Press, page 170.

21. Raghe, Abdirahman O. *Trade Union Movement in Somalia 1960–69,* Proceedings of the 3rd International Congress of the Somali Studies, I1 Pensiero Scientifico Editore, Roma 1988, p. 315.

22. Africa Contemporary Record, *Annual Survey and Documents* 1969–70, Holmes and Meir Publishers, New York 1987, p. B183.

23. Traditionally Somali non pastoral nomadic were mostly saved their wealth through "Bakaaro" if their product is agricultural harvest, if they are in the urban area they save through "Dukaanley" small traders unless they would like to invest or partner with traders.

24. *Xisaabi xil ma leh:* Was anti-corruption campaign launched by the military regime in the early days of the coup d'etat.

25. Ibid. Africa Contemporary Record, p. B182.

26. Somali National Bank, *Annual Record,* Mogadishu 1971.

27. Laitin, David and Samatar, Said - *Somalia Nation in Search of State,* Colorado 1987, Westview Press, page 111.

28. Ibid. Africa Contemporary Record 1975–76, p. B312.

29. Siyad Barre used public-owned enterprises' resources as nas-nuujin (funds for clientelist politics) to reinforce loyalty to him.

30. In the early days of the coup d'etat, the military regime abolished the workers' right of strike and the trade union was under its control. When the black market and inflation adversely affected the standard of living and the working classes remained helpless, the great poet Abdi Muhumed Amin, performed a play called "Muufo" (bread). Muufo was performed in 1978 and openly advocated the rights of the working classes.

31. Somalia: A Country of Study (May 1992). The Library of Congress, Federal Research Division. Edited by Helen Chapin Metz.

32. The author in 1972–81 was a member of the Foreign Department staff of the Central Bank of Somalia. In 1978–80 he personally supervised the foreign reserves of the bank. Although the regime introduced the Franco Valuta system, the decision-makers of the Central Bank and Finance Ministry were against the measure.

33. Galaydh, Ali K. Notes on *the State of the Somali State*, Horn of Africa volume

34. Serious delinquencies began to occur when a check from a certain branch, which had been cashed by anther branch, was returned to the original branch. The manager of the original branch fraudulently excludes the check instead of allowing it to go through standard accounting procedure. This practice led some branches of the commercial bank to keep two sets of records, one for official scrutiny and one for illegal private transactions.

*   Ok funds: Is banking terminology used to indicate that the drawee of a check does have sufficient funds on deposit to cover the amount of the check issued. The bank cannot dishonor a check with "Ok fund". Two officers of an issued bank as guarantee endorse the check.

35. Despite the mobilization of domestic resources, the state owned businesses were deteriorating because of mismanagement. In March 1975, a penalty law was introduced. The law stated that anyone who misappropriated government funds would be subject to death if the amount were over 100,000 Somali Shillings. A merchant, Mohamed Abdi M. Siyad and two officers of the Health Ministry were accused and sentenced to death. Nevertheless, the death penalty law was abandoned without being officially abolished. This encouraged misappropriation of government resources. In addition, a resolution was presented at the third general meeting of the central committee of the Somali Revolutionary Socialist Party. The resolution stated that all personal property owned by its members should be transferred to the Party. The confiscation was intended to discourage wealth accumulation by a privileged elite. The resolution failed. That drive endorsed the use of public office for private gain, looting and corruption.

36. Gray, Albert Jr. *The Economy of the Somali Democratic Republic in the 1980s*, Ufabamu Volume XVII – No. 11, Los Angele 1989, p. 128.

37. Adam, Hussein M. *Militarism and Warlordism: Rethinking the Somali Political Experience*, Paper presented at 36th Annual Meeting of African Studies, Boston 1993, p. 9.

38. In 1982, for the first time, the Somali Commercial and Savings Bank was designated a new executive position "President". This created a power conflict between the central bank and the commercial bank. The top executive position "President" of the Somali Commercial and Savings Bank was covered between 1982 to 1990 by the following executives: Said Mohamed Ali "Sheef" 1982/85, Osman Haji Yusuf 1985/87, Ali Nuur Isaaq 1987/89, Mohamed Ali Hirzi 1989/90, Abdirahman Duale Mohamed January to December '90.

39. Awes, Maho A.H. and Bechtold, Karl-Heinz W. *The Debit Crisis of the Developing Countries and IMF Conditionality. Potential Economic and Social Consequences in Somalia*, 3rd International Congress of Somali Studies, 11 Pensiero Scientifico Editore, Roma 1988, pp. 481 -82.

40. Mansur, Abdalla O. *Contrary to a Nation: The Cancer of the Somali State*, The Invention of Somalia, Edited by Ali Jimale Ahmed, New Jersey 1995, the Red Sea Press, pp. 113–4.

41. Somali Elders, Manifesto I, Horn of Africa volume XIII, New Jersey 1990, p.112.

42. When the Somali Commercial and Savings Bank became unable to pay its depositors, the Somali Central Bank presented a plan of repayment in order to restore the bank's confidence. The project was designed to repay each depositor Sh. So 50,000.00 per day in order to reduce the insolvency. However, the regime was unwilling to repay the claims of depositors. Consequently, the central bank's project was short-lived due to the absence of governmental support and an economic rescue plan.

43. Fanon, Frantz, The Wretched of the Earth, Grove Weidenfeld, New York, p. 183.

44. UNIDO Regional Country Studies Branch, *Somalia Industrial Revitalization through Privatization,* Industrial Review 1988, p. 61.

Contributors

Ladan Affi is a Ph.D student at the University of Wisconsin-Madison. Her interests lie in failed nation-states, gender, and impact of the diaspora on their home countries.

Ahmed Q. Ali is a native of Bakol in the Interriverine region. He is a Civil-hydraulic engineer and has worked in the Land & Water Department, the Ministry of Planning, and the Ministry for Juba Valley Development. From 1986 to 1991, Ali worked for a major local civil contractor in Somalia, Juba Enterprises. He participated in the engineering design, execution and supervision of flood protection, irrigation, and land reclamation works in the Interriverine region. Ali has lived in Phoenix, Arizona since 1992. He taught mathematics at North High School and has published several papers analyzing various aspects of Somalia. He currently lives in Zanzibar, Tanzania.

Mohamed Nuuh Ali is a lecturer in the Department of History at Carleton University, Canada. He earned M.A. and Ph.D. degrees in history at the University California, Los Angeles. He is also the former Dean of the College of Education (Lafoole) at the Somali National University.

Cedric Barnes was an undergraduate and masters student in the Africa department of the School of Oriental and African Studies (SOAS), University of London. He undertook post-graduate research at Trinity College and the Faculty of History at the University of Cambridge, and gained his Ph.D. (entitled 'The Ethiopian State and its Somali Periphery, *circa* 1888–1948') in 2000. His British Academy funded post-doctoral project is entitled 'Poets, politicians and pastoralists – national and clan identity in the northern Somali-lands', hosted by the Department of Languages and Cultures of Africa, SOAS. He has undertaken two periods of fieldwork (1998 and 2002) in the eastern Somali speaking areas of Ethiopia, collecting oral and documentary material.

Omar A. Eno is a Ph.D. candidate in African history at York University. Currently, he is the Director of the "National Somali Bantu Project" at Portland State University-Oregon. He has extensively written on many aspects of Somali history and culture.

Abdi M. Kusow is a sociologist trained in international migration and racial identities. His main area of research interest is the contemporary African diaspora in North America. His recent work appeared in *Symbolic Interaction*, the official journal of the *Society for the Study of Symbolic Interaction*. His chapter on "East African Immigrants in the United States" will appear in Mary Waters & Reed Ueda (eds.), *The New Americans*. Cambridge: Harvard University Press. He has written on the social and political disorganization of the Nation-State in Somalia. His works on those topics appear in edited volumes and regional journals such as *Northeast African Studies* (1994), *UFAHAMU: Journal of the African Activist Association* (1994), and in *The Invention of Somalia* (1995).

Hassan Mahadallah is Assistant Professor of Political Science in the Nelson Mandela School of Public Policy and Urban Affairs. He received his Ph.D. from Tulane University. His interests lie in African International Relations, American Government, and International Relations.

Rima Berns-McGown, Ph.D. is managing editor of the International Journal. She is the author of Muslims in the Diaspora: The Somali Communities of London and Toronto, as well as two novels.

Mohamed H. Mukhtar is Professor of African History at Savannah State University He received his Ph.D. from al-Azhar University, Cairo, Egypt. Dr. Mukhtar has written scholarly works on a number of topics: Historiography, "Arabic Sources on Somalia." In *History in Africa*, 14, (1987). On spread of Islam in Africa, "Islam in Somali History: Fact and Fiction." In *The Invention of Somalia* (1995). On the social history of modern Somalia, "The Plight of Agro-pastoral Society of Somalia." In *Review of African Political Economy*, 70, (1996). He co-authored with Mrk DeLancey, *Somalia, World Bibliographical Series* (1988). Dr. Mukhtar is the author of the new *Historical Dictionary of Somalia* (2002).

Abdul Qadir Arif Qassim was born in Mogadishu, Somalia. He has been educated in both Somalia and the United States. He received a B.A. in Economics at Somali National University in 1977. He was a member of the Central Bank staff from 1972 to 1981. He had been a CEO at HAPLAS, a limited private manufacturing company in Mogadishu, from 1983 to 1990. Currently, he is the Refugee Programs Supervisor at Catholic Social Service of Phoenix. He received his M.B.A. in Global Management at the University of Phoenix, Phoenix in 2002. Presently, he is pursuing a Master of Nonprofit Management at Regis University, School of Professionals at Colorado, Denver. He is a member of African Studies Association.

Index

Index

P

Paradigms, xiii, 1–2, 9
Patriarchy, 107, 111, 115
Paul Ricoeur, xiii, xvii, 13
Plantation slavery, x, 135, 140, 148, 152
Power Shifts, 126
Priorities, xiii, 1, 6, 8–9, 11

Q

Qur'an Schools, 122

R

Racialization, xii
Rajis, 9
Reewing, 5
Reewing-Speaking, 7
Reserved Areas, 33, 35, 37–38, 40, 43–45, 49–50,
    52, 171

S

Scientific Socialism, 166–167, 185
Segmentary, see also segmentary stratification,
    segmentary inclusion and exclusion, 7
Self-same Thesis, xi
Shabelle, 4, 13, 77, 79–80, 83, 87, 136, 137–143, 145,
    149, 151–152, 154, 156, 157–164, 167, 170–171,
    174, 176
Sheikh Uways Ibn Muhammad Al-Barawi, 79
Simultaneous inclusion and exclusion, 3, 5–7
Siyad Barre, xiv, 10, 148, 185–188, 190–191, 193
Slavery, x, xvi, 76, 82, 88–89, 135–136, 140, 142–145,
    147–154, 176
Social boundary of *Somaliness*, xiii, xvi, 1–12

Somali Historiography, xi–xiv, 12, 37, 75
Somali Nationalism, ix, xii–xv, 6, 13, 33, 51, 59–60,
    61–73, 75, 85, 88
Somali Youth Club, see also Somali Youth League,
    34, 44–45, 47, 71, 85, 98
Somaliness, xii–xiv, xvi, 1–12, 171
Supreme Revolutionary Council, 166

T

Tacabwadaag, 168
Teenagers, 120, 123–124
Territorial-based narratives, 8
The Social Boundary of Somaliness, xiii, xvi, 1–12
Toleyn, 8
Toronto, 10, 12, 121–133, 151, 176, 193, 198
Tumaal, 3
Tunni, 22, 26, 82
Turbulent Republicanism, 8

U

Ujeeddobadan, 168
'Ulama, 120, 125

X

Xisaabi xil ma leh, 193

Y

Yibir, 2–3

Z

Zanzibar, 76, 77, 135, 137, 141–143, 146, 149, 152, 178,
    179, 197